Episcopal Vision/American Reality

Episcopal Vision/American Reality

HIGH CHURCH THEOLOGY AND SOCIAL THOUGHT

IN EVANGELICAL AMERICA

Robert Bruce Mullin

Yale University Press
NEW HAVEN AND LONDON

*Published with assistance from the Frederick W. Hilles Publica-
tion Fund of Yale University.*

Designed by Margaret E. B. Joyner and set in Bembo
type.
Printed in the United States of America by Cushing-
Malloy, Inc., Ann Arbor, Michigan.

Library of Congress Cataloging-in-Publication Data
Mullin, Robert Bruce.
  Episcopal vision/American reality.

  Bibliography: p.
  Includes index.
    1. Episcopal Church—History—19th century.
2. Evangelicalism—United   States—History—19th
century. 3. Sociology, Christian—United States—
History—19th century. 4. United States—Church
history—19th century. 5. Anglican Communion—
United   States—History—19th   century. I. Title.
BX5882.M85 1986   283'.73   85-17782
ISBN 0-300-03487-3 (alk. paper)

*The paper in this book meets the guidelines for permanence and
durability of the Committee on Production Guidelines for Book
Longevity of the Council on Library Resources.*

10   9   8   7   6   5   4   3   2   1

To my father and to the memory of my mother

Contents

Introduction

IN THE BLOODY OCTOBER OF 1862 THE AMERICAN CIVIL WAR HUNG IN A
delicate balance. The leading New York City newspapers, however,
whose concerns until so recently had been directed toward recounting
the terrible losses at Antietam and reporting on the still more recent
encounters at Corinth (Mississippi) and Perryville (Kentucky), began
to center their attention on, of all things, an ecclesiastical gathering.
During the first two weeks of that month lay delegates and clergy of
the Protestant Episcopal Church gathered for their triennial convention, which in that year met in New York City. Eyes throughout the
nation, both within and outside of the church, watched in wait for the
outcome of the convention, since its agenda included the formulating
of the church's official position concerning the war that was then
raging. The question of whether the Episcopal Church would join
with the other northern Protestant churches in condemning the southern secession and firmly back the Union became the stuff of daily news
stories and the grist of countless editorials. "Unless we can admit the
idea," warned an editorial writer for the *New York Times,* "that the
Convention now sitting at St. John's Chapel includes among its members a majority of sympathisers with secession, or partisans of their
northern allies, it is difficult to understand how a church with such
historic memories and traditions . . . should hesitate to declare in this
hour of trial its unaltered devotion to the American constitution."[1]
Always mercurial, Horace Greeley stated the problem even more suc-
cinctly: "The issue cannot be shirked—the Church is on trial, and the
nation and the world are looking on."[2] The debate in the convention

1. *New York Times,* October 9, 1862, 4.
2. *New York Daily Tribune,* October 8, 1862, 4.

over the war, however, and the response it provoked in the public at large was simply the culmination of a long story that stretched over six decades—that story is the subject of this book.

When modern students of American religion stop to consider H. Richard Niebuhr's discussion of the tension between Christ and culture or ponder Sidney Mead's "old religion in the brave new world," they often think first of the history of American Catholics or of the different traditions of Judaism or even of the so-called non–main line Protestant denominations, but almost never of the Episcopal Church. Indeed, the standard image of the successful and socially prestigious average Episcopal congregation seems to fly in the face of any talk of the travail of assimilation. Yet first glances are not always accurate. As any student of theology can attest, Episcopal theology has always marched to a drummer far different from that of the rest of Protestantism; and particularly within that branch of Anglicanism known as the high church there has been a long-standing resistance to any identification with wider Protestant theology and culture. The historic question for American Episcopalians has always been how to keep their church intellectually distinct while being socially assimilated.

At no time was this question so pressing as during those six decades from 1800 to 1860 which historians refer to as the antebellum period, an era that has long fascinated students of American religious history. During these years the creative energy of American Protestants not only responded to an expanding western mission field, but also, through countless cooperative ventures, left its mark on the national life and character. During the last thirty years an impressive amount of scholarly work has surveyed the religious landscape of this era. Some have described this period as the "Golden Day of Democratic Evangelicalism."[3] Others have chronicled the triumph of the Evangelical United Front in transcending denominational divisions and uniting in battle against infidelity, barbarism, and immorality.[4]

3. Sydney E. Ahlstrom, *A Religious History of the American People* (New Haven, 1972), 385 ff.
4. For such an interpretation, see particularly Clifford S. Griffin, *Their Brother's Keeper: Moral Stewardship in the United States, 1800–1865* (New Brunswick, 1960), and Charles I. Foster, *An Errand of Mercy: The Evangelical United Front, 1790–1837* (Chapel Hill, 1960). For a more recent caveat regarding a simplistic use of this interpretation, see Lois Banner, "Religious Benevolence as Social Control: A Critique of an Interpretation," in *Religion in American History*, ed. John M. Mulder and John F. Wilson (Englewood Cliffs, 1978), 218–35.

Still others have gone further and have suggested that the cooperative ventures eventually became a "nationalizing force that created a 'common world of experience.'"[5] Most interpreters agree that the antebellum period witnessed theologically the de facto triumph of an Arminianized Calvinism and that it saw socially not only the flowering of the institution of the voluntary society as the prime vehicle of organized benevolence, but also a tendency to interpret the Republic as the "ark of God's redemptive work in the world."[6]

Yet it was during this very period that high church Episcopalians set off in their own direction, out of step with the great evangelical concerns of the religious public at large. They saw their church as an alternative to the rest of the religious milieu. Their willingness to shun any identification with the dominant American Protestant ethos made them a unique religious group in the antebellum period and placed them at the center of decades of controversy. To the modern reader so much controversy involving such a numerically small community may seem strange, yet numbers alone do not tell the story. The issues centered on a historical matrix of questions that was two hundred years old, and as such struck deeply into the psyche of American Protestants. High church Episcopalians seemed to represent the American flowering of the old bete noire of both Puritans and Evangelicals—they were the spiritual descendents of Archbishop William Laud in the land of the Pilgrims. The long-standing suspicion of prelatical pretensions was not easily forgotten, and the sentiment summed up in the famous Plymouth Rock Society toast, "To a church without a bishop and a state without a king," expressed the often voiced fear that the high church system was antithetical to American freedom.[7] The decades-long battles between high church and Evangelical spokesmen often evolved into a debate over the meaning of the American nation.

This study then is not a denominational history nor even a formal history of the high church movement, but rather an imaginative reconstruction of a lost world view via an exploration of the high church vision in the context of the rest of the American religious milieu. In seeking such a goal, the study also aims at bridging a number of

5. Donald Mathews, "The Second Great Awakening as an Organizing Process," in Mulder and Wilson, *Religion in American History*, 218.

6. Sidney Mead, *The Nation with the Soul of a Church* (New York, 1975), 72.

7. The toast was made by the Presbyterian minister George Potts in 1844. For the controversy it provoked, see *No Church Without a Bishop: or the Controversy Between the Revs. Dr. Potts and Wainwright . . .* (New York, 1844).

heretofore separate scholarly fields. General religious historians have usually concentrated on such transdenominational issues as revivalism, temperance, and slavery, while denominational historians have more often shied away from these questions, preferring to explore the internal histories of their respective communities. The problem with such a neat bifurcation, however, is that a large proportion of the American religious public did not live their lives by means of *either* the general religiocultural attitudes *or* by means of a denominational synthesis but precisely by trying to deal with *both*. The tension between these two visions provides a central intellectual theme in antebellum religious history, and in the case of these Episcopalians goes far toward explaining certain enduring historical issues. Social questions such as why Episcopalians were so notoriously silent on the question of slavery and intellectual questions such as why the antebellum high church synthesis declined so rapidly after midcentury both become clearer when the tension between general religiosocial and more narrowly denominational issues is kept in focus.

The period to be considered begins with the emergence of John Henry Hobart and ends with the collapse of the old synthesis after midcentury. These sixty years witnessed such a revolution in theology that toward the end of the period high church apologists found themselves responding not simply to American evangelicalism but to modern intellectual, social, and cultural trends as well. Hence the three goals of this book will be to explore the theological, devotional, and social synthesis offered by these high church figures; to examine the chief points of contention between this high church vision and the rest of the Evangelical enterprise; and finally to speculate as to some of the factors behind the decline of the traditional high church position in the decades after 1845.

The structure of the study reflects certain peculiarities in the history itself. Since most of the denominational events and cast of characters are unfamiliar to the majority of readers, an attempt has been made to fill in this background material without losing sight of the main issues at hand. Furthermore, the first thirty years of the movement is largely a history of the revival of the high church apologetical tradition in New York (a revival largely due to the labors of John Henry Hobart and his associates). New York not only possessed onefourth of the nation's Episcopalians, but also, as will be shown, provided a unique combination of dynamic leadership and ample physical resources. For this reason the smaller high church movements that occurred in Maryland and North Carolina will not be treated. After

1830, however, the multiplication of high church voices makes the movement no longer so easy to characterize either theologically or geographically, and instead it necessitates an examination of a number of figures from different parts of the North.

The book is accordingly divided into six chapters, three dealing with the period of John Henry Hobart and three with that of his intellectual successors. The first chapter sets the stage both socially and intellectually and introduces the protagonists of the first period. The second chapter explores the public controversies of the Hobartian period, the forging of a distinct apologetical vision, and the clash over participation in the American Bible Society, perhaps the most popular of the Evangelical endeavors. Chapter 3 goes beneath the surface of the public controversies and strives to delineate the key theological, devotional, and social principles undergirding the movement. The fourth chapter discusses how these principles were employed in the 1830s to provide a platform for an extensive critique of the "excesses" of democratic evangelicalism—as they were theologically manifested in the debate over questions such as the New Measures of Charles Grandison Finney, and socially as shown in the issues of temperance and slavery—and the positing of the Episcopal Church as an "ark of safety" in this sea of strife. Chapter 5 considers the challenges posed to the older high church synthesis by the new religious impulses as reflected in the philosophy of Samuel Taylor Coleridge and in the Oxford Movement. Finally, chapter 6 analyzes and assesses the various intellectual and social factors that contributed to the decline of the Hobartian synthesis of theology, devotion, and social vision in the decades after 1845.

A note about the term *high church* is necessary. In order for us to truly understand the phenomenon of the American high church movement during these years, two misconceptions must be guarded against. The high church vision in this period should not be confused with modern, post-Tractarian Anglo-Catholicism. High churchmanship in the modern sense of advanced ecclesiastical ceremonialism, and a theology that closely parallels Roman Catholic models, did not begin to emerge until the end of the period under consideration. Nor must the American high church movement be considered as a simple transferring of the older English ecclesiastical party to the American scene. The older English High Church tradition had two distinct aspects. In the sphere of theology it favored an elevated view of episcopacy (usually buttressed by the idea of apostolic succession), a strong emphasis on baptism and the ordinary workings

grace (in contrast to both enthusiasm and latitudinarianism), and a
dislike for Calvinism in general and Puritanism in particular. In the
realm of politics it was committed to a firm support of the religious
establishment, which ensured episcopal privileges and prerogatives.
Along with this it was strongly opposed to the comprehension of
nonepiscopal dissenters. The English High Church tradition before
1830 had two claimed bases of authority: a theological one grounded
in the authority of the early church and a political one grounded in the
heritage of the English religious establishment. The American Revolution and the loss of any claim on the English religious establishment,
it will be suggested, reversed the political thrust of American high
church thought and shifted it 180° from the English pattern. From the
American high church perspective the great need was not the maintenance of a privileged status but rather the defense of the uniqueness of
the Episcopal claims and practices in a theologically inhospitable environment. Hence what led English high churchmen into a Tory,
church–state marriage produced in the American environment a wariness of the political process.

What characterized American high church individuals was their
adoption of the theological heritage of the English High Church tradition and their merging it with social corollaries peculiar to the American situation. Not the Christian state but the vision of the church as a
visible society, "made by Divine appointment the regular and ordinary channel by which the blessing of mercy, and grace, and eternal
life, in Jesus Christ, are conveyed to a fallen world," lay at the center of
their schema.[8] The church provided a framework for the rest of the
Christian experience; through it theology was constructed, a warm
piety was instilled, and service to the world took place.

Furthermore throughout this study it will be suggested that the
internal elasticity of American high church attitudes prevents any
overly narrow theological definition of the movement. Even on such a
question as whether episcopacy was absolutely essential for the existence of a true church (*esse*) or simply necessary for its well-being (*bene
esse*), no unanimity of opinion can be found; to assume arbitrarily that
the former is to be the defining characteristic of high churchmanship
would be necessarily to exclude from consideration such important
figures as John Bowden, professor of belles lettres at Columbia College, and John Henry Hopkins, bishop of Vermont. Rather than by

8. John Henry Hobart, *The High Churchman Vindicated* . . . (New York,
1826), 3.

absolute agreement on all theological articles, the high church writers considered in this study were united by a common assumption and approach. All accepted the normative importance of the primitive church for all modern theological and ecclesiological issues. Second, as will be shown, they emphasized the identification of the present Episcopal Church with the primitive church and saw in this identification the key for defining the position of the Episcopal Church both to the other evangelical churches and to the society at large.

This definition is not an artificial one but reflects the real point of division between high and low church Episcopalians in the antebellum period. Scholars for a number of years have noted that little true theology divided these two groups.[9] High church writers would not deny the evangelical claim of *sola gratia* nor would low churchmen dispute the value of the bishops and ordinances. Rather, they differed as to whether the role of the Episcopal Church in antebellum America was to emphasize its points of commonality with the rest of the religious milieu or instead to emphasize the points that distinguished it from the wider religious environment. On this key attitudinal difference all of the persons considered under the rubric *high church* would have concurred—the Episcopal Church was an alternative to evangelical theology and culture and not part of it.

Such a floating definition of *high church* has two distinct advantages over a more rigid or theological approach. The first is that it allows one to consider individuals such as the minister/journalist Calvin Colton, who is usually not treated in a formal study of the high church movement, yet who as a convert to the Episcopal Church offered an important critique of the theology and practices of the evangelical churches. The second advantage is that this definition allows one to see the high church movement in the Episcopal Church as an Old School, or confessional, movement, acting like other Old School movements of the period with its concern for protecting the peculiar denominational tradition against the demands for transdenominational unity.

All of these issues emerged in the half century of disputation that pitted high church writers against such leading Protestant spokesmen as Charles Hodge, Albert Barnes, Samuel Miller, Horace Bushnell,

9. Perhaps the most recent advocate of this position is Robert W. Prichard, "Nineteenth-Century Episcopal Attitudes on Predestination and Election," *Historical Magazine of the Protestant Episcopal Church* 51(1982): 23–51 (hereafter referred to as *HMPEC*). Although some scholars prefer to distinguish between the terms *low church* and *evangelical,* in this study they will be used interchangeably as was largely the custom at the time.

INTRODUCTION

Edwards Amassa Park, Nathaniel William Taylor, and numerous others. For them the emergence of an invigorated high church apologetic in republican America seemed strangely out of step with the rest of the society. For modern observers the thoughts and visions of these Episcopal spokesmen provide a fascinating insight into the intellectual diversity and richness of antebellum America.

Like all works of this nature, this project could never have been completed without the help and encouragement of many. The library staffs at the New York Public Library, the New-York Historical Society, Harvard Divinity School, General Theological Seminary, and Princeton University were all helpful in ferreting out obscure manuscripts and texts. Special thanks must be given to the staff of the Archives of the Episcopal Church for their hospitality and cooperation during a summer visit there. Most of all, the staffs of the Yale University libraries, and in particular the Divinity Library, gave much expert assistance, and in the latter's case much personal encouragement as well.

This book owes its chief academic debt to Sydney E. Ahlstrom, whose breadth of vision and insatiable intellectual curiosity inspired me continually to broaden the study's implications. Leslie Higgins-Biddle, Emmet McLaughlin, Hans Frei, and J. Robert Wright all read various drafts of this work and helped considerably in clarifying key points. Furthermore, after the death of Sydney Ahlstrom, Hans Frei, in manifold ways, gave much help and support, without which this book might never have been completed. In the transformation from dissertation to book both Charles Grench and Lawrence Kenney of Yale University Press have given great assistance, and the manuscript has benefited considerably.

A special thanks must be given to two colleagues here at Yale, William Silva and Ann Braude, for their encouragement and insightful suggestions along the way. Scholarship, at its best, is a collegial endeavor, and their support helped this project through many a rough period.

Finally, my greatest debt is to my wife, Viola, who aided this work in more material, psychological, and spiritual ways than I can ever thank her for. Her patience and encouragement helped turn what might have been an impossible burden into a labor of love.

Episcopal Vision/American Reality

THE FORGING
OF A GROUP IDENTITY

1

Setting the Stage

IN THE YEAR 1798, AS TIMOTHY DWIGHT BUSILY TRIED TO STIR THE FIRES
of revival at Yale College, Samuel Provoost, the Episcopal bishop of
New York, sat translating the poet Tasso. The contrast between these
two images, the vigor of Dwight and the languor of Provoost, perhaps
best reflects the troubled state of the Episcopal Church in the closing
years of the eighteenth century.

Any historical generalization is necessarily hazardous, and the
above is no exception. For decades, students of this period of Episcopal
history have debated the veracity of Charles Tiffany's characterization
of these years as a period of "suspended animation."[1] Yet any examination of the American Episcopal high church movement must begin by
examining the peculiar exigencies confronting the postrevolutionary
Episcopal Church, since these very problems and challenges were to
be the seedbed for many of the later intellectual and institutional
developments.

The peculiar makeup of the colonial Anglican church made it
inevitable that it would be markedly affected by the American War of
Independence. Anglicanism had experienced a period of rapid growth
in the late colonial period. Factors contributing to this growth in-

1. Tiffany uses this notion in *A History of the Protestant Episcopal Church in the
United States of America* (New York, 1895), 385 ff., a volume in the important
American Church History Series, edited by Philip Schaff. At least since the publica-
tion of George DeMille, *A History of the Diocese of Albany, 1704–1923* (Philadelphia,
[1946]), the issue has been debated. For a bibliographic summary of the controversy,
as well as perhaps the most recent contribution to it, see Frederick V. Mills, Sr.,
"The Protestant Episcopal Churches in the United States 1783–1789: Suspended
Animation or Remarkable Recovery?" *HMPEC* 46 (1977): 151–70.

cluded the establishment of the church in the southern colonies, a vigorous missionary program funded by the English Society for the Propagation of the Gospel, the natural attractiveness of the church to political and cultural anglophiles, and the role it served as a haven for individuals in revolt from the enthusiastic disturbances of the Great Awakening. All of these attractions lost their glitter in the aftermath of the war. The southern establishments were quickly terminated, while in the north missionaries and missionary funds were withdrawn. Indeed, many of the mission churches had been closed since early in the war on account of their clergy's unwillingness to violate their oath to uphold the liturgy by omitting the required prayers for King George. Furthermore the old asset of anglophilism became transformed into the liability of Toryism. In some areas this allegation was close to reality: north of Philadelphia only a handful of the colonial Anglican clergy had chosen to support the colonists in the Revolution.[2]

Many challenges faced the scattered Anglican congregations in the postwar period, but none was more pressing than that of institutional survival. Numerous historians have related at great lengths the story of how this was achieved, of the compromise between the high church Connecticut Episcopalians, led by their bishop, Samuel Seabury (who favored a strong episcopacy, clerical control of the church, and a theology emphasizing sacramentalism and apostolic succession), and the more moderate Episcopalians of the middle and southern states. The availability and quality of the secondary literature makes it possible to pass over the intricacies of the compromise by simply noting that through the establishment of bishops elected by both clergy and laity as well as the granting to the laity a membership in ecclesiastical conventions the institutional structure of the Episcopal Church was reformulated in order to adapt better to a republican society.[3]

2. Frederick V. Mill, *Bishops by Ballots* (New York, 1978), 3–34. On the attraction of English culture, see John Murrin, "Anglicizing an American Colony: The Transformation of Provincial Massachusetts" (Ph.D. diss., Yale University, 1966), and Joseph Ellis, *The New England Mind in Transition* (New Haven, 1973), 55–81. On the role of the Anglican Church as a bastion against religious enthusiasm, see the letters of Samuel Johnson published in *Samuel Johnson . . . His Career and Writings,* ed. Herbert and Carol Schneider, 4 vols. (New York, 1929), 1:111. For a recent account of the effect of the American Revolution upon the Episcopal Church, see David L. Holmes, "The Episcopal Church and the American Revolution," *HMPEC* 47 (1978): 261–91.

3. Perhaps the two best accounts of this period are Mills, *Bishops by Ballots,* and Clara O. Loveland, *The Critical Years: The Reconstitution of the Anglican Church in the United States of America, 1780–1789* (Greenwich, Ct., 1956). Mills and Loveland

Thus institutionally the Episcopal Church had responded creatively to a new situation. Yet institutional adaptation was only half of the challenge; the question of self-identity in large part still lay unanswered. Why would anyone want to join this new church? If before the war the colonial Anglican Church had gloried in its identification with England, such an association was no longer advisable.[4] If, as some have argued, the shift in the American church in the 1780s was a shift from being an English church to being an episcopal one (that is, understanding its primary defining element to be its possession of bishops and not its association with the English establishment), there remained the issue of working out the real practical value of such bishops. Decades of antiepiscopal broadsides had made many people wary of granting large amounts of power to bishops.[5] As one historian has noted, "In dissociating the new bishops from all the undesired aspects of the English episcopate, Americans were slow to allow the accrual of new, to say nothing of old prerogatives."[6] The power of the new bishops was so carefully circumscribed that until 1808 four-fifths of the House of Deputies (composed of laymen and lower clergy) had the power to overrule any opposition by the House of Bishops.[7]

The travail of the Revolution had dealt the young Episcopal

---

disagree, however, in interpreting William White's contribution to the compromise. For a bibliographic summary and a third view, see John F. Woolverton, "Philadelphia's William White: Episcopalian Distinctiveness and Accommodation in the Post-Revolutionary Period," *HMPEC* 43 (1974): 279–96.

4. Mills, *Bishops by Ballots,* 288–307. This is not to deny that anglophilism continued to exist during the early national period nor that colonial Anglicans, particularly in the North, failed to emphasize the importance of the episcopacy and lamented its absence in the colonies. Still, such a shift in understanding, it will be shown, does seem to lie beneath much of the apologetical discussion that burst forth in the first decades of the nineteenth century. A sociological analysis of this shift is attempted in William Swatos, *Into Denominationalism: The Anglican Metamorphosis* ([Storrs, Ct.], 1979). Swatos, however, never really discusses the peculiar sense of self-understanding that emerged in the early nineteenth-century apologetical literature.

5. On the episcopacy debate, see Arthur L. Cross, *The Anglican Episcopate and the American Colonies* (New York, 1902); Carl Bridenbaugh, *Mitre and Sceptre* (New York, 1962), as well as Ellis, *New England Mind in Transition,* 244–56; and Edmund S. Morgan, *The Gentle Puritan: A Life of Ezra Stiles* (New Haven, 1962), 210–25.

6. Raymond W. Albright, *A History of the Protestant Episcopal Church* (New York, [1964]), 142.

7. *Journals of the General Convention of the Protestant Episcopal Church in the United States of America; From the Year 1784 to the Year 1814 Inclusive* (Philadelphia, 1817), 76 (hereafter referred to as JGC).

Church one more blow. As in every war, to the victors belonged the spoils, in church as well as state. Following the Peace of Paris, thousands of Anglicans, both lay and clerical, flocked from their homes to either Britain or British Canada. The few clergy in the northern colonies who had advocated the cause of the colonists accordingly began to assume leadership in the new church. For many a staunch Whig it was a time for rejoicing. Looking back on the event in his own church, one old Whig reflected, "It was a glorious occasion, and many friends of their Country met that day for the first time in years. There were no rascally Tories there that morning."[8] Yet as many would slowly learn, there was no inherent connection between political opinions and the ability to inspire a diocese. Sometimes, as in the case of William White, chaplain of the Continental Congress and Episcopal bishop of Pennsylvania, the men proved to be fine leaders. In other cases, however, as for example that of Samuel Provoost, they had little more than their politics to recommend them.

When one moves from the macrocosm of the entire nation to the microcosm of the diocese of New York, one finds only slight variations in these common themes. New York was one of the stronger centers of the Episcopal Church at the time. It derived its strength neither from an effluence of piety nor a surfeit of learning but rather from a historical accident. In 1705 a parcel of land, then known as Queen's Farm, was granted for the support of Trinity parish, the only congregation of the English Church on the island of Manhattan.[9] As the city grew, this tract of land, stretching from what is now Vesey Street all the way to Christopher Street, became increasingly valuable. Thus the patrimony of Trinity parish was able to furnish something that few other parts of the Episcopal Church possessed to any great extent—money that could be used to help support a diocese.

The end of the war brought on the question of who should control this wealth. New York City had been the center of Tory America, and perhaps the center of Tory New York had been Trinity parish. Among the seven thousand Loyalists abandoning the city in 1783 was Charles Inglis, rector of Trinity, who resigned his office November 1, 1783. On that very day, only weeks before the triumphant Whigs reentered New York for the first time since 1776, Trinity's vestry chose as

8. Cited in James Grant Wilson, ed., *The Centennial History of the Protestant Episcopal Church in the Diocese of New York* (New York, 1886), 134.
9. Morgan Dix et al., *A History of the Parish of Trinity Church in the City of New York*, 6 vols. (1898–1962), 1:467. See also William Berrian, *An Historical Sketch of Trinity Church, New York* (New York, 1847), 134.

Inglis's successor Benjamin Moore, an assistant at Trinity and a moderate Tory. This election was soon challenged by a group of laymen calling themselves "Whig Episcopalians," who argued against the legality of Moore's election. Through the intervention of a council appointed by the legislature of New York for the temporary government of the southern part of the state, the vestry was reorganized, and instead of the Tory Benjamin Moore, the Whig Samuel Provoost was inducted as rector of Trinity.[10] The wealth of Trinity was thus rescued out of politically obnoxious hands. Yet the wounds of this state action never completely healed, and many among Trinity's members would remember it. Fifty years later, the then rector, commenting upon the legislature's action, icily recorded, "In what way the Council could have come to this conclusion it is difficult to conceive, except on the grounds of might overcoming right."[11]

Much of Trinity's financial resources during the 1780s had to be directed toward rebuilding the main parish church, which had been destroyed in the fire of 1776, and not until 1795–96 could its wealth begin to be used for the benefit of the entire diocese. The rambling diocese of New York certainly could have used the help. It stretched all the way from Manhattan Island to the shores of Lake Erie and the St. Lawrence River, and it contained the lush, comparatively rock-free soil of the upstate region, which was increasingly becoming a lure for land-hungry New Englanders. The need to extend the Episcopal Church upstate was seen as a priority both by the vestry of Trinity and by many of its individual parishioners. The account of Daniel Burhans, one of the few active Episcopal clergymen upstate, of the spiritual destitution of Episcopal families in Genesee County (near the Massachusetts border) had prompted the diocesan convention of 1796 to establish a committee of six, all of whom were associated with Trinity, to assist in the missionizing of the state of New York.[12] In the same year Trinity instituted its practice of generously sharing its bounty, through grants and loans, with other Episcopal congregations around the state.[13]

Yet money alone could not revive the Episcopal Church. The case of Duanesburgh in Schenectady County helps illustrate this. The vast

10. For an account of this dispute, see Dix, *History of Trinity*, 2:1–19, and Berrian, *Sketch of Trinity*, 162–63.

11. Berrian, *Sketch of Trinity*, 202.

12. Arthur Lowndes, ed., *The Archives of the General Convention . . . The Correspondence of John Henry Hobart*, 6 vols. (New York, 1911–12), 2:242–44.

13. For a list of Trinity's contributions, see Berrian, *Sketch of Trinity*, 366–86.

inland empire of upstate New York could not help but attract the notice of those whom Dixon Ryan Fox has labeled the "aristocracy of New York." The desire of this group was not simply to profit, but also to reproduce familiar institutions, "and in no particular was its expression more clear than in its cherishment of 'the Episcopal mode of worship.'"[14] James Duane, first mayor of New York and a vestryman at Trinity, who had acquired 50,000 acres of land in Schenectady County, was one such "aristocrat." He contributed eight hundred pounds for the construction of Christ Church, Duanesburgh, in 1793. A rector was soon acquired, and through the generosity of Trinity (three hundred pounds) and Duane's heirs (three hundred pounds) a parsonage was quickly provided. Yet a missionary report in 1803 showed that of the two thousand people in the town only twelve or fifteen were Episcopalians. The Presbyterians, Quakers, Universalists, Methodists, and Baptists were all larger in numbers than the moribund Christ Church, now with a decaying parsonage and no clergyman.[15] What appeared to be lacking in Duanesburgh was not material resources but rather a clear sense of the self-identity of the church and an understanding of its purpose and role, particularly in relation to the other denominations.[16]

Even in places where the church revived and grew in the years following the war, this broader question of the role of the Episcopal Church, both in relation to other religious groups and also to the newly established republic, had to be faced. One of the few upstate churches to revive was St. Peter's, Albany, under the leadership of Thomas Ellison, a native Englishman and Cambridge graduate. Under Ellison's tutelage two important figures of the antebellum republic were to be educated: William Jay, the great abolitionist, and James Fenimore Cooper, the novelist. The accomplishments of Thomas Ellison should not be underestimated.[17] Yet the recollection of Ellison found in Cooper's *Sketches of England* illuminates the limitations of his ministry. He was the "epitome of the national prejudices, and in some respect the national character" of England—a man who scorned dissenters and all "ungentlemanly sects." He was "particularly severe on

14. Dixon Ryan Fox, *The Decline of Aristocracy in the Politics of New York*, (New York, 1919), 137.

15. *Archives*, 3:148.

16. This is clearly implied in further correspondence, where a missionary reported that the church suffered from the "indefatigable industry of the Presbyterians." *Archives*, 4:350.

17. For an account of his labors, see DeMille, *Diocese of Albany*, 26–31.

the immoralities of the French Revolution, and though eating our bread, was not especially lenient to our own; . . . [He was] particularly tenacious of the ritual and of all the decencies of the Church; detested a democrat as he did the devil; cracked his jokes daily about Mr. Jefferson . . . prayed fervently on Sunday, and decried all morals, institutions, churches, manners, and laws but those of England from Monday to Saturday."[18] In short, Ellison was a good English vicar transported to the wilds of upstate New York. Quaintly attractive as it might appear, Ellison's English vicar, however, did little to reflect the political and institutional changes that had recast both the nation and the church since the 1760s. A clergyman such as Ellison could never serve as an adequate model of ministry for the young Episcopal Church.

If the concept of "suspended animation" is to have any value in describing the state of the Episcopal Church in the last decade of the eighteenth century, then perhaps it should be understood as referring not simply to institutional reorganization but rather to a paucity of ideas, models, and metaphors that could hold a group together and provide them with a perceived identity and a vision of their role in the new society. Viewed from this perspective the concept accurately describes the troubled state of affairs.

II

In that same year of 1798, while Timothy Dwight preached and Samuel Provoost translated, William White ordained to the diaconate a young man of only twenty-two years of age, John Henry Hobart. Since so much of the high church revival revolved around the lives and thoughts of Hobart and his associates, a discussion of their early life and education can shed important light on later questions and controversies.

White had known Hobart for most of the latter's twenty-two years and had both baptized and confirmed him. Indeed he would live long enough to also consecrate him to the episcopacy and finally to mourn his death. Hobart was born September 14, 1775, in Philadelphia, of old Puritan stock. His family had been Episcopalian for two generations, in large part through the influence of a Swedish Lutheran grand-

18. Cited in Bayard Tuckerman, *William Jay and the Constitutional Movement for the Abolition of Slavery* (New York, 1894), 2–3.

mother.[19] His father, Captain Enoch Hobart, a West Indies merchant, died only a year later, leaving the infant to the care of his mother, Hannah Pratt Hobart.

Hannah Pratt Hobart provided the earliest and perhaps the deepest lesson of religious instruction for the young Hobart. A notebook of her favorite hymns has survived which provides an insight into the household piety of the family. Anglicanism in the eighteenth century was not known for its piety; it has been characterized as an age that was "unpropitious for the development of religious ardor and adoration" and that sought to reduce revelation to the limits of the rational and to emphasize morality.[20] Yet such generalizations have little to do with the devotional rhythm of the Hobart family. Hymns such as "Jesu who from thy Father's throne / To this low vale of tears come down" and "Jesu how soon didst thou begin / to bleed and suffer for our sin" reflect an emotional and personal intensity foreign to the rounded tones of a Tillotson or an Addison. Such sentiments could have been the products of the Wesleys or the German pietists, but they actually reflect an earlier spirit of English devotionalism. These lines are probably the product of John Austin's *Devotions,* a seventeenth-century English convert to Roman Catholicism, and were likely transcribed from an edition revised in 1696 by Theophilus Dorrington.[21] The hymns share the emotional appeal of Wesleyan and pietist hymnody, yet through them the listener is directed not to a conversion but rather to perceive a web of grace operating particularly through the ordinances of the church. Thus the eucharist is described

> Praise him who has thy pastor's bid
> ever to do what he once did,
> and thankfully his gifts receive.

19. *Archives,* 1:cii. Swedish Lutherans shared with Anglicans an episcopal polity, and in the colonial period not only individual Lutherans but even entire congregations became Episcopalian.

20. Horton Davies, *Worship and Theology in England: From Watts and Wesley to Maurice* (Princeton, 1961), 59. For a discussion of the more positive elements of eighteenth-century English church life, see Norman Sykes, *Church and State in England in the Eighteenth Century* (1934; Hamden, Ct., 1962), 231–83.

21. Hannah Pratt Notebook, Miscellaneous Correspondence, New-York Historical Society, New York. Austin's *Devotions* were frequently republished, often in the edition edited by the English Nonjuror George Hickes. On some themes in seventeenth-century English devotionalism, see G. W. O. Addleshaw, *The High Church Tradition: A Study in the Liturgical Thought of the Seventeenth Century* (London, [1941]).

Sing loud that to this bounteous feast,
each hungry soul must be a guest,
And from his death may life derive.

These themes in the language of piety—a fervent appeal to the affections of the heart and a holiness that grows through grace by means of
the church's ordinances—would constantly sound in the works of the
mature Hobart. Throughout his career, critics would fault him for the
emotionalism of his piety, and many would dismiss it as methodism,
without ever realizing where its true roots were to be found.

His formal education was begun by the Rev. John Andrew at the
Episcopal academy of Philadelphia. One of the fine classicists of his
day, Andrew carefully taught the young man the rudiments of a logic
that appeared to have little in common with the piety Hobart had
earlier absorbed. Instead Hobart learned that ideas were derived from
sensation and reflection and that simple ideas existed in the mind under
one uniform appearance without variety or composition, while complex ideas were derived arbitrarily from without or formed by the
understanding itself.[22]

In 1788 he entered the College of Philadelphia, and in 1791 he
transferred to Princeton, then often referred to as Nassau Hall. He
graduated in 1793. The Princeton of John Witherspoon and Samuel
Stanhope Smith was at the time probably the most influential college
in the middle or southern states, a bastion of both Calvinistic Presbyterianism and the new Scottish Common Sense philosophy
brought over by Witherspoon.[23] Smith and Hobart became good
friends, yet how much the former's philosophy influenced Hobart is
difficult to assess. There is little evidence that he rejected the philosophical instruction at Princeton, and indeed he even read Thomas
Reid, yet his later career and writing manifest little of the lines of
Smith's moral philosophy.[24] If the influence of the Princeton philo-

22. John Henry Hobart, Lecture Notes on John Andrew's Elements of Logic
[Dec., 1789], Miscellaneous Correspondence, New-York Historical Society.

23. On Smith's philosophy and the influence of Scottish Common Sense on
American education, see Elizabeth Flower and Murray G. Murphey, *A History of
American Philadelphia,* 2 vols. (New York, 1977), 97 1:310–11, 318–29. On Princeton during this period, see Thomas J. Wertenbaker, *Princeton 1746–1896* (Princeton,
1946). Howard Miller, *The Revolutionary College: American Presbyterian Higher Education 1707–1837* (New York, 1976), has some astute observations on the shifting
concept of Presbyterian education during this period.

24. On Hobart's reading of Reid, see William Berrian, ed., *The Posthumous Works
of the Late Right Reverend John Henry Hobart . . . with a Memoir of his Life . . . ,* 3 vols.
(New York, 1832–33), 1:53 (hereafter referred to as *Works*).

sophical heritage was minor, the effect of its theological tradition was not. His contact with Calvinism and Presbyterianism only confirmed him in his loyalty to free will and episcopacy. Writing a decade later, he recalled how the conflict between the respect in which he held his instructors and his loyalty to episcopacy "excited in my bosom a painful struggle between the most amiable impulses of feeling and the strong demands of duty."[25]

After an unsuccessful attempt at working in his brother-in-law's business office, Hobart accepted an invitation to return to Princeton as a tutor. While at Princeton this second time, Hobart became close friends with two other persons who along with him would play an active role in the revival of Episcopal apologetical theology.

Frederick Beasley, born in North Carolina in 1777, entered Princeton in 1793. He is now best remembered for his spirited loyalty to the philosophy of John Locke and his pointed dismissal of Scottish philosophy because of "its pretensions to have corrected the eminent Locke."[26] His career, however, was long and varied. He was ordained to the Episcopal priesthood in 1801, after having studied theology with Stanhope Smith and having been a Princeton tutor for two years. Later he would serve numerous pastorates, a fifteen-year stint as provost of the University of Pennsylvania, and as editor of the posthumous works of Stanhope Smith. What would draw Beasley and Hobart together was not a love of Locke but a common desire to defend episcopacy.

Thomas Yardley How completed this triumverate of young Princetonians. Perhaps the most brilliant of the three, he was clearly the most controversial. He possessed Hobart's intensity, yet his sharper mind was quick to push subtle distinctions further, often ignoring propriety and tact. His sharpness was offset neither by Hobart's warmth of piety nor by Beasley's academic donnishness, and it continually left him open to the charge of Pharisaism. One of his contemporary critics described him as standing "preeminent as a polemical

25. John Henry Hobart, *An Apology for Apostolic Order and its Advocates,* 2d ed. (New York, 1844), 35.

26. Flower and Murphey, *American Philosophy,* 1:306. For a biographical sketch of Beasley, see William Sprague, ed., *Annals of the American Pulpit,* 9 vols. (New York, 1859–69), 5:477–84. Any mention of Hobart's Princeton friends must also include Charles Fenton Mercer (1778–1858), whose long and varied career included military and political service as well as an active role in the Colonization Society. His correspondence with Hobart sheds important light upon the thought world of the young Hobart. Much is reprinted in John McVickar, *The Early Life and Professional Years of Bishop Hobart* (Oxford, 1838)

writer but void of every principle of religion or decorum."[27] Unfortunately an inopportune sex scandal involving his servant girl not only
cut short his ecclesiastical career but also has robbed us of many
important biographical details.[28] He was probably a native of Princeton, who entered Nassau Hall in 1790. There he began his friendship
with Hobart and Beasley. Although having an early predilection for
the ministry, How instead chose law for a profession, and he probably
studied with Alexander Hamilton. A business venture led him to
Brownville, a town in Jefferson County in upstate New York. From
there he would add his pen to those of Hobart and Beasley in the
opening apologetical clashes in the first decade of the nineteenth
century.

From as early as June 1794 Hobart had pondered entering the
ministry, though always with a degree of self-doubt as to his own
worthiness.[29] He used his tenure as tutor to carry out his theological
studies. At Princeton the young candidate for Episcopal orders dutifully led Presbyterian chapel service (an action that would have
brought down the wrath of the later bishop), attended the theological
lectures of Stanhope Smith, and through hours of informal disputation drilled himself in the apologetical defense of episcopacy.

Hobart naturally had to look outside of Presbyterian Princeton for
instruction in the peculiarly Anglican aspects of his theological education. For this purpose William White in 1798 gave him a list of books
to aid him in the study of divinity. Through this list Hobart gained a
window into the wide spectrum of Anglican thought.

The preceding century had not been a placid one in the history of
English theology.[30] From the very beginning of the Restoration differ-

27. John Pintard, *Letters from John Pintard . . . 1816–1833*, 4 vols. (New York,
1940–41), 1:113.

28. Contrasting contemporary accounts of the scandal can be found in Pintard,
Letters, 1:113, and in a letter from John Henry Hobart to Rufus King, 30 March
1818, Rufus King Papers, New-York Historical Society. The closest thing to a
biography of How is the sketch of him found in *Archives*, 5:435–37. Most of the
biographical details included here come from that source.

29. See the letters printed in McVickar, *Hobart*, 103.

30. The literature concerning English religious trends of this period is immen-
se. In addition to the Sykes and Davies volumes cited above, perhaps the best
surveys of the period are: Gerald Cragg, *From Puritanism to the Age of Reason: A Study
of Changes in Religious Thought Within the Church of England, 1660–1700* (Cambridge,
1950); John Hunt, *Religious Thought in England from the Reformation to the End of the
Last Century . . .* , 3 vols. (London, 1870–73), particularly volumes 2 and 3; and
Leslie Stephen, *History of English Thought in the Eighteenth Century*, 2 vols. (New

ent understandings of the nature of Anglicanism quickly emerged. Many of the bishops and divines who returned to power with the restoration of Charles II desired to create an intellectual bulwark that would once and for all protect their church from any assault upon either its Arminianism or its polity. To this end they often elevated the normative importance of the early church—particularly the eastern branch, where they could have their episcopacy untroubled by those gnawing questions of grace and free will found in the western Augustine, and in which they saw the seeds of the noxious Calvinism. The works of John Pearson on Ignatius of Antioch and George Bull on the Nicene Creed, in which patristic scholarship effortlessly fades into apologetics, best reflect this approach. Yet competing with this High Church patristic theology was another quite different approach, with another vision of the Church of England. Revolting from the intolerance and violence of the preceding decades, the Cambridge Platonists saw a church that could be comprehensive in its nature and that, while shunning the materialism of a Thomas Hobbes, might be open to the new trends in science and philosophy. Their successors, the Latitudinarians, represented in a person like John Tillotson, readily accepted their emphasis upon reasonableness, moderation, and comprehension, yet eschewed the metaphysics of the Platonists. They were aided in their task by the philosophical principles outlined by John Locke in both his *Essay Concerning Human Understanding* and his venture into Christology, the *Reasonableness of Christianity,* which led them away from a defense of religion and morality on the grounds of any innate propensity and into an empirical search for evidences.[31] The presence on their theological left of a party of Deists, who found

York, 1876). Norman Sykes, *From Sheldon to Secker: Aspects of English Church History, 1660–1768* (Cambridge, 1959), and *Edmund Gibson, Bishop of London, 1669–1748: A Study in Politics and Religion in the Eighteenth Century* (London, 1926), are both important for any understanding of the period. John H. Overton and Frederic Relton, *The English Church, From the Accession of George I. to the End of the Eighteenth Century* (London, 1906), still provides much useful information. Owen Chadwick, *From Bossuet to Newman: The Idea of Doctrinal Development* (Cambridge, 1957), 74–95, has some useful reflections on the High Church patristic position; John Tulloch, *Rational Theology and Christian Philosophy in England in the Seventeenth Century,* 2 vols. (London, 1872), is illuminating on the Cambridge Platonists; and Martin Griffin, "Latitudinarianism in the Seventeenth-Century Church of England" (Ph.D. diss., Yale University, 1963), is a good treatment of the Latitudinarian movement.

31. John Yolton, *John Locke and the Way of Ideas* ([London], 1956), 115 ff. On this issue, see also Margaret Jacob, *The Newtonians and the English Revolution, 1689–1720* (Ithaca, N.Y., 1976).

no value in revealed religion at all, gave further impetus for gen
tions of divines to harp upon the themes of the reasonablenes;
revealed religion and the manifold evidences of the Christian faith.

The political history of England only further complicated the
scene. Many of the stricter High Church bishops and writers continued in their loyalty to the house of Stuart and became Nonjurors
after the Revolution of 1688. Except during the reign of Queen Anne
(1702–14), the Latitudinarian party, with its emphasis upon reasonableness, morality, and a pragmatic rather than principled defense of
episcopacy, held sway in the most influential pulpits and sees of the
English church. The Bangorian controversy, with its debate over the
authority of the church, manifested to all who had eyes to see where
the true power in the Church of England lay. George I's decision to
suspend convocation (the legislative assembly of the church) rather
than see it condemn the doctrines of one of his ecclesiastical favorites,
Benjamin Hoadley, was a serious blow to the lingering High Church
understanding of the nature of the Church of England.[32] For much of
the century the few high churchmen to rise to the episcopacy were
political Whigs like John Potter, who did not allow ecclesiastical theory to interfere with the day-to-day working of the church.

An awareness of the nuances of the English theological scene is
necessary in order to make sense of some of the later American debates, but the divisions should not be overemphasized. Two basic
principles undergird the thought of almost all of these individuals.
The first was a rejection of Calvinism. However little they might have
had in common, John Tillotson, the great Latitudinarian, and Charles
Leslie, the great Nonjuror, both would have gladly danced on the
grave of John Calvin. Until the rekindling of interest in Calvinism that
accompanied the midcentury Evangelical revival, major Anglican religious figures were largely united in their defense of the freedom of
the will and their opposition to the five points to which Calvinism had
been reduced. They criticized Calvinism for its tendency toward fanaticism, for its undermining of the moral nature, and for its susceptibili-
ty to metaphysics and speculation. The critique of it by an early nineteenth-century Episcopalian, "They labour to be wise above what is
written; they boldly attempt to fathom the unrevealed counsels of the

32. On the Bangorian controversy, see Sykes, *Church and State*, 332–78; also
his, *William Wake, Archbishop of Canterbury, 1657–1737*, 2 vols. (Cambridge, 1957),
1:141–46; and George Every, *The High Church Party, 1688–1718* (London, 1956),
which presents a good discussion of ecclesiastical politics during the period.

Godhead," only echoed a century of Anglican criticism.[33] Further-more, most of these Anglican writers agreed on the necessity of basing religious authority on reasoned consent and in opposing any hint of fideism, or reliance on unreasoned faith. Decades of responding to a distinct genre of Catholic apologetic that argued that there could be no middle ground between Catholicism and scepticism had made most Anglican writers defensive of the power of human reason.[34] Tillotson perhaps gave the most succinct formulation of this sentiment: "All revelation from God supposeth us to be men and to be endued with reason, and therefore it does not create new faculties within us, but propounds new objects to that faculty which was in us before." Yet even the Nonjuring Leslie could gladly affirm, "I receive the Scrip-tures upon the testimony, not authority of the Church; and I examine that testimony as I do other facts, until I have satisfied my private judgement there is no other way."[35]

William White attempted to impress upon Hobart both of these principles, since he personally had little sympathy for either the Cal-vinistic propensity toward system building or for any faith grounded on unreasoned consent.[36] The evidence suggests that the student Hobart learned his lesson well. Writing to a friend he remarked, "Dr. [Stanhope] Smith, who is very attentive to me, seems to wish that I should begin to study his system of divinity; but I am entirely opposed to studying any system whatever, till I understand more of that sacred volume from which all their conclusions, if just, must be drawn. . . . Dr. White earnestly recommends to me to study the Bible, to form my opinions."[37]

In the context of eighteenth-century Anglicanism the theological book list that White supplied in 1798 becomes a revealing document. It

33. Thomas Y. How, *A Vindication of the Protestant Episcopal Church* . . . (New York, 1816), 229.

34. On the influence of this sceptical argument on Catholic apologetics, see Richard C. Popkin, *The History of Scepticism from Erasmus to Descartes* (Assen, 1960), 66–87. For an analysis of the classic Anglican answer to this argument, see Robert R. Orr, *Reason and Authority: The Thought of William Chillingworth* (Oxford, 1967), 45–70.

35. Tillotson, *The Works of Dr. John Tillotson* . . . , 10 vols. (London, 1820), 2:257; Leslie cited in Stephen, *English Thought*, 1:196, who also emphasizes Leslie's rationalism.

36. On White, see Sydney A. Temple, Jr., *The Common Sense Theology of Bishop White* (New York, 1946), particularly 86–104.

37. McVickar, *Hobart*, 144.

provided Hobart with a spectrum of what was for White the acceptable Anglican theological tradition. John Woolverton has astutely noted that White was particularly concerned with forging a broadly unified view of the history or Anglicanism that could hold under a common umbrella of continuity the separate theological distinctions.[38] Nowhere is this striving for unity more clearly seen than in his course of study recommended to Hobart. In all the chief foci of theological education—scriptural study, systematic divinity, church history, liturgy—ox and ass are yoked together in a way that would have made even Odysseus pause. The second generation Cambridge Platonist Simon Patrick is coupled with the radical Latitudinarian Daniel Whitby, and both are listed along with the Nonjuror Leslie, the Caroline High Churchman George Bull, and the Erastian Benjamin Hoadley. Representatives of nearly all of the movements in Anglican religious thought since the Restoration were eclectically, if not blithely, united in White's list. Anti-Calvinism based on a fear of fanaticism, a concern for the moral nature of man, a distrust in metaphysics, and a shared agreement on reasoned consent are the only common principles holding the list together. For this reason it is significant that the only figure from the English Reformation that White included is Richard Hooker. The moralistically grounded anti-Calvinism, which was a shared presupposition of most eighteenth-century Episcopalians, allowed for little sympathy with the actual teachings of the English Reformers and their preoccupation with Reformation era questions of grace. The Great Awakening and the Methodist schism had made American Episcopalians not only less tolerant of enthusiasm than ever, but also more anxiously protective of the freedom of the reasoned will. The Reformation perspective of a John Whitgift in the Lambeth Articles, which defended predestination, or in the views of other sixteenth-century English Reformers seemed strange and foreign to post-1660 Anglicans. For White, the intellectual heritage of the Anglican communion was more a product of the seventeenth and eighteenth centuries than of the sixteenth.[39]

38. Woolverton, "Philadelphia's William White," 284–87, 295. A copy of White's list is printed in *Archives,* 2:128–31.

39. White of course was not alone in this preference for post-1660 writers over Reformation sources. It was a common attitude among Connecticut Episcopal writers of the eighteenth century. See in particular John Beach, *God's Sovereignty and His Universal Love to Men Reconciled . . .* (Boston, 1747). For a bibliography of the eighteenth-century evidence, see Hector Kinloch, "Anglican Clergy in Connecticut

In his attempt to form a synthetic Anglican theological tradition White made one of his most important contributions to the intellectual development of the young Episcopal Church. The list given to Hobart became the nucleus of a more complete course of ecclesiastical study approved by the General Convention of 1804. The 1804 list assumed a kind of authoritative status for many Episcopalians and served as the definition of the bounds of acceptable theological opinion.[40] It remained, however, simply an eclectic accumulation of opinions. Many a writer who tried to set forth a consistent Episcopal theological position from the works cited on the list came ruefully to realize that reconciling the creedal teachings of the High Church Pearson and the Erastian Hoadley was a Herculean task. Many an English writer was amused at this eclectic use of the Anglican theological heritage. As one writer explained to an English audience, "[These Americans] think that nothing but good can come from the Church of their fathers."[41]

The eclectic authorities carefully enumerated by White would serve as one strand of the Hobartian theological milieu, yet a second strand would be derived from a group of writers who either were not included in Bishop White's list of 1798 or who, though included, lost their distinctiveness in the eclectic nature of White's canon of authorities. The continuing voice of the strict High Church party that had refused to disband despite the political reverses earlier in the century is now but a footnote in the history of English theology, yet these men had an enormous influence on the developing thought of Hobart and his associates. Their vigorous apologetical defense of episcopacy served well in the rough and tumble world of religious controversy.[42]

1701–1785" (Ph.D. diss., Yale University, 1959), 222 ff. The theological ramifications of this abandonment of the Reformation perspective are ably discussed by C. F. Allison in *The Rise of Moralism: The Proclamation of the Gospel from Hooker to Baxter* (London, 1966).

40. An example of this, from as late as the 1840s, is the use the Episcopal bishop of Vermont, John Henry Hopkins, made of White's list to prescribe the limits of acceptable interpretations of the Articles of Religion. See *A Reply to a Letter of Dr. Seabury . . .* (New York, 1846).

41. "The American Church," *The British Critic and Quarterly Theological Review* 26 (1839):340. Published anonymously, this essay was written by John Henry Newman. See "The Anglo-American Church," in John Henry Newman, *Essays Critical and Historical,* 2 vols. (London, 1901), 1:309–86.

42. The following discussion is necessarily foreshortened. It does not attempt to characterize the whole history of the continuing High Church movement during the eighteenth century, but rather to emphasize those aspects of the wider story that

Four individuals in particular constitute the core of this group.[43] Three of these men were closely associated with each other: George Horne (1730–92), who successively served as vice-chancellor of Oxford, dean of Canterbury, and finally bishop of Norwich; William Jones of Nayland (1726–1800), chaplain and biographer of Horne; and William Stevens (1732–1807), a layman, cousin of Horne, and biographer of Jones. All three shared a common fascination with the linguistic theory of John Hutchinson, which claimed that Hebrew was the most primitive of all the languages and that moreover it could provide the key to natural philosophy. In common with other Hutchinsonians these men shared a distrust of much of the popular confidence in natural religion as an independent vehicle of revelation. Perhaps through the influence of Hutchinson, all of these men were suspicious of speculative theology and chose rather to tie their writings closely to scriptural and early church evidence.[44] More important, however, along with Charles Daubeny (1745–1827), archdeacon of Salisbury, they attempted to keep alive the theological flame of the older, Nonjuror tradition, while carefully dissociating it from political heterodoxy.

Perhaps the most important work emanating from this group was a collection of essays edited by William Jones entitled *The Scholar Armed Against the Errors of the Time* (1792). The work included not only Jones's own "Essay on the Church," but also contributions from George Horne, Charles Leslie, and the Nonjuring mystic William Law. Although *The Scholar Armed* did include defenses of the evi-

---

most directly influenced American development. A case could be made for including John Potter in such a discussion, since his *Discourse On Church Government* (1707) had a wide American circulation during the early decades of the nineteenth century. Yet it was often circulated in a form abridged by William Stevens, under the title *A Treatise on the Nature and Constitution of the Christian Church* (London, 1773). For a more complete account of the English situation, see A. J. Mason, *The Church of England and Episcopacy* (Cambridge, 1914), 227–448.

43. For an affectionate account of this circle, see W. K. Lowther Clarke, *Eighteenth-Century Piety* (London, 1944), 101–17.

44. For a discussion of these themes in Hutchinson and their importance for High Church writers, see William Jones's preface to the second edition of *The Works of the Right Reverend George Horne, D.D. . . . ,* 6 vols. (London, 1830), 1:vi–x, and in particular the suspicion Jones had for metaphysics and speculative theories in general. The most well known American Hutchinsonian was the convert to Anglicanism Samuel Johnson, first president of King's College. See Ellis, *New England Mind in Transition,* 228–32. As will be suggested in chapter 3, this Hutchinsonian emphasis would have a marked effect on American high church theology.

dences of Christianity, the constitution of the church, and the authority of civil government, what actually characterizes this collection is its strong defense of the visible church. The church was not a voluntary society erected by men but rather a society ordained of God, with its authority derived not from men but from God alone:

> The church must have orders in it for the work of the ministry; but no man can ordain himself, neither can he (of himself) ordain another, because no man can give what he hath not. . . . No ambassador ever sent himself, or took upon him to sign and seal treaties or covenants . . . without being sent; that is, without receiving authority so to do from an higher power. The act would be so far from beneficial, that it would be treasonable.[45]

The acceptance of the visible, historical church was as essential for the believer as any right belief. The promise of God was not a general promise but a specific promise to a specific body, his church. As William Law observed, "If there be no uninterrupted succession, then there are no authorized ministers of Christ; if no such ministers, then no Christian sacraments; if no Christian sacraments then no Christian convenant, whereof the sacraments are the stated and visible seals."[46]

The "errors of the time" naturally included the extremes of the French Revolution. Yet in reacting to the French situation, Jones and Daubeny differed greatly with many of their contemporaries. Anglican evangelicals such as William Wilberforce responded by forming organizations such as the Society for the Suppression of Vice, organizing Sunday schools, and generally by emphasizing a spirit of Protestant cooperation that emphasized social outreach rather than traditional points of theological contention.[47] For Daubeny and Jones, however, the solution to the disorder of the French Revolution was not in Wilberforce's new spirit of evangelical cooperation but in a more faithful cleaving to the divine institution of the church. In answering Wilberforce, Daubeny argued that

> The Church is not merely a number of people, agreeing in the same articles of faith, or in the same acts of religious worship; but it is moreover a society, holding one visible communion under the same divinely constituted government: a society not of man's but of

45. *The Scholar Armed Against the Errors of the Time* . . . 2 vols., 2d ed. (London, 1800), 2:19–20.
46. Ibid., 1:286.
47. See the discussion in Foster, *Errand of Mercy*, 28–38; and Ford K. Brown, *Fathers of the Victorians: The Age of Wilberforce* (Cambridge, 1961), passim.

Christ's forming; a society of spiritual incorporation of which he is the head, and all individual Christians, who have been regularly admitted into it, the members.[48]

Anything less than actual membership in the visible church was simply a form of schism for Daubeny. The "error of the time" that most concerned Jones and Daubeny was a perceived loss of the certainty of authority. A continuing theme in their writings was the idea that religious authority must be linearly traceable back to God. Their faith in the historical pedigree of episcopacy buttressed their confidence in the "divinely instituted" church as the best means for bringing order and stability, since through it alone God had promised to act. Throughout the pages of *The Anti-Jacobin Review,* a journal founded in 1798 to defend conservative interests in church and state, Daubeny attacked Wilberforce's and the evangelical movement's deemphasis of the issue of the visible church.[49]

As a group these high church apologists not only kept alive the ideas of the older, Nonjuring tradition, but also materially aided brother high churchmen whenever they could. They befriended the Scottish Nonjuring bishops, when, in 1791, they journeyed to London to plead their case to the royal sovereign, whom they had three years earlier finally recognized; and they assisted the American Anglican expatriates Jonathan Boucher and Thomas B. Chandler during the American Revolution.[50] Furthermore, they took a lively interest in American Episcopal Church life. When Samuel Seabury journeyed to England in 1783 seeking consecration to the episcopacy, they arranged for him an annual income of fifty pounds.[51] It is small wonder that the works of these English writers soon found their way across the Atlantic. In the late 1780s William Stevens began sending to Seabury some of their works.[52] Yet the precise channels through which these works entered American circulation remain unclear. Jones's "Essay on the Church" was known in Vermont as early as 1793–94. Upon perusing it, J. C. Ogden, an Episcopal clergyman, was so impressed by its importance that he sacrificed the money he had set aside for a new

48. Charles Daubeny, *A Guide to the Church* . . . (New York, 1803), 41.

49. On this question, see Brown, *Fathers of the Victorians* 172–76.

50. T. T. Carter, *Undercurrents of Church Life in the Eighteenth Century* (London, 1899), 208.

51. Bruce Steiner, *Samuel Seabury, 1729–1796: A Study in the High Church Tradition* (Oberlin, Ohio, 1971), 362.

52. Ibid., 363.

winter coat and with it arranged for the printing of an inexpensive edition of the essay. Another contemporary testified to the work's appeal: "The little, short, thick tract was printed and much good did it do. It told us what the world is, and what the church of God is—how to find the latter, and how to know the wicked nature of the other."[53] Daubeny's *View of the Church* was introduced to America in 1801 by John Bowden, the head of the Episcopal academy in Cheshire, Connecticut. Writing to Daubeny, Bowden emphasized how important works such as his were: "We are determined that it shall be a standard for all our candidates for holy orders. Clergymen brought up at the feet of Leslie, Horne, Jones, and Daubeny, will not fail to be orthodox in their faith, pure in their lives, and zealous to promote the kingdom of Christ."[54]

Both of these theological streams—the eclectic approach of William White and the apologetic approach of the English high churchmen—would combine in the theological world of the young John Henry Hobart. Together they formed an intellectual-theological milieu that stood in marked contrast with the theological world of the rest of American Protestantism. Hobart's attempt to work out an American high church synthesis from these two theological streams would lead him far astray from the world of Timothy Dwight and Lyman Beecher. Anti-Calvinism and a concern for the church would spur him and his associates onward, in the same way as moral reform and revivalism would inspire the rising evangelical united front. The clash between them would entail a contest between two distinct views of the essence of a common faith.

III

Such was the theological world Hobart entered upon receiving the right of ordination from the hands of William White, June 3, 1798.[55] If there were present at that event any seers into the future they must have smiled at the text chosen for the ordination sermon: Proverbs 3.17,

53. Philander Chase, *Reminiscences* . . . 2 vols., 2d ed. (Boston, 1848), 1:17–18. Chase continued to have a high opinion of Jones and made a special visit to his church during Chase's trip to England in the 1820s, ibid., 1:385–86.

54. Cited in E. Edward Beardsley, *The History of the Episcopal Church in Connecticut,* 2 vols. (New York, 1868–69), 2:23.

55. McVickar, *Hobart,* 152. The date is mistakenly printed as 1808.

"Her ways are ways of pleasantness, and her paths are peace." Hobart's subsequent career was anything but pleasant or peaceful.

For less than a year after his ordination he served two small country churches outside of Philadelphia, and in May 1799 he left to take charge of Christ Church, New Brunswick, New Jersey. Whether he left Philadelphia with a broken heart—having been spurned by a young lady named Sophie Duche, the daughter of a fellow clergyman—is unknown, but if he did his heart quickly mended.[56] He soon became enamored of Mary Goodin Chandler, whom he married in 1800. In Mary Chandler, Hobart found not only a life companion, but also a further connecting link to the wider Anglican heritage. Her father, Thomas B. Chandler (1726–90), had been one of the most important colonial Anglican clerics in the north and a leader in the fight for a colonial episcopate. It has already been mentioned how as an expatriate he had been befriended by the English High Church circle of Jones and Horne. Returning to America in 1785, he reassumed his prewar pulpit and served there until his death five years later. Had Chandler lived to know Hobart, the older clergyman might have taught the young deacon many things. It is not unlikely, however, that Hobart learned from Chandler indirectly, through the memory of Mary Chandler Hobart. Hobart's eventual program for Episcopal church growth parallels Chandler's views of the state of the colonial church written fifty years earlier:

> The church seems to be in a state neither of increasing, nor losing ground, in regard to its numbers. This appears to me to be in some measure owing to that general harmony and good understanding which subsists between the Church and the Dissenters. The points in controversy between us, some years ago, were disputed with warmth and some degree of animosity. Then the Church visibly gained ground. But these disputes have, for some time, subsided, and charity, candour, and moderation seem to have been studied, or at least affected by both sides. The Dissenters have become so charitable as to think there is no material difference between the Church and themselves; and consequently that no material advantage is to be had by conforming to the Church; and, under the influence of this opinion, custom and false notion of honour will be an effectual bar against conformity.[57]

The Episcopal Church could not grow unless its distinctiveness was

56. Albright, too, wonders about this. See *History,* 173. On Hobart's affections for Sophie Duche, see *Archives,* 2:95–108.

57. Cited in Sprague, *Annals,* 5:138.

made clear to the entire community. Through his wife, Hobart also inherited the task of editing his late father-in-law's *Life of Samuel Johnson,* a convert from Congregationalism and the leading high church figure in the colonial church. The editing of this work introduced Hobart to the question of the historical roots of the American Episcopal Church. A concern for the historical continuity of the Episcopal community in America would emerge as an important theme in the apologetical theology of Hobart and his circle.

After serving a few months in Hempstead, New York, Hobart accepted a call as an assistant minister at Trinity Church, New York. In 1801, the year of Hobart's ordination to the priesthood, the statistics of the Episcopal General Convention record 206 known ministers, of which number 19 resided in the diocese of New York. Three Episcopal churches served the more than 60,000 inhabitants of New York City—Christ Church, St. Mark's, and Trinity (although Trinity actually possessed three congregations: that of the parish church and those of the two missions of St. Paul's and St. George's). With the resignation of Samuel Provoost in 1801 for health reasons, both the episcopate and the rectorship of Trinity fell into the hands of Benjamin Moore, and Hobart, along with Cave Jones and Abraham Beach, became one of the three assistants.

In the next year, 1802, a Connecticut clergyman named John Bowden (1751–1817) resigned his position as head of the Episcopal academy at Cheshire and accepted the professorship of moral philosophy, belles lettres, and logic at Columbia College. A native of Britain, Bowden had served at Trinity before the Revolution and had supported the British cause during the war. This did not, however, do much to impede his postwar ecclesiastical career. In 1796 he had been elected bishop of Connecticut, although he declined the honor on account of poor health.

Yet Bowden was more than merely a donnish clergyman. His relationship with William Jones and Charles Daubeny has already been mentioned, and, in his devotion to the cause of episcopal apologetics, he became an enthusiastic participant in what would become the Hobartian circle. He was particularly fond of the writings of Charles Leslie, and as one of his students recalled, "From the reading of Leslie's two folios, (which I remember on the shelves to which he resorted for his chief reading,) Dr. Bowden may have derived, certainly he there strengthened, his controversial powers, his clearness in statement, his acuteness of distinction, and his directness of argument."[58] In addition to being a devotee of the English High Church apologetical tradition, he was also a diligent student of ancient ecclesiastical history. Both of these interests would be put to great use in the decades to come. He was not only the oldest and most accomplished, but also probably the most learned of this small circle of clerics.

With the arrival of Bowden upon the scene the dramatis personae were complete. In the first few years of the new century they found themselves congregating in the state of New York. Beasley in 1803 accepted the rectorship of St. Peter's, Albany. How moved to Brownville on business, while Hobart was at Trinity and Bowden at Columbia. Their common theological and apologetical interests lay ready for any spark of controversy that would ignite their energy and enthusiasm in the cause of the defense of their church.

58. Ibid., 5:307.

2

The Public Controversies

THEOLOGICAL CONTROVERSY IN EARLY NINETEENTH-CENTURY AMERICA
had little of the dry, decorous tone that most modern students of
theology have come to expect. Participants saw their role not so much
as that of disinterested academic scholars, but that of modern-day
Achilleses and Hectors, battling over the gates of one denomination or
another, hurling tracts and broadsides against the other with the force
that earlier generations had hurled spears and arrows. The main bat-
tleground of the theologian was apologetics—here he championed the
claims of his community and defended it from assault. It was in just
such a context that Hobart and his circle emerged in the early part of
the century as the champions of Episcopal claims, and their involvement in a series of important religious controversies helped define the
place of the Episcopal Church in antebellum American society.

I

Hobart was never a man to seek a quiet and retired existence. "Nature
has fitted him for a leader," observed one of his contemporaries. "Had
he studied law he would have been upon the bench; in the army a
major-general at least; and in the state, nothing under prime minister."[1] Having chosen none of these areas, but rather the ministry as his
field of endeavor, Hobart busied himself during his early years at
Trinity with the workings of both the parish and the diocese. He was
considered an oddity at first but eventually became quite popular. The

1. McVickar, *Hobart*, 246.

fervent religion which he had inherited from his mother gave to his preaching style an intensity that was unusual in American Episcopal preaching. Sincerity, earnestness, and affection came together in his sermons in a way that sharply contrasted with the dispassionate style theretofore favored by Anglican preachers.[2] Furthermore, Episcopal preachers read their sermons, both to emphasize their prepared nature and also to distance themselves from the extemporaneous preaching of the more enthusiastic denominations. Hobart's eyes were so bad, however, that he could only with great difficulty read a written sermon, and instead he was forced to memorize his texts and to deliver them without notes. For many, the result of this new style of preaching was electrifying. Elizabeth Seton, the first canonized American saint, was one such parishioner devoted to Hobart. "Give [him] a look and a sigh for me," she requested of her sister-in-law, "such as you will for yourself, but mercy is everywhere and my temple is a large one." On still another occasion she enthusiastically wrote, "Willy carried me to the door where I sat one half hour before the bell stopped—then looking up found [Hobart] in the pulpit—such fervent prayers I never heard before."[3]

Hobart furthermore appears to have been one of those strange and rare creatures who thrives in the environment of official committee meetings. In nearly all of the major areas of importance in which the diocese of New York involved itself, Hobart took an active role. In 1799 he became secretary to the House of Bishops; in 1801 he was named to the board of trustees of Columbia College as well as in the same year being chosen as a delegate to the Episcopal General Convention; in 1802 he helped to establish the Protestant Episcopal Society for the Promotion of Religion and Learning in the State of New York; in 1806 he helped to found the Protestant Episcopal Theological Society, and his role in the forming of the New York Protestant Episcopal Bible and Common Prayer Book Society in 1809 will be discussed below. Throughout his long ministry he would continually organize new committees and societies.

Perhaps Hobart's greatest contribution to the diocese of New York, however, and indeed to the church at large, was his role as ombudsman. For this role Hobart was both constitutionally suited and geographically well placed. Throughout his life he had a gift for

2. Ibid., 185–86.
3. Mary K. Flanagan, "The Influence of John Henry Hobart on the Life of Elizabeth Ann Seton" (Ph.D. diss., Union Theological Seminary, 1978), 159.

accumulating loyal friends (a quality his critics were quick to label as clique or party building). In the early years of the nineteenth century he rapidly built up a large group of correspondents. They corresponded furthermore on the major ecclesiastical issues of the day, and they sought Hobart's opinion on questions of both theology and church practice. In addition, the centrality and wealth of the Episcopal Church in New York attracted various requests for different types of assistance from as far south as Maryland. Books in particular were in high demand. Missionaries and rural clergy regularly requested Prayer Books and catechisms as well as Daubeny's *Guide to the Church* and *The Scholar Armed* and other English High Church standards.[4] Yet from some missionaries came the warning that the standard English theological works had only limited appeal on the frontier. As one missionary noted, "However fond I am in having the Doctrines, Disciplines, and Worship of the Church vindicated, yet I prefer works of piety and devotion. These hit the heart and have a more lasting effect than all the arguments which can be used."[5] The need for both apologetical and devotional literature was regularly voiced by Hobart's many correspondents.

Yet these clerics did more than simply request books: they also shared with Hobart their observations and insights concerning the religious situation in their different regions. The first decade of the nineteenth century witnessed a great period of revival within American Protestantism, labeled by later historians as the Second Great Awakening.[6] From Timothy Dwight at Yale College to James McGready on the frontier in Kentucky, the American churches percolated with a renewed intensity. England experienced a similar revival, reflected in such persons as Hannah More and the members of the

4. For some examples, see *Archives,* 4:376, 453.

5. *Archives,* 3:190.

6. The whole question of the Second Great Awakening is in the process of being reexamined, and there is not a really good treatment of the movement as a whole. Donald G. Mathews, "The Second Great Awakening as an Organizing Process" (first published in the *American Quarterly* in 1969), gives some important guides for any approach to the period. Regarding aspects of it, see Charles R. Keller, *The Second Great Awakening in Connecticut* (New Haven, 1942); Fred J. Hood, *Reformed America: The Middle and Southern States, 1783–1837* (University, Ala., 1980); Joseph A. Conforti, *Samuel Hopkins and the New Divinity Movement* (Grand Rapids, 1981); Robert L. Ferm, *Jonathan Edwards the Younger, 1745–1801* (Grand Rapids, 1976); and John B. Boles, *The Great Revival, 1787–1805: The Origins of the Southern Evangelical Mind* (Lexington, 1972).

Clapham Sect and manifested in a reawakening of both experimental piety and the reform impulse. An important difference, however, distinguished the American from the English experience. American Protestantism of the eighteenth century, with the exception of Anglicanism, was overwhelmingly Calvinistic and rigorously Calvinistic at that. The Second Great Awakening, it is now generally agreed, actually weakened the authority of strict Calvinism among American Protestants. Both by increasing the size and importance of non-Calvinistic denominations such as the Campbellites and the Methodists and by precipitating a drift within the American Reformed theology coming out of such centers as Yale and Andover, the Second Great Awakening eased American evangelicalism out of a strictly Calvinistic orbit.[7] Almost the reverse phenomenon, however, occurred in England. The revival spirit of the late eighteenth century had produced a growing body of persons within the established church who were in sympathy with many of the religious principles labeled as Calvinistic. Although probably not stricter than their American counterparts, they were invariably compared not with the tradition of Edwardsian Calvinism, but with the Latitudinarianism and moralism that had characterized much of eighteenth-century Anglican thought. From this perspective the evangelical revival was seen as a Calvinistic revival, and as such a threat to the theological principles held so dearly by the other Anglican groups. The High Church circle, in particular, responded to the challenge of the Calvinistic revival, and a sporadic fourteen-year debate beginning in 1798 (known as the Calvinistic controversy) pitted Charles Daubeny and the other contributors to the *Anti-Jacobin Review* against defenders of the Evangelical position.[8]

The English debate would have wide ramifications in American Episcopal circles. Hobart and other American Episcopalians were avid readers of the *Anti-Jacobin Review,* and indeed they often reprinted

7. Perhaps the classic studies of this shift are still Frank Foster, *A Genetic History of the New England Theology* (Chicago, 1907), and Joseph Haroutunian, *Piety versus Moralism: The Passing of the New England Theology* (New York, 1932). For an overview, see also H. Shelton Smith, *Changing Conceptions of Original Sin* (New York, 1955), and William McLoughlin, *Revivals, Awakenings, and Reform: An Essay on Religion and Social Change in America, 1607–1977* (Chicago, 1978). Two biographies are also helpful on this shift, particularly vis-à-vis the New Haven theology. See Sidney Mead, *Nathaniel William Taylor, 1786–1858: A Connecticut Liberal* (Chicago, 1942), and Stephen E. Berk, *Calvinism versus Democracy: Timothy Dwight and the Origins of American Evangelical Orthodoxy* (Hamden, Ct., 1974).

8. Brown, *Fathers of the Victorians,* 170–79.

articles from it in their own journals.[9] Their proximity to Calvinistic denominations made them acutely sensitive to the English controversy and particularly to the often debated question of the degree of Calvinism to be found in the Articles of Religion. Yet by following the line of analysis set down by Daubeny and other *Anti-Jacobin Review* writers, they interpreted the Second Great Awakening as a vigorous revival of Calvinism. The fears and concerns of a Calvinist takeover of the established English church became transmuted by these American Episcopalians into a fear of a growing Calvinist threat to their own church.

The pressing need for works of apologetics and devotion prompted Hobart to begin republishing a number of English religious works, modified and adapted for the peculiar needs of the American situation. In 1803 he published an edition of William Stevens's *Treatise on the Nature and Constitution of the Christian Church*. His real fame—or notoriety—emerged, however, with his publication in 1804 of two works: *A Companion for the Altar* and *A Companion for the Festivals and Fasts of the Protestant Episcopal Church*. Both were compiled from older works. *Companion for the Altar* was based upon communion tracts by Edmund Gibson (1669–1748), bishop of London, and Samuel Seabury; and *Festivals and Fasts* was adapted from a work of a similar title by the English Nonjuror Robert Nelson (1656–1715).

Through these volumes Hobart attempted to supply the demand for works of both piety and apologetics. In the process, however, he actually forged a distinctive style of religious literature that blended an appeal for emotional piety and a strong defense of elevated church doctrine. Two principles underlie his work: "That we are saved from guilt and from dominion of sin, by the divine merits and grace of a crucified Redeemer" and that this merit and grace are only with certainty applied to the soul "in the devout and humble participation of the ordinances of the Church, administered by a priesthood, who derive their authority by regular transmission from Christ."[10] *Companion for the Altar,* for example, contained a series of daily meditations

9. *Archives,* 3:55. John Bowden called the English journal a "most admirable publication." See too *The Churchman's Magazine* 3 (1806): 412, for other American opinions of the journal as well as an example of it being reprinted.

10. John Henry Hobart, *A Companion for the Altar* . . . 2d ed. (New York, 1809), iv. Hobart published two other devotional handbooks at this time, *The Companion for the Book of Common Prayer* (1805) and *The Clergyman's Companion* (1809), but the two discussed above were the most important for his contemporaries.

to help prepare an individual to receive holy communion. Readers were reminded of their sacramental obligations; they were urged to consider their natural state and to ponder the means by which sanctification was to be achieved. The sacrament served both as the vehicle of grace and also as the opportunity by which the individual could deepen his understanding and appreciation of the divine promise through introspection and meditation. By means of these meditations Hobart suggested a model of piety and devotion that would enrich the worship life of the church and that would provide, in Hobart's eyes, a middle ground between the "cold, unfruitful, and comfortless system of heathen morals" and the "wild spirit of enthusiasm."[11] Yet included by Hobart was a meditation upon church order. Part of the individual's confidence in the divine promise of grace was connected with a confidence in the ministry. Hobart's emphasis upon the work of divine grace through the ordinances and sacraments rather than through a conversion led him ineluctably to place a far greater emphasis upon the question of *which* church and *which* sacraments. Thus he counseled the penitent to ask,

> Am I a member of the church of Christ, which he purchased with his blood, which he sanctifies with his spirit, and which, according to his sovereign pleasure, is made the channel of his *covenanted* mercies to a fallen world? . . . Do I keep my communion with this church by devout submission to the ministrations of its priesthood in the orders of Bishops, Priests, and Deacons, deriving their authority by regular transmission through Jesus Christ, the redeemer and head of the Church who has promised to be with the ministers of apostolic succession "always, even to the end of the world."[12]

Ecclesiology and piety merged in the devotional message of Hobart.

Hobart was quite open about admitting where he had found it advisable to modify his English sources. In the preface to his *Festivals and Fasts* he noted how he supplemented Nelson's original work by adding a more elaborate discussion of the true constitution of the Christian church, which he derived from the labors of William Stevens, John Potter, and Charles Daubeny.[13] In it, he presented the church as a well-formed and regular society with an officially desig-

11. *Companion for the Altar,* v.

12. Ibid., 31–32. Emphasis in original. In the first edition of this work these questions were part of an introductory treatise on the obligation of receiving holy communion.

13. *A Companion for the Festivals and Fasts of the Protestant Episcopal Church . . .* 12th ed. (New York, 1846), iii.

..ated ministry that traced its pedigree back to its institution by Christ, a society to which all people were required to belong. In emphasizing the visibility, historicity, and authority of such a church, Hobart elevated questions of order to the level of issues of gospel truth. God's promise of grace was not a universal blessing but was limited to that church established by him. The continuing existence of the church throughout history took on a religious meaning; it was viewed as one of the greatest of miracles and an important part of the believer's confidence.[14]

The question of the nature of the church took on an added importance in Hobart's system and became intertwined with issues of personal piety. Hobart's correspondents had only praise for his two endeavors, particularly for his weaving of doctrine and devotion. As one wrote,

> When those doctrines are handled in Controversy with the Dissenters, there are but few who will read them, and scarcely even do they go abroad unaccompanied by reflections which tend greatly to irritate. Your Plan excells, because the mind, by the solemnity of the Prayers and the mode and manner of the Meditations is naturally disposed to receive without prejudice the most important Doctrines."[15]

The persons who saw only little value in abstract questions of theology per se readily perused them when they became intermeshed with a whole system and scheme of devotion.

II

Hobart's labors did not go unnoticed outside of the confines of the Episcopal Church. In 1805 Samuel Miller, one of the leading lights of the Presbyterian Church, wrote darkly of these Episcopal treatises in a letter to another important Presbyterian, Ashbel Green. Miller noted that the Episcopalians had been growing rapidly in both the city and the state of New York, "not so much in numbers as in arrogance,

14. A practical ramification of this change was a far greater interest among high church Episcopalians in chronicling the evidences of the historic church than in discussing the question of the evidences for Christianity. The discussion of the former question is over four times longer than the treatment of the latter in the twelfth edition of Hobart's *Festivals and Fasts*.
15. *Archives*, 3:451.

insolence, and high church principles. . . . Within the last year they have made many publications, in the form of sermons, tracts, and much larger works, in which the high-toned doctrines of Laud and his successors in opinion are exhibited, and most strenuously contended for."[16] Indeed, the publication of *Companion for the Altar* and *Festivals and Fasts* sparked a decade of theological disputations between Presbyterians and Episcopalians. The apologetic emerging from this debate sheds important light upon the theological self-understanding of this group of high church writers.

The Presbyterian Church in New York was far larger and more important than the Episcopal Church at the time, and during the early years of the nineteenth century it was continuing to grow both in numbers and importance. In part, demography lay behind this steady growth. "The expansion of New England," to use Lois K. Mathews's well-known phrase, resulted in thousands of new migrants moving into the upstate area. The flow of settlers was so great that it was recorded that 1,200 persons passed through Albany alone in a single three-day period in 1795.[17] In the race to missionize this burgeoning population the New York Presbyterians had two decided advantages. The bulk of the immigrants were Congregationalists and were hence far closer theologically and ecclesiastically to the Presbyterians than to the Episcopalians. A Connecticut Congregationalist such as Jonathan Edwards, Jr., who as an organizer of the Connecticut Missionary Society was closely associated with the New York missions, could feel equally at home in either Congregationalism or Presbyterianism.[18] To further facilitate this cooperation and to better answer the need for missionaries, Congregationalists and Presbyterians established in 1801 the famous Plan of Union. Particularly when the Plan of Union

16. Samuel Miller to Ashbel Green, 12 March 1805, Samuel Miller Papers, Princeton University, Princeton, New Jersey.

17. Lois K. Mathews, *The Expansion of New England* (New York, 1909), 139–69. See too William Warren Sweet, *Religion on the American Frontier, 1783–1840;* Vol. 2: *The Presbyterians* (1936; New York, 1964), 40 ff. That group which Episcopalians simply called Presbyterians in fact was composed of three separate groups: Presbyterians, Dutch Reformed churches, and the Associate Reformed synod, the American branch of the Scottish convenanters of the eighteenth century. Of the three great opponents to the high church movement, Samuel Miller was a Presbyterian, William Linn was Dutch Reformed, and John M. Mason was Associate Reformed. On the interrelationship of these groups at the time, see John T. McNeill and James Hastings Nichols, *Ecumenical Testimony: The Concern for Christian Unity within the Reformed and Presbyterian Churches* (Philadelphia, 1974), 127–36.

18. See Ferm, *Jonathan Edwards the Younger,* 164–69.

was further strengthened through the Accommodation Plan of 1808, which granted to Congregational consociations parity with Presbyterian presbyteries, the new arrangement left the New York Presbyterians in a strong position to capitalize on the influx of New England settlers.[19] Furthermore the fires of revival were beginning to flame among the Presbyterians, though always controlled to prevent excess. "In most of the northern and eastern presbyteries," it was reported to the General Assembly of 1803, "revivals of religion, of a more or less general nature have taken place. In these revivals, the work of divine grace has proceeded, with a few exceptions, in the usual way. . . . In this calm and ordinary manner many hundreds have been added to the church, in the course of the last year; and multitudes of those who had before joined themselves to the Lord, have experienced times of refreshing and consolation from his presence."[20]

Such was the vitality of the Presbyterian Church in New York at the commencement of the Episcopal–Presbyterian controversies. From the historical perspective such a clash was almost inevitable. For generations, beginning in the days of Elizabeth I, Episcopalians and Presbyterians had struggled over control of the Church of England, and from the seventeenth century had struggled over control of the Church of Scotland. First one group gained ascendency and then the other, until finally the ecclesiastical armistice of the Glorious Revolution acknowledged Presbyterian control north of the river Tweed and Episcopal control south of it. The group memories of this struggle were dutifully and partisanly kept alive—among Anglicans in such works as Peter Heylyn's *Aerius Redivivus* and Edward Hyde's *History of the Rebellion,* and among Presbyterians in the various works of Edmund Calamy and in Daniel Neal's *History of the Puritans.*

Neither the Scots, the Scotch-Irish, nor the descendents of the Puritans felt any great love for the established Church of England, and the history of the relationship between Presbyterians and Episcopalians during the colonial period did little to correct the situation. The two groups had come to rhetorical blows over the episcopate question in the decade before the American Revolution. Many Presbyterians perceived the elevated theological claims of the Episcopalians to be a stalking horse for their real aim of political domination. Particularly in New York, where the colonial Anglican church had been quasi-estab-

19. Robert H. Nichols and James H. Nichols, *Presbyterianism in New York State* (Philadelphia, [1963]), 78–86.

20. *Extracts from the Minutes of the General Assembly of the Presbyterian Church in the United States of America, 1803* (Philadelphia, 1803), 10.

lished in the lower counties, the association between Episcopal theological claims and the threat of political domination was not easily
forgotten. As late as 1840, a semiofficial Presbyterian account of the
late colonial period played upon this theme of domination and reminded its readers of that time when "the Presbyterians, feeble and
oppressed, were compelled for the greater part of the century, besides
supporting their own church, to contribute their quota towards the
support of the Episcopal Church, already enriched by governmental
favour."[21] Even after the war a number of church buildings and glebes
were claimed by both Episcopal and Presbyterian congregations, and
in one of the confrontations that resulted an Episcopal minister attempted to conduct a service from the reading desk while simultaneously, in the same church, the Presbyterian minister tried to
preach from the pulpit.[22] Although Episcopal–Presbyterian tensions
had abated in the decade and a half after the Revolution, Presbyterians
continued to remain sensitive to any Episcopal claims that impugned
the authority of their ministry.[23]

Any impetus toward controversy not supplied by history and
group memories of the denominations was probably provided by
demographic, sociological, and personal considerations. Throughout
the first half of the nineteenth century the backbone of Episcopal
Church membership was primarily the upper-middle-class professional and business community, drawn in large part because of the
educational level of the clergy and by the restrained emotionalism and
high literary decorum of Episcopal worship.[24] In many parts of New
York, both Episcopal and Presbyterian ministers competed for the
religious loyalty of this group.[25] Furthermore Hobart, How, and

21. Samuel Miller, *Memoir of the Rev. John Rodgers, D.D.* . . . (1813; abridged
ed., Philadelphia, 1840), 94. This edition was sponsored by the Presbyterian Board
of Publication.

22. DeMille, *Diocese of Albany*, 29.

23. Samuel Miller [Jr.], *The Life of Samuel Miller, D.D., LL.D.*, 2 vols. (Philadelphia, 1869), 1:206–10.

24. William Manross has argued as much from evidence derived from a survey
of antebellum Episcopal laymen. See *The Episcopal Church in the United States, 1800–
1840* (New York, 1938), 180–86. His conclusions are supported by George DeMille
in his discussion of the social makeup of the first vestry of St. Thomas Church, New
York City: see *St. Thomas Church in the City and County of New York, 1823–1954*
(Austin, Tex., 1958), 6–9.

25. Richard J. Wertz, "John Henry Hobart, 1775–1830: Pillar of the Episcopal
Church" (Ph.D. diss., Harvard University, 1967), 283 ff., makes this point. Wertz
goes on to note that in Episcopal high church apologetics Presbyterians alone were

Beasley all had close personal associations with Presbyterianism, since they all had been students at Princeton under Stanhope Smith. It is not hard to imagine why for them Presbyterianism came to be seen as the principal obstacle standing in the way of the growth of the Episcopal Church in New York. Nor were the Presbyterian writers in a position to be particularly charitable. The theological position of the Episcopal high church party not only flew in the face of traditional Presbyterian claims, but also indirectly threatened the success of the Presbyterian–Congregationalist union. The Plan of Union presupposed that the minor differences in the traditional understandings of the nature of ordination that existed between Presbyterians and Connecticut Congregationalists paled in significance when contrasted with their unity in doctrine and the exigencies of the missionary situation. A revival of high church apologetics that brought to the public eye questions concerning the validity of ordinations and the true ground of ministerial authority could possibly damage the new union.[26]

The Episcopalian–Presbyterian debates can be divided into two phases. The first began with the debate found in the pages of the *Albany Centinel* over the issues raised in Hobart's *Companion for the Altar* and *Festivals and Fasts* and culminated in the debate over Hobart's most famous work, *An Apology for Apostolic Order and its Advocates*. The second phase concerned the publication by Samuel Miller of the first of his two volumes of *Letters Concerning the Constitution and Order of the Christian Ministry* and includes the responses to Miller's tomes by John Bowden and Thomas Y. How. Although their endeavors are not as well known as Hobart's, both Bowden and How did much to correct and refine some of Hobart's arguments.

In a letter requesting Bibles, Prayer Books, and volumes of Daubeny, an upstate missionary wrote to Hobart,

> It was but one day before yesterday that I met with the first and last number of the Centinel of Albany, attacking the episcopacy of the Church, in the last of which I found a direct application to you. . . . [The author's] abusive language, with prudent management on our

---

singled out for individual critique, while all the other Protestant groups were lumped together.

26. Some traditions in Presbyterian theology, for example, were far more emphatic about the absolute necessity of Presbyterian ordination. See the examples How cites in *Vindication of Episcopal Church*, 20–21. For background to traditional Reformed teachings concerning ordination, see James L. Ainslie, *The Doctrines of Ministerial Order in the Reformed Churches of the 16th and 17th Centuries* (Edinburgh, 1940), 155–90.

part, will do us more good than his argument can do us hurt. The latter, it will be easy to refute, but it will be difficult to make that refutation generally understood while his abuse cannot be mistaken; and patience and forbearance on our part will be equally clear. In short, I should suppose from the two numbers I have seen, that providence has permitted the church to be attacked in a manner more favorable to her interest and cause of truth than her state of peace and security.[27]

Hobart and his circle did not enter the *Albany Centinel* controversy naively concerned with simply an abstract defense of truth but fully hoping that such a controversy might give wider circulation to their ideas and positions.

In 1805, William Linn, minister of the Dutch Reformed congregation in Albany and a man known in New York City Reformed circles, began publishing a series of "Miscellanies" in the *Albany Centinel* in which he attacked the elevated ecclesiological assumptions behind Hobart's two volumes.[28]

For Linn the issue at hand was very simply one of Episcopal aggression. "It is their proclaiming themselves to be the only true Church," he explained, "and condemning all others, in imperious and insolent language, which has given offense. It is their reviving exploded doctrine about *divine right and uninterrupted succession,* and claiming an *exclusive right* to the administration of the word and ordinances, which has excited both opposition and contempt."[29] Underlying this question of ecclesiology, however, lay other issues central to the question of church life in early national America.

Perhaps the first thing that strikes the modern reader of these debates is their strange preoccupation with the question of charitableness. On the most superficial level of rhetoric the charge of uncharitableness served as little more than a "tar pit" into which to cast one's opponents. Thus the Episcopalians hoped that Linn's abusive language would prove counterproductive and give rise to a sympathy that ultimately would prove beneficial to the Episcopal cause. Much ink was therefore spilled in the *Albany Centinel* controversy, as it so often was in the various religious debates of the period,

27. *Archives,* 4:461–62.
28. On Linn, see Philip J. Anderson, "William Linn, 1752–1808: American Revolutionary and Anti-Jeffersonian," *Journal of Presbyterian History* 55 (1977): 381–94 (hereafter referred to as *JPH*).
29. *A Collection of Essays on the Subject of Episcopacy* . . . (New York, 1806), 80. Emphasis in original.

trying to prove who was the aggressor and who the defendant. In addition to any rhetorical importance, however, the debate over the limits of charity in fact hinted at a fundamental disagreement over the proper limits of the denominationalism that was then slowly defining itself within the context of the American religious scene. Historians and sociologists are not unanimous in their understandings of denominationalism, yet Sidney Mead's definition of it as "a voluntary association of like-hearted and like-minded individuals, who are united on the basis of common beliefs for the purpose of accomplishing tangible and defined objectives"—that is, as a noncoercive and nonexclusive body—may be taken as a starting point.[30] Unlike the classic model of the European church, which claimed an exclusive right over the individual believer on both theological and political grounds, in American denominationalism churches tended to shy away from such exclusivity. For example, membership in the Presbyterian Church rather than the Methodist Church (or vice versa), it was generally agreed, did not radically affect one's standing as a citizen of America or of the kingdom of heaven.[31] The high church writers, however, believed that to have such an attitude was to sell their theological birthright for a mess of denominational pottage. Hobart in *Festivals and Fasts* had proclaimed, "The Christian Church is not a mere *voluntary* society; but one whereof men are *obliged to be members,* as they value their everlasting happiness: for it is a *society appointed by God,* with enforcements of *rewards and punishments.*"[32] Whereas Hobart, How, and Beasley raised no objections to the sociological aspect of denominationalism, they denied its theological implications. The question of which was the true church was central to them. God had endowed his church with both a true message and a true order, and the abandonment of either had serious implications. Other American Protestants erred when, in the name of charity, they underestimated the importance of divine order. Charity, properly understood, was a

30. Sidney Mead, *The Lively Experiment* (New York, 1963), 104. For an extended discussion of the historical approach to denominationalism, see the essays included in Russell E. Richey, ed., *Denominationalism* (Nashville, Tenn., 1977).

31. Whitney Cross in his now famous *The Burned-Over District: The Social and Intellectual History of Enthusiastic Religion in Western New York* (New York, Harper Torchbook ed., 1965), 40–43, discusses the social forces behind this tacit acceptance, yet, as he adds, the consensus did not include nonevangelical denominations such as the Universalists and often fell short in practice.

32. *Festivals and Fasts,* 19. Emphasis in original.

virtue that could operate only between individuals; it had no business in the realm of truth and error.

This elevation of church order, however, threatened the other Protestant churches, both theologically and practically. If a true church were to be defined by its order as well as by its faith and if the Episcopal claims that episcopacy was the apostolic order could be proven, all other religious groups were implicitly unchurched and became by implication only voluntary societies. To further heighten Protestant concerns this exclusivity was not merely preached but also practiced. Episcopalians reordained other Protestant ministers, much to the consternation of the wider religious community, and they even debated in convention the issue of the validity of nonepiscopal baptisms.[33] The theological exclusivity of the high church theory of the church challenged both the ministerial status of nonepiscopalian clergy and even the possible validity of their sacraments. An important part of the denominational compromise was undermined by their implication that membership in a particular church could possibly affect an individual's future state. Both theologically and socially the exclusive high church claims challenged the reigning assumptions in antebellum Protestantism.

In their elevation of the historic episcopacy, these writers confronted a basic problem. If episcopal polity were the mark of the true church, what in fact was the actual state of nonepiscopalians? Here they found themselves in a dilemma. They had raised in importance the visible church by claiming that through it alone God promised the covenant of salvation. One possible conclusion from such a premise might have been that outside of the church there could be no salvation. Such an admission, however, would have been disastrous for their cause, since it would have bound it to the extreme argument of Roman Catholic writers, immortalized in Boniface VIII's papal bull *Unam Sanctam,* which Protestants universally found offensive. It most served their purpose to raise the question of validity without binding themselves to any dogmatic conclusion. Hence in lieu of the extreme position of Boniface, the high church writers generally adopted a different

33. Linn, *Essays on Episcopacy,* 85–87. For the question of rebaptism, see William E. Martin, "The Question of the Validity of Lay Baptism: Its Antecedents, Theological Foundations, and Influence in the History of the Church of England" (Ph.D. diss., Notre Dame, 1977). Hobart and Bishop White discussed the question in a series of letters. See Bird Wilson, *Memoir of the Life of the Right Reverend William White . . .* (Philadelphia, 1839), 364–70.

answer to the question of the state of those outside the church, probably derived from the writings of Charles Daubeny.[34] They argued that
although the promise of God's mercy was limited to his church and
although nonepiscopalians could have no claims to these promised or
covenanted mercies, they might still benefit from the general, or "uncovenanted," mercies of God. As How, for example, explained, although those who departed from episcopacy were in great error, there
always remained the hope that allowance might be made for error by
the righteous judge.[35] In part this appeal to a hope in the mercy of God
was a curious inversion of the seventeenth-century Anglican argument, popularized by William Chillingworth, which held that a mer-
ciful God would never condemn an individual who sincerely tried to
understand the Bible and that on the practical level no sincere believer,
even though possibly in error, need ever fear for his own salvation. Yet
the concept of uncovenanted mercies was extremely unfortunate and
easily misunderstood, ranking along with a term like "immediate
emancipation" in its propensity to generate more heat than light.
Other evangelical Protestants took small solace in the uncovenanted
mercies offered to them by How and the others. For them the idea that
true believers would find themselves formally barred from the divine
promise was perverse, and an attack upon the concept of uncovenanted
mercies continued to be a standard part of the critique of the high
church movement long after the term had been abandoned by many
Episcopal theologians. The phrase became a lightning rod attracting
and channeling evangelical resentment of the exclusive ecclesiology of
the high church movement.

Linn also questioned the appropriateness of such an exclusive high
church theology in republican America. William White twenty years
earlier in a tract entitled *The Case of the Protestant Episcopal Churches
Considered* had attempted to defend the republican nature of episcopacy, yet the elevated doctrine of the Hobart circle raised anew the question of the traditional link between episcopacy and tyranny. For Linn,
Companion for the Altar and *Festivals and Fasts* were possibly the first
trumpet blast of the return of the bigotry, superstition, and old preju-
dice that characterized the days of William Laud. An appeal for author-

34. The linking of this argument to Daubeny was fairly common in antebellum
episcopal circles. See the letter, Henry Ustick Onderdonk to Samuel Seabury, 21
May 1836, Samuel Seabury Correspondence, General Theological Seminary, New
York, New York; and John Bristed, *Thoughts on the Anglican and American-Anglo
Churches* (New York, 1822), 11.
35. Linn, *Essays on Episcopacy*, 158–59.

ity in the realm of the church could all too easily become a justification for state authority. "If we can prove from the writings of the fathers, merely because they relate facts, that Bishops are a superior order to Presbyters," he asked, "may we not also prove, from the writings of the Old Testament, that kingly government is of *divine right?*"[36]

In 1807 the *Christian's Magazine,* newly formed and under the editorship of the Associate Reformed minister John M. Mason, entered the fray in defense of "that Ecclesiastical government which contains the visible unity of the Church Catholic with perfect equality of rank among her ministers; and the chief of those tenets which are known as the *doctrines of the Reformation,*" and in strong opposition to the revived high church apologetic.[37] In an extended review of Hobart's edition of the *Albany Centinel* debate, he chided the Episcopal writers for their feigned innocence to the charge of aggression: "Verily, if this is no attack upon non-episcopalians, it is so like one, that we need a shrewd interpreter at our elbow, to prevent our mistaking it. 'I never,' said Jack, of Lord Peter's brown bread, 'saw a piece of mutton in my life so nearly resembling a twelve-penny loaf!' "[38] Mason broached two questions, both integrally connected with the exclusive Episcopal claims: was any aspect of external church order so essential to the being of the church that its absence would unchurch a religious body, and second, if the Episcopal Church were indeed a truer church than the other Protestant bodies, why did it possess no signs of greater spirituality?

Mason's review prompted Hobart to publish yet another work, his *Apology for Apostolic Order and its Advocates.* Hobart's *Apology* is noteworthy neither for the power of its reasoning nor for the originality of the individual components that made up its argument. From seventeenth- and eighteenth-century English high churchmen he inherited the apostolic form of argument; from the Jones–Daubeny circle he inherited a heightened view of the importance of ecclesiology and a repugnance for schism; and from the Anglican anti-Calvinist tradition he derived the standard antipredestinarian arguments and the traditional defense of the Church of England against the charge of Cal-

36. Ibid., 131–33.

37. "Introduction," *Christian's Magazine,* 1 (1807), xii–xiii. Emphasis in original. On Mason, see Jacob Van Vechton, *Memoirs of John M. Mason, D.D., S.T.D.* . . . (New York, 1856); and on the founding of the *Christian's Magazine,* see Miller, *Life,* 1:217.

38. Ebenezer Mason, ed., *The Writings of the late John M. Mason, D.D.* . . . 4 vols. (New York, 1832), 3:21.

ism. What Hobart did to all these threads was to join them by weaving them into an overarching new model of the purpose and action of the Episcopal Church. He united them with a new "story" that gave meaning to the church's present embattled existence, both by emphasizing a history that linked the small community to a glorious past and also by stressing its continuity with the broader state of world Christianity.[39]

The new model of understanding that Hobart set forth was the model of the pre-Constantinian church. Although the association of the young American Episcopal Church with the primitive church had been made previously, and William White himself had hinted at it in his *Case of the Protestant Episcopal Churches Considered,* the analogy had usually functioned only negatively by serving simply to distance the American episcopate from the established bishoprics of England.[40] Hobart, however, favorably identified the New York religious scene with the pre-Nicene church in order to justify Episcopal exclusive teachings:

> I . . . have the consolation of having faithfully borne my testimony to the principles of the Apostolic and primitive Church; to principles which "the noble army of martyrs" confessed in their writings, in their lives, in the agonies of those cruel deaths to which their persecutors hunted them; to principles which in every age have ranked among their advocates some of the brightest ornaments of science, and intrepid champions of divine truth."[41]

The model of the church inspiring Hobart was the vision of the small but pure ancient church, surrounded by a hostile population, loyally cleaving to the apostolic truth. For Hobart, the primitive church of the confessors and martyrs continued through history and was purged but not destroyed in the English Reformation. This body was the true mother of the small, struggling Episcopal Church. Through this continuity the Episcopal Church inherited the stature of an 1,800-year heritage, and Hobart would let none of its opponents forget it. For Hobart it was impossible that such an august succession of saints, scholars, and confessors could be anything less than a sure

39. Hobart's originality should not be overemphasized here. Many of these themes are also found in Thomas Y. How's contributions to the *Albany Centinel* debate, and How's *Vindication of the Protestant Episcopal Church* is probably the finest example of this style of apologetic. However, the wide popularity of Hobart's *Apology* assured that the apostolic argument was invariably linked with Hobart and not with How.

40. See, for example, William White, *The Case of the Episcopal Churches Considered,* ed. Richard G. Salomon (n.p., 1954), 31.

41. Hobart, *Apology,* 16.

and trustworthy witness of the true teachings of Christ, and he eagerly wrapped himself in their moral authority. Indeed, it is somewhat amusing to hear such grandiose rhetoric emanating from these minor clerics in a small corner of a vast continent:

> Episcopacy has the sanction of *ancient universal* usage; while Presbyterianism sprang up but a few centuries ago. . . . [Bishops] hold their rights therefore by *prescription, by long immemorial usage.* This is a title which has peculiar claims to the respect and obedience of all friends to institutions santioned by the wisdom of the ages.[42]

It was to such a glorious primitive church that the Episcopal Church was connected, and Hobart carefully traced its pedigree through the period of the English Reformation, the colonial experience and the conversion of Samuel Johnson at Yale, up to the present. It is impossible to understand Hobart's vision of the Episcopal Church without acknowledging the powerful reality for him of this analogy in particular and the continuity of the visible church in general. The overwhelming reality and importance of this model dwarfed all other concerns for Hobart and dictated for him its present responsibility. Its chief task in 1807 was the same as it had been in the time of Irenaeus— to be true to its inherited message and order. In answer to Mason he emphasized that as important as individual piety might be, it was not as essential to the church as was the cleaving to apostolic unity and the avoidance of error. Thus he emphasized,

> I strike into no new paths. I advocate no new principles. I arrogate no new discoveries. The GOOD OLD PATH in which the Fathers of the primitive church followed their blessed Master to martyrdom and glory; in which the venerable Fathers of the Church of England found rest to their souls—is the path in which I would wish to lead, to a "rest eternal in the heavens," myself and those that hear me.[43]

As a model this analogy of Hobart's possessed great power and appeal and gave meaning to an isolated religious community. Yet it also deeded to these writers a wariness and suspicion of all that surrounded them. The famous maxim of the apostolic era, "What has Athens to do with Jerusalem?" might have had a certain flourish in third–century Carthage, when Tertullian first uttered it, yet in Hobart's New York such a spirit of separation both from the surrounding religious bodies and from the state would lead to real problems.

42. Ibid., 89. Emphasis in original.
43. Ibid., 261. Emphasis in original.

Hobart's devotion to the vision of the historic church led him boldly into one of the great quagmires of Anglican theology. Elizabethan churchmen had generally defended episcopacy either on pragmatic grounds or as simply the most beneficial organization to meet the peculiar needs of the English situation. Not until Richard Bancroft, in his St. Paul's Cross sermon of 1588, did the divine right of episcopacy find a major English advocate, and not until the Restoration did the Church of England uniformly require the reordination of foreign Protestant ministers.[44] Within Anglican circles it had never been clearly defined whether bishops were part of the nature (*esse*) of a church or simply part of its well-being (*bene esse*), and such an important English divine as Richard Hooker had argued simply for the latter. This ambiguity within Anglican ecclesiology had been played up in White's *Case of the Episcopal Churches Considered*. White had written this work during the post–Revolutionary War struggle to organize American Episcopalians, and in it had suggested that in times of dire emergency episcopacy was not essential to the nature of the church.[45] Hobart's fascination with the idea of the visible church, however, led him (perhaps with more fervor than foresight) to take an extreme position on the issue. If not more rigid than the position set forth in the *Albany Centinel* debates, Hobart's discussion of episcopacy in the *Apology* was certainly more unequivocally put. Instead of hedging on the question of unchurching other Protestants, Hobart met it squarely. Episcopalians had the logical responsibility of denying the validity of nonepiscopal ordinations. He wrote, "If any person can point out to me by what method I can maintain that Bishops alone have the power of ordination, and at the same time concede the power to Presbyters, he shall have my warmest thanks."[46]

Hobart, however, did more than link his church to a glorious past. Evangelical writers had regularly criticized high church ecclesiology for its audacity and presumption in prescribing the limits of the true

44. On this shift within Anglicanism, see William Lamont, *Godly Rule: Politics and Religion, 1603–1660* (London, 1969), 28–56.

45. White, *Episcopal Churches Considered*, 33–47. For a discussion of White's thoughts on this issue, see Temple, *Common Sense Theology of Bishop White*, 21–29; Mills, *Bishops by Ballots*, 183–89; and Walter H. Stowe, ed., *The Life and Letters of Bishop William White* . . . (New York, [1937]), 63–76. Although never criticizing him publicly, in private Hobart's circle had little patience with White's views. As one wrote, "It is pretty difficult to defend Dr. White . . . but what is the opinion of one of our clergy?" *Archives*, 4:533. See too 5:189.

46. Hobart, *Apology*, 45.

church to the borders of such a minor denomination within the American scene. To answer this charge Hobart sought to connect his church not only with the heritage of the primitive church, but also to the practice of the universal church. The relative strength of episcopal and nonepiscopal churches outside of America interested Hobart, and he continually argued that it was the Presbyterians and not the Episcopalians who were the "comparatively small sect." The vast number of episcopalians in the Latin, Greek, English, Irish, Swedish, Danish, and Moravian churches gave witness to the fact that episcopacy, far from being an eccentricity, was the norm.[47]

Having elevated the importance of ecclesiology and the apostolic understanding of the office of the bishop, Hobart had finally to explain how an office so conceived could fit into early national America. If the lawn sleeves of an English lord bishop bespoke a foreign figure for American society, the gaunt, ascetic figure of an apostolic bishop was perhaps an even more foreign sight. Would not such absolute divine power be an unsettling tendency in the society? To answer this practical question Hobart emphasized a sharp, if not arbitrary, distinction between episcopacy as a divine institution and episcopacy as a form of church government. The sacral authority of episcopacy emanated from its divine institution, but its juridical power was derived from the laws of each church. In the case of the American church the government was pointedly republican and popular. Bishops were elected, could legislate only with the concordance of a council of lower clergy and laity, and hence could never be an unstabilizing political force since they governed only by consent.[48] Hobart's answer may have indeed been only a paradox at best and an evasion at worst, since it never really addressed the question of the indirect power of bishops based on their moral suasion, yet it was a paradox that Hobart would return to throughout his ministerial career, regularly invoking it to reconcile the idea of the historic episcopacy as a theological truth and the political reality of early nineteenth-century America.

Episcopalians generally praised Hobart's *Apology,* and some went so far as to call it a "masterpiece."[49] Presbyterians found the work less

---

47. Ibid., 100. On this point as well, How parallels Hobart. See Linn, *Essays on Episcopacy,* 4–5. See too Wilson, *Memoir of White,* 366–67, for White's thoughts on the evidence of worldwide episcopacy.

48. Ibid., 218–20.

49. See, for example, John Jacob Tschudy [?] to John Henry Hobart, 3 April 1816, Hobart Correspondence, Archives of the Protestant Episcopal Church, Austin, Texas. Charles Daubeny also spoke highly of it. See *Works,* 1:123.

convincing. John M. Mason wrote a highly critical review of it in the *Christian's Magazine*. Yet Mason was not the only Presbyterian to take offense at the revival of high church Episcopal claims. Samuel Miller, one of the leading Presbyterian clergy in New York City and author of *Retrospect of the Eighteenth Century,* the first intellectual history written in America, also wrote two series of letters defending the Presbyterian ministry. The first volume, published in 1807 only a month and a half after the publication of Hobart's *Apology,* in particular strove to defend the veracity of Presbyterian ordinations in the face of extravagant claims by Episcopal writers. Justifying the need for his volume, Miller admitted,

> The late Mr. *Burke* has somewhere said, "Let us only suffer any person to tell us his story morning and evening but for one twelve-month, and he will become our master." Many zealous advocates of Episcopacy have been so long in the habit of saying, and of hearing it said, that the Scriptures "clearly," "strongly," and "unquestionably" declare in favor of their system; and some of them so little in the habit of reading the refutations of this error, that they unfeignedly believe it, and scruple not to stigmatize all who do not see it, as given up to blindness and prejudice.[50]

He used three tacks in answering the high church writers. First, he rehearsed the traditional Presbyterian arguments denying the existence of episcopacy in the New Testament and challenging the Episcopal hermeneutic that used the early church to determine the right reading of Scripture. Second, he attempted to isolate the high church apologetic from the main currents of Anglican thought. The *iure divino* episcopal advocates had always been but a small minority within the Anglican communion, and "19/20" of English and American Episcopalians had opposed it. Finally, Miller hammered upon the theme already raised by Mason: if the Episcopal Church were the only true church why did it not manifest more fruits of holiness?

Three Episcopal champions responded to Miller. James Kemp, a clergyman from Maryland and eventually its second bishop, published a minor work, *Letters in Vindication of Episcopacy,* that was reprinted in the *Churchman's Magazine* of 1808. More important than Kemp's contribution, those of John Bowden and Thomas Y. How took the form of extensive critiques of Miller's *Letters.* In their volu-

50. Samuel Miller, *Letters Concerning the Constitution and Order of the Christian Ministry* . . . (New York, 1807), 117. Emphasis in original. Two years later Miller published a second volume, *A Continuation of Letters Concerning the Constitution and Order of the Christian Ministry* . . . (New York, 1809). Both works were reissued in 1830 as a single volume.

minous endeavors one sees an attempt both to continue the Hobartian emphasis upon the identification of the present-day church with the thought and ethos of the early church and to shore up certain weaknesses in the Hobartian apologetic exposed by evangelical critics.

"I am instructed, entertained, and greatly edified by Dr. Bowden's book," confessed one contemporary. "It is I think unanswerable; and yet, I doubt not, the incorrigible pertinacity of Calvinism will induce either Mason or Miller, or more probably both of them, to attempt a refutation."[51] In his own volumes of *Letters* Bowden attempted to grapple with the first two aspects of Miller's critique of the high church position. His long-standing interest in the early church served him well as he dutifully entered into the morass of controversial patristic theology and debated such seemingly abstruse questions as the veracity of Ignatius of Antioch's epistles, St. Jerome's views on the ordination practices in the pre-Nicene church in Alexandria, and the correct dating of the rise of the papal supremacy. These were not, however, abstruse questions but rather part of a long-established debate over the content of the apostolic witness and its authority for the modern church. Little in Bowden's apostolical argument was original, yet what his volumes lacked in originality they made up for with scholarly competence, and he had probably the best knowledge of Anglican patristic theology of all the high church writers. The early church argument was not, however, simply an external one for Bowden. Just as for Hobart, the reality of the primitive church had a personal religious force, yet its appeal was more epistemological than metaphorical. The early church served not so much as a model for understanding the present situation as the only certain basis upon which religious truth could rest. Scripture as interpreted by the witness of the primitive church was the basis for religious truth, and all heresy was ultimately innovation:

> Christianity can admit of no improvements. It was complete the moment the canon of Scripture was closed; and those who lived in or near the apostolic age, had many advantages for understanding what were the doctrines, the constitution, and the discipline of the Christian church, which we have not. The Holy Scriptures, expounded and elucidated by primitive and universal belief and practice, will effectually secure us from the delusions, the heresies, and schisms of later ages.[52]

51. *Archives*, 6:105.
52. John Bowden, "Letters to Dr. Miller . . ." in *Works on Episcopacy*, ed. Benjamin T. Onderdonk, 2 vols. (New York, 1831), 1:222.

The apostolic witness provided a sure basis for religious truth in a world of change and decay.

Bowden also had the more practical task of answering Miller's charge that the elevation of episcopacy in the high church apologetic violated the Anglican theological tradition. Miller's error, according to Bowden, lay in his confusing two questions: was episcopacy of divine order, and if so what were the consequences? Virtually all Episcopalians, argued Bowden, answered yes to the first question, and it was only concerning the latter question that a controversy existed. Within episcopacy differences of opinion did exist vis-à-vis nonepiscopal churches. Bowden acknowledged that whereas some held that episcopacy was essential to the visible church (though he was quick to emphasize that episcopacy was never deemed necessary for salvation), others saw it only as necessary for the well-being of the church, and that nonepiscopal ministrations, though irregular, were not necessarily invalid.[53] Bowden furthermore shied away from the Daubeny–Hobart view of uncovenanted mercies and instead suggested a middle ground in which nonepiscopal churches were considered to be in that particular (*quod hoc*) imperfect or defective, but with no opinion hazarded concerning their accessibility to the divine covenant.[54] Yet on the practical or apologetical level this theological admission had little force. The implicit thrust of Bowden's prose still aimed at shaking loose Presbyterian loyalties. Bowden acknowledged as much and questioned whether a conscientious nonepiscopalian who was convinced that episcopacy was a divine institution "can derive any comfort from the concession, that this principle does not go so far as totally to *unchurch* or whether he can continue a member of such a church consistently with the duty of being a member of a complete, sound, scriptural and serious Church."[55]

As might have been expected, Thomas Yardley How was never a man to compromise. His two volumes in response to Samuel Miller bristle with the logical implications of the exclusive ecclesiology sketched out by the high church writers, and the Hobartian model of the church surrounded by hostile powers is, if anything, stronger in How than in Hobart himself. Just as the planets would immediately rush to the sun from the force of gravity if no force stood to counteract it, so too for How, "the Church would infallibly have merged in the

53. Ibid., 1:295–97.
54. Ibid., 211–12.
55. Ibid., 212.

Key

larger religious societies around her, if she had pursued the poli
of . . . seeking peace, by forgetting every circumstance of distinctic __
between them and her. No body of men will grow without contend-
ing for their principles; nor will any attachment be preserved for principles which it is made an object to keep systematically out of sight."[56]
Much of How's work reiterated the themes of apostolicity and universality that Hobart had earlier emphasized.

Yet the most interesting aspect of How's treatises is the defense of
the Hobartian discussion of grace. How possessed a peculiar sensitivity to questions of grace, and indeed he almost succeeded in making Daubeny's and Hobart's awkward category of covenanted mercies
take on coherence and clarity. Presbyterian misunderstandings of the
formulary stemmed from an erroneous understanding of grace. The
Episcopal belief in the general atoning work of Christ, far from bot-
tling up the hope of salvation within one group, actually spread it
throughout the world. Not even faith was an absolute condition for
salvation:

Imp̄t

> [We] believe that the blood of Christ was shed for all mankind;
> extending not less to such as have never heard of his name, than those
> who live under the full light of his Gospel. The uninstructed pagan
> will be tried by the law of that reasonable nature which God has
> given to the whole human race; and a merciful Judge will make all
> proper allowances for the difficulty of the circumstances in which
> they may be placed.[57]

Yet this is far from denying that episcopacy is a divine institution,
obligatory upon all, and that its absence constitutes an error. The core
of How's critique of Calvinistic evangelicalism was that it lowered too
far the demand of divine truth while it underestimated the breadth of
divine mercy.

Key

This analysis of the contributions of Hobart, How, Bowden, and
Beasley to this first apologetical skirmish clarifies the point that their
coherence as a group did not stem from their theology per se. Not one
of them agreed with all of the others on the formal theological question in the background of the debate—to what extent must a true
church be episcopal in polity?[58] What seems to have held these men

---

56. How, *Vindication of Episcopal Church*, xv. How's first attack on Miller is his
Letters Addressed to the Rev. Samuel Miller, D.D. . . . (Utica, N.Y., 1808).

57. How, *Vindication of Episcopal Church*, 106.

58. Their theological differences did not go unnoticed by their contemporaries.
See Samuel Miller's contrast of Bowden and How, *Continuation of Letters*, 21–22.

together was both a common story and a common theological presupposition. The story separated out the fledgling Episcopal Church from the rest of the American religious environment and linked it to both the primitive and universal church. The theological presupposition led them invariably to see the source of religious truth in the scriptures as interpreted through the witness of the primitive church.

III

In February of 1811 Bishop Moore of New York suffered an acute attack of paralysis which necessitated the election of an assistant bishop. In the special convention of the diocese Hobart was elected over the opposition of a small but vigorous minority. Hobart was so young upon assuming the office that he occasionally resorted to powdering his hair white to give himself greater solemnity.

The election of Hobart cast the high church party in a new situation: after this point they were not simply apologists for a vision of the Episcopal Church and its relation to the other denominations and the state, but could now begin to implement this vision. Yet they did not operate without opposition, in large part stemming from Hobart's attempt to place his mark upon his diocese. He was single-minded in his attempt to control the church, and it is indeed hard at times to be certain where his vision of the distinct role of the Episcopal Church in antebellum society ended and where a personal monomania and inability to tolerate opposition began.[59] From early in Hobart's episcopate only those clergy who agreed with the general tenets of Hobart's high church program were appointed as missionaries, and diocesan patronage in general fell into high church hands. His consolidation of power, however, did not go unresisted. Hobart's attempt to purge Cave Jones, an opponent, from the staff of Trinity led to a large public protest and threatened another legislative reorganization of Trinity.[60]

Probably the most important controversy that marked Hobart's young episcopacy was the extended debate over Episcopal involve-

59. This point is convincingly argued in Wertz, "John Henry Hobart," 308. Wertz, however, is less convincing in his discussion of the social ramifications of Hobartian high churchmanship. See chapter 3.

60. Ibid., 144–229. Wertz provides by far the most complete discussion of the Cave Jones affair in particular and of Hobart's attempts at consolidating the diocese in general. For a critique, however, of some of his conclusions, see chapter 3.

ment in the Bible Society movement. It is hard to overestimate the importance of the Bible in the development of American life and culture. Particularly during the antebellum period it was both a book and a symbol—a talismanic force to ward off both Deists and Catholics. In large part this was the result of what Nathan Hatch has characterized as a crisis of authority within American culture during the period, a crisis that affected popular religion.[61] The popular cultural movement away from authority by deference and toward authority by popular consent produced a religious corollary in giving to the concept of *sola scriptura* a fundamentally new meaning. In place of creeds, systematic theologies, and to some degree even an official clerical interpretation of the Scriptures, the Bible alone, "without note or comment" (to use the popular phrase of the time), became the final basis of authority. Furthermore even among those evangelical Protestants who did not jettison theology and creed, the authority of the Bible increased for two reasons. On the practical level cross-creedal discourse could take place only with a common theological denominator—which invariably became the Scripture itself. Second, the unadulterated Bible became an important symbol of unity for American Protestants, a reality that united them despite apparent differences. Through distribution of the Bible "the rough edges of bigotry and superstition are wearing off, and Christians are coming gradually nearer and nearer together."[62] Finally the Bible gave meaning not only to the present existence of the church, but also to a vision for the state. The vast flowering of scholarly literature in the last decade that has stressed the importance of millennialism and biblical typology in the formation of an American national self-understanding is only a belated recognition of a central theme in American thought.[63] In particular,

61. Nathan Hatch, "*Sola Scriptura* and *Novus Ordo Seclorum*," in *The Bible in America*, ed. Hatch and Mark O. Noll (New York, 1982), 62, 67.

62. Matthew Larue Perrine to the Presbytery of New York, 1816. Quoted in Hood, *Reformed America*, 123. On the general question of the voluntary societies as harbingers of Christian unity, see Lefferts A. Loetscher, "The Problem of Christian Unity in Early Nineteenth-Century America," *Church History* 32 (1963): 7–15, in particular.

63. The literature on this question is voluminous and still growing. For representative viewpoints, see Ernest L. Tuveson, *Redeemer Nation: The Idea of America's Millennial Role* (Chicago, [1968]); Conrad Cherry, ed., *God's New Israel: Religious Interpretations of American Destiny* (Englewood Cliffs, N.J., 1971); Sacvan Bercovitch, *The Puritan Origins of the American Self* (New Haven, 1975); Alan Heimert, *Religion and the American Mind: From the Great Awakening to the Revolution* (Cambridge, Mass., 1966); Nathan Hatch, *The Sacred Cause of Liberty: Republican*

the historic identification of America as God's new Israel, and the typology surrounding it that cast America in the role of the holy nation, suggested that evangelical action could play an important role in the national destiny.[64]

The impulses behind the Bible Society movement were manifold. According to legend, the story of a young Welsh girl, who having labored long and traveled far in order to purchase her own copy of the Scriptures only to be informed that none were available, so pricked the conscience of England that local societies began to arise to aid in the free distribution of the Bible.[65] There were other impulses, however, that were not quite so otherworldly. In the politically and socially tense English society of the time the distribution of the Bible was hoped to stymie the growth of immortality, scepticism, and political discord. For all of these motives the British and Foreign Bible Society was founded in 1804, on nonsectarian principles and under lay control.[66]

In America, the Philadelphia Bible Society was organized in December of 1808, the Connecticut Bible Society in May of 1809, and in rapid succession state societies were organized in Massachusetts, New York, and New Jersey. By 1816 more than one hundred Bible Societies were organized in the United States.[67] Yet by 1814–15 it was becoming increasingly clear that such a multiplication of societies could not serve the needs of the rapidly expanding population, and that one united national society was needed. In 1816, largely through the efforts of Elias Boudinot, head of the New Jersey society, a convention of representatives from local societies was called. The convention, which included Nathaniel William Taylor, Gardiner Spring, Jedediah

Thought and the Millennium in Revolutionary New England (New Haven, 1977); and J. F. MacLear, "The Republic and the Millennium," in *The Religion of the Republic,* ed. Elwyn A. Smith (Philadelphia, 1971).

64. Note, however, that Mark O. Noll voices some important cautions about making any simple identification of evangelical purpose and national destiny. See "The Image of the United States as a Biblical Nation, 1776–1865," in Hatch and Noll, *The Bible in America,* 39–58.

65. Arthur Lowndes, D.D., *A Century of Achievement: The History of the New-York Bible and Common Prayer Book Society . . .* 2 vols. (New York, [1909]), 1:8.

66. On the origin of the British Bible Society movement, see John Owen, *The History of the Origin and First Ten Years of the British and Foreign Bible Society,* 2 vols. (London, 1816). Both Foster, *Errand of Mercy,* 82–100, and Brown, *Fathers of the Victorians,* passim also discuss its rise. Foster, in particular, argues that the founding of the Bible Society reflected a desire for social control.

67. Henry O. Dwight, *The Centennial History of the American Bible Society* (New York, 1916), 9.

Morse, James Fenimore Cooper, and numerous other luminaries, founded the American Bible Society and elected Boudinot as its first president.

It was just such a distinguished organization, rooted in all of the intellectual, cultural, and social forces discussed above, from which Hobart tried to distance the New York Episcopal Church. Not that Hobart was completely alone in his opposition. A number of important English high churchmen—including Herbert Marsh, Margaret Professor of Divinity at Cambridge; Christopher Wordsworth, brother of the poet and dean of Bocking; John Randolph, bishop of Oxford; and Henry H. Norris, curate of Hackney—all voiced opposition to the British and Foreign Bible Society and supported the more narrowly ecclesiastical alternatives.[68] Yet key differences between the English and American scenes made Hobart's task a far more difficult one. Rather than the power and prestige of a rich and established church, Hobart had only the small Episcopal community to offer as an alternative vehicle for scripture distribution. Furthermore antidemocratic rhetoric was a major part of the English critique. Norris, writing in pre–Reform Bill England, often voiced the fear of an ignorant but literate populace, unwilling to accept the authority of its betters. Such an appeal would have been largely counterproductive in Hobart's New York. Incorrigible ignorance was something that might be found on the foreign mission field, but never did Hobart attribute it to the population of the Republic.

Although the New-York Bible and Common Prayer Book Society was technically organized by Benjamin Moore, there seems little reason to doubt the claim of his biographer that Hobart was the "originator and soul" of the association.[69] Organized in the spring of 1809, more than six months before the New-York Bible Society would be organized, its structure reflected many of the high church objections to the organization and purpose of voluntary societies in general and the Bible Society movement in particular. The bishop of the diocese was to be the president, each New York City clergyman was ex officio to be a member of the board of managers, and the entire board was to consist of more clergy than laity. More important, however, the soci-

68. On the English opposition, see Owen, *History of Bible Society*, 1:213–14, and Lowndes, *Century of Achievement*, 1:10–15, 28–29. American high churchmen were well acquainted with the English debate. See the *Churchman's Magazine* 8 (1810): 353 ff. See also *Works*, 1:205, 252–56, etc., for the later correspondence between Norris and Hobart.

69. McVickar, *Hobart*, 286–87.

Prayer

ety took as its aim the distribution of both the Bible and the Book of Common Prayer. As Hobart explained, "What better method . . . can be adopted to disseminate the truths of the Bible, than by dispersing a book which, exhibiting these truths in the affecting language of devotion, impresses them on the heart as well as on the understanding?"[70]

The distinctiveness of such an approach can be seen by contrasting it with the response of the Episcopal Church in Pennsylvania to the Bible Society movement. There, Bishop William White openly supported the interdenominational Philadelphia Bible Society and served as its first president. In praising it, White noted with approval that the Bibles "shall be separated from all notes and commentaries whatsoever, and, except the contents of the Chapters, shall contain nothing but the sacred text. It is therefore manifestly a design in which all denominations of Christians, without exception, may unite."[71]

In 1815 Elias Boudinot wrote to Hobart, the president of the Bible and Common Prayer Book Society, requesting that he send delegates to the upcoming organizational meeting of the American Bible Society. Hobart responded by issuing a pastoral letter—the very first such letter in the history of the American Episcopal Church—that strongly urged New York Episcopalians to support their own denominational endeavor. The next year he attempted to strengthen the Bible and Common Prayer Book Society by creating a lay auxiliary—perhaps recognizing belatedly that despite the lack of apostolic succession among laity, only their financial support could ensure the success of the society.[72]

The Bible Society controversy entailed eight years of sporadic pamphlet warfare, which acutely illuminates the intraepiscopal disagreement over the vision and role of the church offered by Hobart.[73] Where did the division lie?

70. Hobart, "Address Before the New York Bible and Common Prayer Book Society" (1809), excerpted and reprinted in Lowndes, *Century of Achievement,* 1:23–24.

71. White, "An Address of the Bible Society Established in Philadelphia," excerpted and reprinted in Lowndes, ibid., 1:35–36. For a discussion of White's views concerning the Bible Society, see Stowe, *Life and Letters of Bishop White,* 140.

72. Despite the Auxiliary Society, the New-York Bible and Common Prayer Book Society was never in strong finanical shape during its early decades. In 1838 the society and auxiliary merged. On its later history, see Lowndes, *Century of Achievement,* 1:73–480.

73. The number of pamphlets contributed to this debate is quite large and many were of a very occasional nature. The debate can be divided into two phases. The first concerned the controversy over Hobart's pastoral letter of 1815. It was answered, anonymously, by William Jay, *Strictures on a Pastoral Letter to the Laity of the*

Episcopalians, maintained Hobart, ought to support Episcopal benevolent societies rather than general societies. In part his motivation was purely practical. Often in his writings he lamented for all the "Episcopal" money flowing into the coffers of the national societies while the denominational societies starved. Similarly part of his attitude cannot be separated from his peculiar personality. Hobart seemed constitutionally unable to support a society he could not control. But in addition to these factors, the vision and model out of which Hobart operated left almost no room for the concept of general societies. The dominant evangelical typology, it has been noted, saw the nation in the role of the new Israel. Implied in this as a corollary was that one of the functions of the church was like that of the priests and prophets of ancient Israel—to rehearse the need for national holiness and national righteousness. The adoption by Hobart and his circle of the model of the early church rather than that of ancient Israel had far-reaching implications. In the model of the primitive church God did not work either through a nation or even through a collection of Christians but through his self-appointed vessel, the church. One is hard-pressed to find in Hobart any sympathy for a concept of the body of Christ above that of the visible church and its bishops. There was no sense for Hobart that in inter-Christian cooperation God was actually creating something new in sacred history. The gospel had to lead to the church or it had not been properly understood. The notion of "general" evangelism, of communicating the Christian truth while omitting all divisive issues of order, was meaningless.

While the vast majority of American Protestants saw hope and expectation in the Bible Society movement during the first two decades of the nineteenth century, Hobart saw only cause for worry. Not only did general societies serve no positive good, they were fraught

---

Protestant Episcopal Church . . . (New York, 1815), and includes Hobart's and Jay's responses to each other. The second phase began with Hobart's return to the question of the Bible Scoiety in his Diocesan Address of 1822. To this phase Jay contributed *A Letter to the Right Reverend Bishop Hobart* . . . *by a Churchman* (New York, 1823); *A Letter to the Right Rev. Bishop Hobart, in Reply to a Pamphlet Addressed to Him by the Author* . . . (New York, 1823); and *A Reply to a Second Letter* . . . *From the Right Rev. John Henry Hobart* . . . (New York, 1823). Hobart's contributions were: *A Reply to a Letter Addressed to the Right Rev. Bishop Hobart* . . . *by Corrector* (New York, 1823); *A Reply to a Letter to the Right Rev. Bishop Hobart by William Jay* . . . *By Corrector* (New York, 1823); and *A Note from Corrector to William Jay* (New York, 1823). Lowndes, *Century of Achievement,* 1:55–70, 198–249, summarizes most of the main arguments.

with perils. They separated the word of God from the church of God.
The Bible Society, for Hobart, seemed to be based on the principle of
functional unity, that in spite of differences Protestants could unite to
undertake common projects, without uniting on questions of ministry and fellowship.[74] It assumed that only subordinate and nonessen-
tial points divided Christians and that these could be easily dismissed.
Such a predicament could only weaken the Episcopal Church, the
most distinctive of the Protestant religious groups, and would
eventually result in the amalgamation of the weaker Episcopal community into the mass of evangelical Protestantism. "In all these associations," he warned, "the minority will glide insensibly into the
larger mass, unless they are constantly on their guard; and then their
safety can be secured only by a tenaciousness which may incur the
stigma of bigotry and interrupt unity and harmony."[75] Hobart saw the
threat of amalgamation everywhere—even in the minutes of the Bible
Society meetings, which he construed as a form of Presbyterian
preaching. The identity of the church would be threatened by any
cooperative endeavor that did not first attempt to deal with divine
principles.

If Hobart was the great proponent of the vision of the Episcopal
Church as the primitive church, carefully distancing itself from all
other churches, his arch–Episcopal critic was William Jay (1789–
1858), the patrician, judge, and moral reformer. A proud member of
the respected Jay family that included the first Supreme Court justice,
William Jay was not one to allow the Episcopal Church to separate
itself from the wider concerns of antebellum evangelical Protestantism without a fight.[76] Furthermore, as an individual deeply involved
in the Bible Society, he had little sympathy for Hobart's criticisms of
it.

Hobart's fundamental error for Jay was his confusing of the function of the Bible and that of the Prayer Book. Although admiring the
Episcopal liturgy, Jay adamantly maintained that any formal coupling
of the Bible and the liturgy was an slap at the authority of Scripture.
"Why," he asked, "if the Scripture be the perfect rule, insist on the
necessity of a *digest* to accompany it? nay, more, contend for the con-
nexion [sic] as indispensable, and represent the separation as 'un-

74. [Hobart], *Reply to "An Answer to Bishop Hobart's Pastoral Letter . . ."* (New
York, 1815), 27.
75. *A Pastoral Letter to the Laity of the Protestant Episcopal Church . . . on the
Subject of the Bible and Common Prayer Book Societies . . .* (New York, 1815), 18.
76. Tuckerman, *William Jay,* 10–13.

natural!' "[77] He scoffed at the fear of amalgamation, so real for Hobart, since it implied a lack of confidence in the laity. He reminded both Hobart and his readers of the origin of this charge in the English debate, and its connection with a strong antirepublican sentiment. Furthermore Hobart's call to limit charity to church endeavors smacked to Jay of substituting self-interest for charity. It seemed that one was to do good to his neighbor from Hobart's perspective only if it would benefit the giver by increased church membership.[78]

Jay reserved his sharpest critique of Hobart for a private letter written in 1818 that explained why he chose to support the Bible Society rather than the Bible and Common Prayer Book Society. What Hobart failed to see was that with the founding of the first British Bible Society a new era had opened in the Christian world. "A union unparalleled since the days when believers were of one heart and one soul, had been formed by the Christians of Britain," Jay explained, "influenced by a wisdom too wonderful to be of human origin, its efforts were directed to the single end of blessing the poor, the ignorant, and the sinful, with the knowledge of their God and Saviour."[79] The failure of the Episcopal Church to support wholeheartedly such a reform was heavy with consequences. Not only did it divide a common labor and hence weaken the general effectiveness, but it also threatened the bonds of fraternal union that were slowly resulting from voluntary cooperation. Hobart's exclusivism cast the church into the role of a sect, unconcerned with the claims of Christianity except where they might benefit its own small fellowship. "This principle must forever render us passive spectators of every effort to enlarge the Redeemer's Kingdom, unless we can at the same time extend 'the protestant episcopal church.'"[80] For Jay the proper attitude of the Episcopal Church was not exclusiveness and separation but active involvement in the general religious concerns of the age since these concerns did not reflect simply the desires of the churches nor even of the nation but were part of the divine plan. Hobart's reticence and seeming-sectarianism both frustrated and puzzled a person like Jay, who shared in the hope that general societies like the Bible Society might actually be products of a dispensation of divine grace poured out in the new century.

77. [Jay], *Strictures on a Pastoral Letter*, 9.
78. [Jay], *A Letter to the Right Rev. Bishop Hobart*, 9.
79. William Jay to John Henry Hobart, December 1818, Hobart Correspondence.
80. Ibid.

Perhaps the most succinct formulation of this critique of Hobart's opposition to the Bible Society, from the perspective of the millennial hope that was more or less a shared assumption in evangelical Protestantism, was provided by an anonymous Congregationalist writer. Hobart's opposition only reflected his failure to perceive the spirit of God working in the present age:

> It is our happy lot to live and act in an age when God is calling into action that vast system of means by which he is to introduce his Millenial [*sic*] Glory, in which the kingdoms of this world are to become the Kingdoms of our Lord and his Christ, . . . and if we find these means resisted, and decried from various sources and from various motives, this is only what is to be expected: and from the very character of the opposition when compared to that of former times, we may gain a strong argument, that the work in which we are engaged "is the doing of the Lord."[81]

Whereas Hobart conceived of the church as the primitive community holding the true faith and order while surrounded by a hostile community, and as a direct result of this saw the Bible Society as simply a challenge to its identity, the mass of antebellum evangelical Protestants saw the Bible Society as a vehicle of the kingdom of God.

The combination of theological distinctiveness and apologetical pugnacity precipitated this conclusion among the high church circle. Their theological presuppositions were a residue and remainder of an older world and different from those that undergird the rest of antebellum Protestant America. Their immediate concern was apologetical; that is, they felt the need to defend the peculiarities of their system. Yet in order to do so they found themselves forced to dig more deeply into their theological tradition in order to resurrect better arguments. Out of this tradition they derived not only theological arguments, but also a vision of history and society that placed them in sharp contrast to the mass of their religious contemporaries. Following the inner logic of their apologetic on a question such as the Bible Society movement, they found themselves out of step with the tune to which the rest of American Protestants marched.

On the practical level, however, the storm over the Bible Society was one of great intensity and threatened the fine theory crafted by Hobart, Beasley, Bowden, and How upon the rock of ecclesiastical

---

81. "Bishop Hobart's Strictures on Bible Societies," *Quarterly Christian Spectator* 6 (1824): 37.

reality. Numerous important Episcopalians such as Rufus King and John Pintard crossed Hobart on this issue and continued to support the Bible Society.[82] Hobart's correspondence is peppered with letters from individuals who shied away from the extreme position outlined by Hobart, and indeed Hobart himself expressed private doubts as to the wisdom of the course of action.[83] Yet he also received an equal number of letters supporting his course. As one missionary wrote, "In regard to Geneva, they may do as they may think fit. It is a divided place at least. I have not heart that any besides the Colonel and the Judge are in opposition, and (in strict confidence) I little heed them— they may remain so and receive a lesson from Episcopalians which may shew them that they overrate their influence:—they may as well learn this at one time as another."[84] The issue of support of the Bible Society catapulted an ecclesiastical theory into the practical social question of religious cooperation.

This examination of the two great theological debates of the Hobartian period, the Presbyterian and Bible Society controversies, has given evidence that the high church apologetic, firmly grounded as it was upon the model of the early church, was not simply an abstruse theological issue. By means of it these writers elaborated a vision of the church and its relation with society that was a far cry from the predominant view of their religious contemporaries.

82. *Letters of John Pintard*, 1:39, 44–45.

83. See the following letters from the Hobart Correspondence: Henry U. Onderdonk (6 March 1817), James Robertson (12 June 1816), and John Nicholas (12 March 1817). For Hobart's own doubts about the wisdom of his course, see John Henry Hobart to Nathaniel Williams, Nathaniel Williams Papers, typescript copy, Archives of the Episcopal Church, Austin, Texas.

84. Henry Ustick Onderdonk to John Henry Hobart, 24 February 1817, printed in Dix, *History of Trinity*, 3:145.

3

The Hobartian Synthesis

THE FOREGOING "PUBLIC" HISTORY OF THE HOBARTIAN CIRCLE AND examination of their apologetical schema and the controversies resulting from it can go only so far, particularly since Hobart was far more than a controversialist. "[His] great contribution to the Church was not in anything he wrote or said, . . ." one historian has suggested, "but in the leadership he brought to a very imporant diocese at a critical period in its history."[1] It was not simply as a theoretician but as a leader, giving practical meaning to a theory of the church, that Hobart most decisively affected his diocese. His nineteen-year episcopate (1811–30) was characterized by a continuing directing and instructing of the religious life of the New York church. Through these instructions and directions arose a theology, a piety, and a social perspective that were unique in antebellum America and that served as a basic alternative to the religious and social assumptions of American evangelicalism.

I

The theological platform that supported the high church system had its foundation in the eclectic and high church traditions inherited by Hobart and his circle. In the conclusion of an *Apology for Apostolic Order* Hobart boldly announced, "My banner is, EVANGELICAL TRUTH, APOSTOLIC ORDER," and both of these principles are central for any understanding of Hobartian high church theology. Yet from the per-

1. Manross, *Episcopal Church in the United States*, 54.

spective of the broader study of American religion Hobart's claim is easily misleading.[2] On the surface Hobart did share the basic *sola gratia* assumption of the Reformers, agreeing that salvation could be a gift only of God. Even the greatest of human endeavors "can neither merit pardon for the past, nor procure favour for the future."[3] All grace had to be given by God through Christ, and it was the divinity who freely pardoned and accounted the sinner righteous. Yet a closer analysis suggests that Hobart's "evangelical truth" owed more to seventeenth- and eighteenth-century authorities of the eclectic tradition like George Bull than to Evangelical writers like George Whitefield. Most American Protestants at the time (at least among those who would have considered themselves evangelicals) would have united behind the idea, stemming from the Great Awakening, that divine grace dramatically and forcefully encountered the individual, provoking a conversion and an instantaneous regeneration that manifested itself in faith, repentance, and benevolence.[4] Hobart, however, operated from a tradition that abhorred the solafidean excesses of the Great Awakening and the apparent separating of the experience of faith from any willful desire for personal improvement. Evangelicals erred in that they constantly sought to divide and distinguish the regenerate community, or those in whom virtue had begun its work in the soul, from the mass of the unregenerate. Hobart and his circle suggested a fundamentally

2. Hobart, *Apology*, 262. Emphasis in original. Hobart's use of the term *evangelical* is technically correct and reflected the customary usage of eighteenth-century English High Church writers who argued that evangelical could only properly mean, pertaining to the gospel. Yet among American religious historians it has had a far broader use. On an attempt to define its usage in the American context, see Sydney E. Ahlstrom, "From Puritanism to Evangelicalism: A Critical Perspective," in *The Evangelicals,* ed. David Wells and John D. Woodbridge, 2d ed., rev. (Grand Rapids, 1977), 289–309.

3. John Henry Hobart, *Sermons on the Principal Events and Truths of Redemption,* 2 vols. (London, 1824), 2:94.

4. This is not of course to imply that perfect harmony by any means existed within American evangelical Protestantism on this question. New Divinity men such as Samuel Hopkins and later revivalists such as Charles G. Finney tended to place a far greater emphasis upon the experience itself, while New Haven divines such as Timothy Dwight tended to unit regeneration and sanctification. Yet whatever their individual differences, they would have all opposed the movement in Anglican theology away from solafideanism as represented in George Bull, bishop of St. David's, *Harmonia Apostolica* . . . (1669–70), which attempted to reconcile Paul and James on the question of justification. On the broader English background to this shift in the notion of evangelical, see Allison, *Rise of Moralism,* 118–37.

different model from that of conversion for the understanding of the working of divine grace. Grace functioned regularly and continuously, and metaphorically it operated more like a fine dew than like a violent shower. It cooperated with individuals rather than overpowering them by making them passive.[5] Following the lead of the important eighteenth-century Anglican theologian Daniel Waterland (1683–1740), Hobart eviscerated the inner dynamic of American evangelicalism by simultaneously removing the locus of justification from the individual soul by placing it with the divine action and by emphasizing the external means by which this grace was to be appropriated.[6] Whereas for a person such as Timothy Dwight justifying faith was a "confidence in God" or an "emotion of the mind," for Hobart it was rather a persuasion of the truth of the promises of God.[7] In its essence, justifying faith was made more intellectual; it was no longer an emotion of the mind but instead a truth to be accepted. Furthermore there existed an even more important difference between evangelical and high church theologies. For an individual like Dwight regeneration was seen as a change in heart consisting in a new, heartfelt relish for spiritual objects. Thus faith and good works were connected as it were ontologically in the new regenerated character.[8] The Hobartians, in conformity with the traditional moralistic emphasis within Anglicanism, tied justification to the fruits it produced not ontologically but volitionally. The individual willfully, in cooperation with grace, concerned himself with good works, since true faith ought to lead to a spirit of humble reliance upon God. By deemphasizing the nonvolitional aspects of justifying faith, while at the same time emphasizing its volitional interconnection with love and action, "faith formed by love," the centrality of the conversion experience melted away, leaving only an undifferentiated web of grace. At all points grace cooperated without ever overwhelming the individual. Sharing the criticism of

5. See, for example, "The Church of England Defended . . . ," *Churchman's Magazine* 5 (1809): 102.

6. Waterland makes these changes in "A Summary View of the Doctrine of Justification," in *The Works of the Rev. Daniel Waterland, D.D.* . . . . 6 vols. (London, 1856), 6:1–38. On Waterland's theology of justification, see R. T. Holtby, *Daniel Waterland, 1683–1740: A Study in Eighteenth-Century Orthodoxy* (Carlisle, U.K., 1966), 128–39. Hobart explicitly acknowledged his indebtedness to Waterland. See *Truths of Redemption*, 2:91.

7. Contrast Timothy Dwight's lectures on justification and regeneration in *Theology Explained and Defended in a Series of Sermons* . . . 12th ed., 4 vols. (New York, 1851), 2:326–33, with Hobart, *Truths of Redemption*, 2:98.

8. Dwight, *Theology Explained*, 2:418–27.

eighteenth-century opponents of the Wesleyan and evangelical re
vivals, the high church clergy faulted American evangelicalism fo
both its emotionalism and its subjectivism. The evangelical reliance
upon experience made it oblivious to differences in temperament
among individuals. People, argued Hobart in his *Truths of Redemption,*
are of different psychological temperaments, and accordingly, "It is an
error to require of both of the descriptions of persons [the ardent and
susceptible and the grave and sedate], the same pungency of penitential
feeling, and ardour of penitential expression."[9] True justifying faith
avoided both this emotionalism and an overriding of the human will.

When called upon to define the true nature of the evangelical faith,
high church writers stressed the external rather than the internal. An
evangelical was one who held the doctrine of the Trinity, accepted the
fall of man, believed that Jesus Christ had become the mediator between God and man, and finally trusted that redemption was for all
humankind but that it would be effectual to the salvation only of those
who availed themselves of it.[10] The evangelical truth that Hobart
preached was largely formal and external. Whatever importance individual fervor might have it did not define the nature of evangelical
faith. Just as it was observed in Hobart's answer to Mason, at the
height of the Presbyterian controversy, that the marks of the true
church were formal (for example, apostolic order) and not pietistic, so
too on the individual level the core of assurance was in an assent to a
series of claims and not an experience.

The practical ramifications of this attitude can be seen in the question of baptism. From their very origins the baptismal offices of the
different Anglican liturgies all claimed that "none can enter into the
kingdom of God except he be regenerate and born anew of Water and
the holy Ghost"; and spoke of the newly baptized child as "regenerate
and grafted into the body of Christ's church."[11] With the appearance
of Whitefield and the interest during the middle years of the eighteenth
century in the conversion experience, Waterland and other Anglican
writers found themselves defending the authenticity of the traditional
view of regeneration and the new birth of baptism and distinguishing
it from the new birth of conversion advocated by Whitefield. Waterland did this by stressing the connection between baptism and the

9. Hobart, *Truths of Redemption,* 1:332.
10. *Christian Journal* 3 (1819): 138.
11. For a background to this service, see Archibald John Stephens, ed., *The Book of Common Prayer . . . with Notes Legal and Historical,* 3 vols. (London, 1849–54), 2:1278, 1299–1302.

change of state that regeneration entailed, while at the same time distinguishing between the act of regeneration and the process of renovation.[12] Hobart very early adopted this regeneration/renovation distinction, since it provided an alternative to the conversion model of piety favored by most evangelical Protestants and successfully held in tandem an elevated view of the church ordinances and a demand for sanctification. For Hobart the new birth came via the sacrament of baptism: "In a certain sense . . . every baptized person undergoes a change of spiritual condition—is born again."[13] Hobart was never completely consistent as to what this change actually entailed. At times he saw it primarily as an entrance into the church, the community of grace, but at other times (particularly in his early writings) he elevated the importance of the sacramental regeneration and saw it as an actual moral change.[14] The analogy he most often used was that grace was received by title in baptism, but not actually. God offered justification conditionally in baptism, yet for the gift to be consummated the grace had to lead to a real progress within the Christian life, which Hobart understood as renovation. Through renovation the affections were transformed; a change in heart and life was affected; and salvation and justification were actually achieved. Renovation entailed the movement from the sacramental presentation of the new life to the actual. Although on one level this simply reshuffled the order of the same elements that made up the evangelical notion of salvation, this change in order had tremendous practical importance in daily life. Because it was grounded in an external formal action, the question of the new birth or regeneration never became a source of personal anxiety among high church Episcopalians the way it often was among evangelicals. Regeneration was firmly encased within an objective rite, and no personal sentiment or action could ever lead one to question it.

12. Daniel Waterland, *Regeneration, Stated and Explained* . . . (Philadelphia, 1829). Published in England in 1740, the work quickly crossed the Atlantic and was used by colonial Anglicans as an important critique of the Great Awakening emphasis upon conversion. Jonathan Dickinson, first president of Princeton College, strongly attacked Waterland's distinction: see "Remarks on a Discourse by Dr. Waterland . . ." in *Sermons and Tracts* (Edinburgh, 1793), 373 ff. Waterland's work was published in America in the early nineteenth century and for decades continued to be a favorite among high church clergy. See Clifton H. Brewer, *A History of Religious Education in the Episcopal Church to 1835* (New Haven, 1924), 314–18.

13. *Works*, 2:60–61.

14. This inconsistency was known by his contemporaries, some of whom despaired of ever reconciling Hobart's different positions. See Henry Ustick Onderdonk to Samuel Seabury, 6 Dec. 1833, Seabury Correspondence.

Although they willingly admitted that not all who were grafted onto Christ would remain in the end, they adamantly maintained the truthfulness of the sacramental grafting. Whereas evangelicals often perceived a lack of sufficient fruit as a sign that the moral change promised in regeneration had not in fact occurred, this was never necessary for the Hobartian. Viewed from the distinction between regeneration and renovation a lack of sufficient fruit was seen simply as a squandering of a divine gift.

How this view clashed with the dominant evangelical system can be seen in the response it evoked from Nathaniel William Taylor, the great theologian of the New Haven theology. The question for Taylor was not one of baptism, but rather of the need to preserve the reality of the change in conversion. His basic theological critique stemmed from his axiomatic assumption "that those and those only, who are regenerated by the spirit of God possess moral excellence."[15] Both the high church identification of baptismal regeneration and the new birth and their further distinction between regeneration and renovation suffered from the same basic errors. First, the high church position made an external state a necessary component of the spiritual state by claiming that "men have faith and repentance, and *if* baptized, they are children of God, in a state of salvation so far as they can be in this life and entitled to all the counsels and blessings of the gospel covenant."[16] It limited the working of the spirit of God to the public ministrations of the church. Such a position failed to account for the existence of faith and repentance before the regeneration of baptism. But the most important error Hobart and the other high churchmen fell into was their perversion of the real importance of the new birth. For Taylor, as for most antebellum evangelicals, the world was divided into two classes, those who possessed holiness and those who did not. They saw the new birth as a real change, a genuine transference from one class to the other. The high church suggestion that the new birth could exist independent of a real moral change implied to them that an individual could be in a salvable state without holiness. Although no Episcopalian would have argued that salvation without holiness was possible, a fundamental difference in the understanding of nature and grace did divide high church and evangelical understandings of holiness. For Taylor, holiness was superadded to ordinary human nature, a

1)

Errors

2

---

15. Nathaniel William Taylor, *Regeneration, The Beginning of Holiness in the Human Heart* (New Haven, 1816), 5.

16. Ibid., 18. Emphasis in original.

gift to be received, while for the high church writers it was viewed more as a fact to be appropriated by habitual effort.[17]

The fact that high churchmen, following their liturgy, continued to refer to baptismal regeneration as a new birth, while the rest of evangelical America reserved the term to describe their own call for a change in heart, led to continuing misunderstandings. For evangelicals, high churchmen lacked godly discipline, particularly with regard to the sacraments. Although they encouraged personal preparation, high church pastors generally did not require any experience of a pious change as a prerequisite for communion, and this separation of sacrament from spiritual change was a scandal for many. As one indignant writer asked, "How can you come [to communion] with those, who spend the night following dancing in the very room where they so lately received the sacrament: or played cards on the very table from which but just before they received the sacramental bread and wine?"[18] Indeed, in private even some high church theologians feared that the radical distinction between regeneration and renovation resulted in the divorcing of the sacrament from sanctification. As we shall see, by the 1830s there was a general movement away from the Waterland–Hobart formulary in favor of approaches that while preserving sacramental efficacy tried to elevate the importance of moral regeneration. Despite these technical problems, however, during the early decades of the century the regeneration/renovation distinction did serve as a fundamental alternative to the conversion-centered evangelicalism of antebellum Protestantism.

Of far greater importance to the core of high church theology than issues of grace was the question of apostolic order. The vision of the early church to which American high churchmen appealed was not the growing and dynamic tradition of Herder that would become so important in Western thought, but a finely defined and crystallized tradition inherited from generations of English writers. This preromantic, static view of history led them to view the early church more as a mine of information than as a living and vital community in its own right. The history of the early church was primarily important apologetically, and in no area more so than in buttressing Episcopal ministerial claims. Missionaries often wrote to Hobart requesting a list of the succession of bishops and their consecrators in order to

17. Wertz, "Hobart," 117–18.
18. William Bacon, *Regeneration, The New Birth: A Sermon* . . . (Waterloo, N.Y., 1818), 19.

better emphasize the historic continuity of the church.[19] Apologists such as Bowden, Hobart, and How went to great lengths linking current Episcopal practices with the record of the primitive church. An American edition of the works of Barnabas, Ignatius, Clement, Polycarp, and Hermes appeared in 1810. On an even more popular level Episcopal journals such as the *Churchman's Magazine* and the *Christian Journal* regularly included short lives of and excerpts from the writings of such luminaries as Ignatius and Irenaeus. Many an Episcopalian took solace and strength from the moral authority implicit in this unbroken tradition. Yet equally as important, the primitive church served as a rock of epistemological certainty. The primitive church was for them what the Augsburg Confession was to Lutherans and the Westminster Confession was to Presbyterians, the classic locus of true doctrine. Yet the very difference in nature between a confession and a corpus of history led to a different theological spirit. The appeal of the primitive church made high church writers rigidly certain on issues such as church polity and questions such as the nature of the Trinity and the person and work of Christ, since the primitive witness seemed clear and certain on these questions. Yet on many other questions, such as justification and abstruse debates over grace, they were remarkably flexible and critical of the dogmatic tendencies among some of their contemporaries.[20] They had little patience with the speculative aspects that tended to characterize much of the Presbyterian and Congregational theology of the period.[21]

Rather than a theological confession, these men offered a method of analysis derived from the great age of Anglican high church patristic

19. *Archives,* 4:342.

20. This idea is fruitfully played out in G. V. Bennett, "Patristic Tradition in Anglican Thought, 1660–1900," in *Oecumenica: An Annual Symposium of Ecumenical Research, 1971–2* (Minneapolis, Minn., 1972), 66–67, who also provides a good background on the question of tradition.

21. Theodore Dwight Bozeman in *Protestants in an Age of Science: The Baconian Ideal and Antebellum American Religious Thought* (Chapel Hill, 1977), has noted that Old School Presbyterians often expressed concern over the use of metaphysics and speculative theology. See, in particular, 132–59. There were, however, key distinctions between the antimetaphysical biases of the Old School and the high church movements. Bozeman has shown how the Old School bias stemmed from the Baconian emphasis on inductive reasoning and that it was directed largely against rationalistic Unitarianism. My research suggests that the high church bias had its roots more in Hutchinsonianism than Baconianism and that it was directed as much against Calvinistic views on predestination and schemes of grace as against rationalism.

scholarship as represented in John Pearson and George Bull.[22] Scripture as interpreted by the early church and as refocused, if necessary, by the English Reformers became the standard high church theological approach. The linchpin of the entire argument was the myth of the pure church. Virtually every high church writer shared the belief that a period of centuries existed during which the church accurately reflected the true teachings of the scriptures and hence could be used as a sure interpreter of scripture. During this primitive and pure age, stretching from the death of Christ to the growth of papal supremacy, the scriptures were finalized, the doctrines of the Trinity and person and work of Christ were defined, and the polity and life of the church were finally worked out. It was a three- or four-century period of brilliance in the dark and murky history of the church. The witness of this pure church was the hermeneutic by which both nonepiscopal Protestants and Roman Catholics could be answered, since it attested to the apostolic nature of episcopacy while excluding papal supremacy.

So important was the concept of the pure church that high church writers were always quick to defend it. Unfortunately, the growing trend toward what is now known as modern church history implicitly threatened the assumptions of the pure church argument. Since the middle of the eighteenth century, historians such as Johann Lorenz von Mosheim (1694–1755), often called the father of modern church history, had indirectly challenged the pure church argument through their attempt to separate church history from the realm of apologetics. Troubled by this trend, one high churchman lamented,

> Most ardently do we join in the wish for a good Church History. A history which should bring the progress and fruits of the Gospel in the foreground, giving us only a distinct yet clear view of human errors and abuses, and which, withal, should have been written in the vein of true Christian philosophy. . . . Not the least of its excellencies would be that it would go far to put an end to the controversies on Church government, and supercede the necessity of much that is written on the Evidences and Systematic Theology.[23]

22. Pearson (1613–86) was best known for his study of the epistles of Ignatius of Antioch and also for his *Exposition of the Creed* (1659). Bull (1634–1710), in addition to his writings on the question of justification, was also famous for his defense of the orthodoxy of the pre-Nicene church in his *Defensio Fidei Nicaenae* (1685). For background, see H. R. McAdoo, *The Spirit of Anglicanism: A Survey of Anglican Theological Method in the Seventeenth Century* (London, 1965).

23. "Church History," *Churchman* 4 (November 8, 1834): 759. Questions concerning Mosheim were first raised in *Christian Journal* 2 (1818): 120.

Having rested their theology on a view of history that presupposed that the hand of God was clearly active preserving his truth in the primitive church, they could only respond with alarm at attempts such as Mosheim's that tended to cloud their clear evidence by removing God from active participation in history.

For the practical ramifications of how this witness of the primitive church was to be employed Hobart and other high church writers relied heavily on principles set down by the eighteenth-century English writer William Reeves (1667–1726). Defending the appeal to the early church against the contemporary attacks of Jean Daille, Reeves attempted to define the proper authority that the apostolic evidence possessed. "But for us," he observed, "we look upon the Divinely-inspired Writings only, as binding in themselves; and upon the Fathers, as much better qualified for the Interpretation of the Scriptures, than the Moderns; who tho' in truth such Pigmies, are yet so tall in Imagination, as to fancy they can take a nicer view of the Sacred Text merely upon their own Legs, than upon the Shoulders of the Ancients."[24] Reeves went on to answer two popular objections to the use of the fathers: that some of their individual views were strange and that they disagreed among themselves. In response to the former he emphasized that their authority lay in the facts they conveyed concerning the life and practice of the early church and not in the peculiar opinions and theories which they held. In answer to the claim that they disagreed among themselves Reeves elevated the rule of Vincent of Lerins, with its famous formula *quod ubique, quod semper, quod ab omnibus* (everywhere, always, and from all things), as a basis for authority. Where the fathers agreed among themselves the truth lay. Hobart found Reeves's "Right Use of the Fathers" and his use of the rule of St. Vincent immensely appealing, and he quickly adopted it. Thus he could proclaim,

> Let it not be supposed that I advocate the papal tenet of the infalli-
> bility of the Church, of the necessity of implicitly receiving her
> interpretations of sacred writ. What indeed the great body of Chris-

24. William Reeves, "Preface Concerning the Right Use of the Fathers," in *The Apologies of Justin Martyr, Tertullian, and Minutius Felix, . . . with the Commonitory of Vincentius Lirinensis Concerning the Primitive Rule of Faith* (London, 1709), lxiv. Reeves was an important source in nineteenth-century Episcopal circles, and Hobart urged every candidate for the ministry to read him. See Hobart, *An Introductory Address on the Occasion of the Opening of the General Theological Seminary . . .* (New York, 1822).

tians in every age, and in all places; what the universal Church, universal as to *numbers,* to *time,* to *place,* has received, may be morally demonstrated, must be founded in the Word of God.[25]

The trustworthiness of the Episcopal theological claims stemmed from the consensus of the early fathers and the factual veracity of their witness. The early church argument gave an objective, empirical, and almost quasi-scientific quality to high church theological discussion that, in certain ways, paralleled the way in which the Scottish Common Sense philosophy was at the same time influencing evangelical thought and pushing it toward objectivity and facticity.[26] Whereas, however, evangelicals found their inspiration in an orderly and regular nature brimming with teleological meaning, the high church writers responded to a vision of history that found God peculiarly present at certain points such as the era of the primitive church. Yet one of the indirect consequences of the high church approach was that it not only set the method for their theology but also defined the scope. Questions not treated directly in the scriptures or by the primitive church were, from the high church perspective, not theological issues and accordingly were not concerns of the church. The high church response to the abolition and temperance movements, for example, displayed an unwillingness to see these as religious questions at all, since there was no precedent from the primitive church to do so. The model of the primitive church shaped the theological agenda among the high church figures.

Because of their rigidity in theological method, so surely anchored upon the vision of the pure church, high churchmen never considered themselves to be liberals. Although their contemporaries saw them as dangerously close to Latitudinarians and Socinians on questions of grace, from their own perspective they saw themselves as bastions of theological order. Rather than viewing their rejection of the conversion experience and total depravity as marks of a liberal religion (as evangelicals suggested), high churchmen considered themselves to be defenders of the apostolic faith, bulwarks against unorthodoxy, and a

25. John Henry Hobart, *An Address Delivered Before the Auxiliary New-York Bible and Common Prayer Book Society . . .* (New York, 1816), 11. Emphasis in original.
26. On the ramifications of this phenomenon in evangelical thought, see Bozeman, *Protestants in an Age of Science,* passim; Herbert Hovenkamp, *Science and Religion in America, 1800–1860* (Philadelphia, 1978), 3–37; and John Vander Stelt, *Philosophy and Scripture: A Study in Old Princeton and Westminster Theology* (Marlton, N.J., 1978), passim.

bastion for tradition in the face of an untraditional spirit within the rest of American Protestantism.

Episcopal rhetoric during this period overflowed with warnings concerning the threat that modern trends within American religion and culture posed to the inherited truth and order of the Episcopal Church. There was a growing fear throughout the 1820s (that was to become even stronger in the 1830s) that the political values of liberty and freedom of individual opinion might threaten to become the rule even with questions of revealed faith. The problem of maintaining both intellectual and institutional authority became an increasing concern in this context, for, as one important high church theologian noted while addressing the annual convention of the diocese of New York, "In civil or social affairs, there is no appeal to any higher authority than men. . . . But in religion all is reversed. The will of God, ascertained from his word, is final; and against this, the united judgement of every man and every angel would be rebellion."[27] The primitive church grounded their faith and protected them against the tendency toward the anarchy of private judgment.

Their self-understanding as traditionalists within an untraditional religious culture was often a stronger impulse than their theology itself and led them enthusiastically to applaud movements toward confessionalism within other denominations. Even though they might theologically deplore the strict Calvinism of the Westminster Confession, as a group they preferred the confessional impulse of the Old School Presbyterians to the more evangelical attitude of the New School. The high church fear of a loss of distinctiveness caused them to view movements toward confessionalism as allies in the struggle against the amalgamating spirit within American evangelicalism. Accordingly, they applauded a lecture by their old bete noire Samuel Miller, published under the title *The Utility and Importance of Creeds and Confessions* (1824). In it Miller emphasized the need for creeds to preserve the harmony and purity of the visible church, and the inability of scripture alone to fulfill this need:

> It is not enough for attaining this object, that all who are admitted profess to agree in receiving the *Bible;* for many who call themselves christians, and profess to take the *Bible* for their guide, hold opin-

27. Henry U. Onderdonk, "Authority and Private Judgement," [N.Y.P.E.C. Convention Address 1821], in *Sermons and Episcopal Charges*, 2 vols. (Philadelphia, 1851), 1:366.

ions, and speak a language as foreign, nay as opposite, to the opinions and language of many others, who equally claim to be christians, and equally profess to receive the Bible, as east is to the west.[28]

The church—depository, guardian, and witness to the truth—had the obligation to seek out a surer base, and for Miller this was the confession. Writing in the *Christian Journal,* an Episcopal correspondent warmly praised Miller's essay and coyly noted the parallels between Miller's position and Hobart's opposition to the general Bible societies.[29] For Episcopalians, movements such as that which Miller's sermon represented confirmed for them that even Protestants were coming to recognize the need for order as a means for preserving truth.

II

Great point

On the practical level, questions of theology often became questions of piety. A standard evangelical criticism of American high churchmen was that they lacked both experimental and moral piety. As one critic claimed, instead of vital piety, all that high church formalists offered was "a little thin sabbatical morality, a miserable deterioration of heathen ethics, of the unsanctioned codes of Plato, or Epictetus, or Seneca."[30] Ironically, however, both his contemporaries and later historians have praised Hobart for his role in vivifying Anglican piety. Such widely contrasting interpretations suggest a fundamental difference in the high church and evangelical understandings of the nature of piety.

The charge of "formalism" directs the student to one of these fundamental differences, since for Hobart and other high church writers piety could never be divided from form. The church and its ordinances were the chief vehicles of piety: the liturgy spurred on the growth of individual piety, while the catechism continued the work of instruction. Baptism, as the regenerative new birth, gave to all the chance of salvation, and the ordinances of the church aided in the

28. Samuel Miller, *The Utility and Importance of Creeds and Confessions* . . . (Princeton, 1824), 11. Emphasis in original.

29. [Robert Croes], "Correspondence," *Christian Journal* 8 (1824): 338. Miller attempted to defend the compatibility between his position and support for the Bible Society in the January 1825 issue of the same journal. For an account of this dispute see, Miller, *Life,* 2:96–102.

30. Bristed, *Anglican and American-Anglo Churches,* 3.

process of making that potential a reality. The eucharist, for example, offered a "lively representation of the sufferings and death of Christ" that aimed at provoking a penitential sorrow out of a "deep sense of the evil of sin, as a *presumptious contempt of the righteous authority of God.*"[31] The liturgical confrontation between the natural human state and the infinite divine love lay at the heart of the church's life of prayer, and the true task of devotional aids was to make this confrontation more explicit through preparation and self-examination. The difference between Hobart and his evangelical contemporaries was that whereas both would agree on the need for faith, repentance, and the work of the holy spirit in the life of a true Christian, for Hobart these were goals to be achieved via the liturgy and from within the church and not requirements for entrance into the community.

A closer examination of Hobart's discussion of the schema of the Christian life reveals an even more important difference. For Hobart, the life of the righteous should be a progression in goodness:

> Daily advancing in all holy virtues and graces, his love to God, his trust in his Saviour, his pious and devout affections should constantly become more sincere and strong, and his active sympathy and benevolence should burn with a brighter and brighter flame. . . . Thus all the divine, social, and personal virtues would be displayed in his life and conversation, with increasing brightness.[32]

Once inside the community the individual should strive to grow in grace by constantly meditating upon the mercy and perfection of God. Yet in this schema of growth one observes a marked personalization of the Christian life. All of the virtues Hobart chose to emphasize—an appreciation for the grace of God, a heightening of personal sympathy—were personal in nature, and none necessarily had a social corollary. Indeed, high church piety as a rule lacked the social dynamic of contemporary evangelical life. The emphasis upon disinterested benevolence that inspired the reform movements of the early national period and the evangelistic spirit that empowered the great missionary endeavors of the first decades of the nineteenth century found little place in high church piety. Even the benevolence that Hobart did see as a fruit of true faith seemed to lead to private charity rather than social reform. Those reform movements such as the Bible and Common

31. Hobart, *Companion for the Altar*, 75, 71. Emphasis in original.
32. *Works*, 3:438–39.

Prayer Book Society that did emanate from the high church movement were products of ecclesiology and not piety. Social means of grace created personal and individual growth in the Hobartian system. The church was a channel of grace, which, although being a social institution, treated its members as individuals and not as members of a common body. The fact that group demands were lowered, at least in contrast to the evangelical churches, allowed ironically for a far greater practical individualism.[33] A fruit of this practical individualism was that the Hobartians saw the church in an almost quasi-therapeutic role. Individuals came to it and made use of what it offered to redirect their own lives. The church as doctor was to help in the healing of as many souls as possible, but it was not to make rigorous demands upon its members outside of that therapeutic relationship. True piety lay not in dynamic group action but in an individual's day-to-day routine.[34]

If the devotional schema outlined by these high churchmen was not evangelical (in the American sense of that term), neither could it be considered Catholic in any traditional sense. Early in his career Hobart had flirted with the doctrine of the real presence, or the notion that in the celebration of the holy communion Christ was actually present to all and not just to believers. From the works of the Nonjurors George Hickes and John Johnson he had learned not only of the doctrine of the real presence but also of the claim that Anglican clerics were actually priests in the levitical sense, that is, offerers of a sacrifice. William White went to great pains to disabuse his former student of these views, and he evidently did his job well. In most of his mature writings Hobart displayed little interest in the classical Catholic notion of the sacraments as conduits of objective grace.[35] The importance of the sacraments was not as conduits but as a pledge or guarantee of the relationship between the individual and the historic community. The issue of sacramental validity for Hobart therefore encompassed little more than the question of proper connection with the church. "It is of the utmost importance," he urged, "to ascertain with whom God has

33. This had been a long-standing point of contention between Anglican and evangelical modes of worship, and John F. H. New sees it cropping up in Puritan criticism of Anglican worship as early as the sixteenth century. See *Anglican and Puritan: The Basis of their Opposition, 1558–1640* (Stanford, 1964), 41–42.

34. See, for example, "An Extract from a Funeral Discourse," *Christian Journal* 2 (1818): 183–84, for a particularly striking instance of praise for this type of piety.

35. For a copy of White's letters to Hobart on this subject, see *A Voice From the Past. Two Letters From Bishop White to the Rev. John H. Hobart, D.D. . . . .* (Philadelphia, 1879).

not as ~~...~~ ch
primitive Augus.

invested authority to administer those sacraments, which derive all
their efficacy from being administered according to his appointment."[36] In addition to cementing the relationship between the individual and the historic church, he suggested further values of the
sacraments and ordinances: they instructed individuals with symbols;
they served as a test of humility and submission (since the connection
between cause and effect was never rationally apparent); they were
pledges of mercy and grace; and finally, when united with awe, reverence, penitence, faith, and gratitude, they could confer salvation.[37]

Perhaps the most surprising aspect of high church piety was the
great importance it placed on both sentiment and nonrational means of
conveying religious truth. For all their criticism of the emotionalism
of evangelicalism these high church writers were well aware of the
value of an appeal to the feelings. They may have disliked the evangelical tendency to let emotion overwhelm reason (particularly in both
revivalism and in the demand for a conversion), yet they did not ignore
the usefulness of nonrational persuasion. As Hobart wrote, "There is
no truth which the consideration of human nature, and the testimony
of daily experience more strongly establish than that man is swayed
more by his *passions* than by his *reason*. By the impressive power of
external rites and emblems, you gain access to his passions; you
awaken, you guide and control them."[38] Indeed, if the message of the
early nineteenth-century revivalists can be characterized as "get religion," the call of these high church writers was to "feel religious."
Much of this appreciation for the power of an appeal to the feelings
should be traced back to Hobart. His household piety as a child
abounded with emotion and feeling, and throughout his life he placed
great weight on the importance of sentiment and the connection between human and divine affections. Even in the face of death he spoke
of the value of such feelings. Writing to his sister after the death of a
close friend, he observed, "[God] has given us virtuous feelings to be
indulged and he separates the objects of our affections from us only
that by being less bound to this world we may love it less, and aspire
constantly after another where we look for the full and perfect fruition
of every virtuous sentiment and feeling."[39] Since for Hobart all learn-

36. Hobart, *Companion for the Altar*, 177.
37. This is a summary of an important sermon Hobart delivered in 1816 at the
dedication of Trinity Church, New Haven. See John Henry Hobart, *The Moral
Efficacy and Positive Benefits of the Ordinances of the Gospel* (New Haven, 1816).
38. Hobart, *Companion for the Altar*, 167. Emphasis in original.
39. *Archives*, 1:301.

ing was effected through the senses, religion as well had to be conveyed in this manner. True religion, accordingly, addressed the whole
individual—feeling as well as intellect, body as well as spirit—and
could never forget the importance of the nonrational. Placed in an
environment that is conducive to religious sentiment, an individual
would feel religious, and this in turn would strengthen the habit of
piety. A chief task of both the clergy and the liturgy was to make the
laity feel religious. The true Christian ought to *feel* in confession the
forgiveness of sin, in thanksgiving *feel* that his prayers have been answered, and finally, "Let him *feel* especially that the 'Lord is in the
place' where he thus worships, and his affections will be awed, his
manner will be solemnized, his whole soul will be occupied in that
homage which he offers to his God, glorious in holiness, fearful in
praise."[40] It is clear that Hobart and his fellow high churchmen had an
ambiguous view of the role of feelings in religion. While rejecting
their use either in determining doctrine or even as a prerequisite for
entrance into the church, the core of their individual piety revolved
around the importance of holy feelings.

Thus the conflict between the differing understandings of the role
of the affections in religion that separated evangelicals and high church
writers reflects the more basic pattern of Hobartian/evangelical disagreement. Evangelicals, following the teachings of theorists such as
Jonathan Edwards, believed that the experience of conversion entailed
the reception of a new set of holy affections. Those natural affections
which the individual possessed before conversion were not treated as
inherently evil but were viewed as corrupt concerning the things of
religion. The new heart and affections came from a gracious act of God
at the time of conversion, when the soul experienced the excellence
and glory of divine things. For the Hobartians, however, religious
affections traced their origin not to conversion but to creation itself.
They served as part of the divine economy of grace, preparing the
individual for the reception of the church's message.

This emphasis on affection and environment may help explain
why so much emphasis was put on form and decorum in worship and
why there arose such an early interest in Gothic architecture, decades
before the founding of the now famous Cambridge Ecclesiastical Society. Of course one must not ignore the social significance of architecture for these individuals. Both as a symbol of their social prominence
and as a response to their numerical weakness, Episcopal congrega-

40. *Works*, 2:37. Emphasis in original.

tions often put great emphasis upon the quality of their church buildings. Yet church buildings had a religious as well as social function. Although they acknowledged that worship could be done in any physical environment, "it is conformable to a law of our nature, that the excitement and the expression of our feelings of devotion, should be aided by those exterior embellishments that delight the eye, and gratify the taste, and thus—for there is an intimate association between all our powers—enlighten the understanding and elevate the heart."[41] Gothic architecture in particular aptly fitted both the apologetical appeal and devotional spirit of the high church movement. Its evocation of an earlier epoch linked the present Episcopal Church to the long, continuous historic church—a visible reminder of continuity. Furthermore the reverential spirit the architecture evoked aided in spiritual nurture.[42]

The open appeal to nonrational means for conveying true religious sentiment hints at an important difference between high church piety and the general tenor of evangelical devotion. The contrast has been likened to the distinction between the idea of "cultural determinism" and that of the "unregenerate soul."[43] Implicit in the Anglican view of prayer and custom, the argument continues, is a fundamentally passive assumption about human psychology, "one nearly behavioristic in its appreciation in the way set and customary forms work upon the mind as if by reflex, to condition it, affect it, and cause it to respond in predictable ways."[44] Part of the rationale behind this devotional emphasis was a purely practical preference for concord over strife. From the very days of Elizabeth I it was recognized that a liturgy that instilled love and loyalty was far preferable to the divisions that resulted from theological discourse. Yet it also reflected a deep confidence in the continuity between the realm of reason and that of grace. High

41. John Henry Hobart, *The Worship of the Church on Earth . . .* (Philadelphia, 1823), 14–15.

42. On the general appeal of the Gothic revival, see Kenneth Clark, *The Gothic Revival, An Essay in the History of Taste,* 3d ed. (London, 1962). On its introduction in America, see Richard K. Newman, "Yankee Gothic, Medieval Architectural Forms in the Protestant Church Buildings of Nineteenth-Century New England." (Ph.D. diss., Yale University, 1949). St. Thomas Church was the first important Gothic building in New York City. See DeMille, *St. Thomas,* 22–23. The first book written in America on Gothic architecture was by a high church Episcopal cleric. See John Henry Hopkins, *An Essay on Gothic Architecture.* (Burlington, Vt., 1836).

43. Alan Kantrow, "Anglican Custom, American Consciousness," *New England Quarterly* 52 (1979): 317.

44. Ibid., 317.

church writers often criticized Calvinists for extrapolating from the doctrine of the fall the idea of total depravity. Whereas Hobart and the others would have agreed that no moral effort of natural man was acceptable to God vis-à-vis salvation, they nonetheless adamantly maintained that these natural instincts were still virtues. Natural virtues such as sympathy were not to be despised but instead nurtured, since they were prime vehicles of divine grace. The world and human nature were not totally alien and separate from God but rather filled with crèches of grace. "If it be a first truth," Hobart explained, "that the infinitely wise and perfect Creator has not made anything in vain, there can be no principle of that nature which he has given us, which is not designed in some degree to form our character, and to influence our conduct."[45] The appeal to the feelings was part of the Hobartian belief that the Christian life had to encompass the whole individual.

Such an appeal to the natural religious feelings had still another important function in the Hobartian schema. The elevating of the importance of natural motive and impulses such as fear, remorse, and gratitude played an important role in extending the perimeters of the high church appeal to include those "to whom it is idle to talk of fathers, and ancient classics, of historical proofs . . . and translations."[46] The positive evaluation of the natural religious impulse did much to counterbalance Hobartian ecclesiastical theology, which, being so tied to the evidences of the primitive church, always ran the danger of lapsing into a narrow fideistic intellectualism. The emphasizing of the importance of the religious intuition extended the appeal of the Hobartian synthesis beyond the confines of the clerical library into the daily life of the laity.[47]

In this context it is easier to understand the issues underlying the final evangelical critique of Episcopal piety, its lack of moral rigor. Much of the rigor of evangelical piety in early nineteenth-century

45. John Henry Hobart, *Christian Sympathy: A Sermon Preached to the Congregation of English Protestants in the City of Rome* . . . (London, 1825), 6. For a similar sentiment, see "On Compassion," *Churchman's Magazine* 11 (1815): 120–24.

46. Gulian Verplanck, *Essays on the Nature and Uses of the Various Evidences of Revealed Religion* (New York, 1824), 59–60. Verplanck was professor of Christian apologetics at General Seminary from 1821 to 1825.

47. One sees the implicit tension between the ecclesiastical theology and the piety of the Hobartians in the praise some of them will bestow on eighteenth-century English figures such as Horne and Jones of Nayland as rigid ecclesiastical apologists, yet the fault they find in these same figures for downplaying the value of religious intuition. See Verplanck, *Essays,* 42. The question of the value of religious intuition would plague Hobartian writers for decades.

America concerned the call for an elevated moral life from its followers. Dueling, horse racing, gaming, theatergoing, and public balls were all eschewed and eventually even drinking would be included under this ban. As one scholar has suggested, however, the vices these evangelicals attacked all tended to have been aristocratic activities, and their rejection reflected as much a rejection by lower-middle- and middle-class individuals of an aristocratic morality as it was a statement of the inherent evils of these activities.[48] Holiness was tied to this social morality. We have seen how a standard critique of high church sacramental thought was that it permitted card players, dancers, and other such participants in worldly amusements to take communion. Yet this was not simply a sacramental worry. One layman, writing to Hobart, lamented the lax morality among Episcopalians: "Such a course . . . seems inconsistent with Christian sobriety, and dangerous to the morals of the members of the church."[49] The issue of "vain amusements" was even debated in the Episcopal General Convention of 1817 and again in that of 1823. In 1817 the House of Bishops issued a general pastoral letter on the question, while the House of Deputies (through the machinations of the Hobartian party) sidestepped the question. An even stricter proposal by evangelical delegates in 1823 to bar from communion all those persons who attended the theater was tabled.[50] Although these attempts bore little fruit, Episcopal evangelicals did attempt to enforce the shared evangelical morality wherever they could.

No single reason explains why other Episcopalians in general and high churchmen in particular rejected this evangelical social piety. One important factor is that the high church social piety was the status quo or traditional teaching. At least since the issuing by James I of the Book of Sports in 1617 Episcopalians had defended the right of amusement. Furthermore much of the theological message of the high church position involved the plea to avoid innovation. A resistance to evan-

48. Donald G. Mathews, *Religion in the Old South* (Chicago, 1977), 39–80. On general American attitudes toward amusements at the time see Anne Hollingsworth Wharton, *Social Life in the Early Republic* (Philadelphia, 1902); Foster Rhea Dulles, *America Learns to Play: A History of Popular Recreation, 1607–1940* (New York, 1940); and Russel B. Nye, *The Cultural Life of the New Nation, 1776–1830* (New York, 1960).

49. Edmund J. Lee to John Henry Hobart, 12 Nov. 1817, Hobart Correspondence.

50. William White, *Memoirs of the Protestant Episcopal Church . . . ,* 2d ed. (New York, 1836), 229, 248.

al social morality became tied to the general concern for resisting changes to the received order. This suspicion of innovation would only become stronger in the decade of the 1830s, when these changes were perceived as occurring at an increasingly quickened rate. Another factor was sociological. Part of the function of evangelical social morality, according to Mathews, was to elevate status. Status concerns seem to have had little importance in Episcopal evangelicalism (for which status was, on the whole, more secure than for other groups). A third factor was that the devotional system of the Hobartians did not need evangelical morality in order to secure a deeper spirituality. It served little purpose in the high church schema of sanctification. But in addition to all these factors, the whole tenor of the Hobartian scheme of nature and grace revolted against it. For Hobartians, nature and grace were as intricately connected in the issue of worldliness as they had been in the earlier question of natural virtue. In Hobart's vision, the individual believer was firmly embedded in the world. And as he continued to explain,

> Religion does not demand, in a certain sense, the sacrifice of the world. She requires the sacrifice of those passions only which are incompatible with our virtue, and thus destroy our peace. She only bestows those hopes which exalt all the virtuous pleasures of life, and administer consolation and support under its numerous trials.[51]

The world was basically a good place, and just as natural virtues were to be directed rather than abolished, so too with much of human nature. Whether this ethical attitude of the Hobartians was nothing more than a form of "cosmic Toryism" is ultimately difficult to conclude. Those most satisfied with their present lot historically have been the strongest champions of a theology that put its trust in God's beneficent working through human nature, and indubitably many accepted the Hobartian toleration of evangelical vices without accepting any more of the schema. Only a case-by-case biographical approach can hope to determine the issue. Yet the sermons and catechetical literature do see this rejection of evangelical social morality as being at one with their rejection of the evangelical distinctions between the saved and damned and nature and grace.

What has become apparent is that the theology and the devotional life of the high church movement pulled in different directions. The

51. John Henry Hobart, *The Candidate for Confirmation Instructed . . .* (New York, 1826), 33.

theology glorified an identification with the pre-Nicene church and methodologically was tied to the scriptures as interpreted by the "pure church." The devotion emphasized a sentimental piety of nonrational forms and a view of personal growth that was almost therapeutic in its nature. What model of ministry, if any, could serve both sides of this high church synthesis? The theology seemed to call for a stern man of the book—an *Athanasius contra mundum,* cleaving to the revealed truth without regard for consequence. The devotional piety seemed to call for a man of feeling—whose heart could intrinsically feel the sentiments of his flock. How these two could be reconciled was the problem confronting high church writers and educators.

One thing they could all generally agree on was that the ministry was a separate caste, if not ontologically at least practically. Ordination into the historic ministry set an individual apart, and high churchmen were always quick to defend the sanctity of their office. They were not alone in this concern. From the early years of the nineteenth century, the Episcopal Church in general had striven to elevate the dignity of the clergy by putting strict limits on the role of lay readers.[52] A true minister was one connected to the visible historic church.

In addition to this concern for legitimacy, ministers were urged to maintain orthodoxy in doctrine and particularly to be able to defend the peculiar teachings of their church. In his address to the opening session of the newly reorganized General Theological Seminary Hobart emphasized to the young seminarians the importance of being true to their theological roots:

> Go back to the first ages of Christianity, and contemplate the learning and the eloquence of an Origen and a Tertullian, a Cyprian and a Jerome, a Basil and a Chrysostom, an Athanasius and an Augustine. Bring often to view the constellation of divines, that adorned and adorns the Church from which you are descended, illustrious in talents, learning and eloquence, and aiming at their learning & eloquence be emulous also, with equal fidelity and zeal, to come forward in the world, the champions of the Christian faith.[53]

The minister, as steward of the apostolic tradition, had the responsibil-

52. Charles N. Brickley, "The Episcopal Church in Protestant America, 1800–1860, A Study in Thought and Action," (Ph.D. diss., Clark University, 1949), 74–77. Hobart and the other high churchmen were particularly adamant in defending clerical prerogative. See the correspondence between Samuel Haskell and Hobart over the authority of lay readers, 31 May 1813 and 25 August 1813, in Hobart Correspondence.

53. Hobart, *Introductory Address,* 34–35.

ity to know and to defend the apologetical story that Hobart and his supporters had established and to cleave to the theological principles they had derived. Every seminarian was to be well versed in Reeves's "Right Use of the Fathers" and if called upon to be ready to defend church principles against any attacker.

Yet the bulk of the actual advice ministers received was not in this apologetical vein but rather urged upon them the need for personal piety and sensitivity. The eighteenth-century Anglican ministerial model that had striven for a balanced reasonableness, untouched by emotional fervor, was clearly abandoned in favor of a more fervent approach. The change in emphasis is not surprising considering the importance of vital piety for Hobart personally. Early in his preparation for the ministry he had decided that as important as knowledge might be, "the improvement of the heart should be the end of all our requirements."[54] Following the teaching of the older Caroline High Church tradition, he emphasized that a true minister must be a man of piety since prayer was the true ornament of the priesthood.[55] But furthermore, the true minister must possess not merely piety but also warmth in spirit and affection. He was to be the man of feeling within his congregation, the model or icon of the mercy of God. As one minister urged in an address to the New York diocesan convention,

> Enlarge, enlarge your bowels of affection. Ye know nothing if ye are only acquainted with the voice of authority, reproof, correction, and with pointing out the letter of the law. Be fathers; this is not sufficient; be mothers; travail in birth again till Jesus Christ be formed in the heart of all your parishioners.[56]

To bring about this change required not simply the disclosure of truth, "but the disclosure of it with a melting pathos, and an overwhelming earnestness."[57]

This heightened appeal to sentiment and the comparison of the minister's role to that of a mother at first glance seem to confirm Ann Douglas's argument concerning cultural shifts among liberal ministers and upper-middle-class women during the first half of the nine-

---

54. *Works,* 1:51.

55. For Hobart's indebtedness to earlier tradition in this regard, see the individuals he cites in *The Clergyman's Companion* (New York, 1806), 109–15.

56. William A. Lacey, "Sermon Delivered at the Opening of the Annual Convention of the Protestant Episcopal Church in the State of New York . . ." in *Christian Journal* 6 (1822): 296.

57. Ibid., 296.

teenth century.[58] In part Douglas's argument is supported by certain trends in the Episcopal understanding of the ministry. A heightening of appreciation for sentiment and feeling did take place during these years. Yet a deep respect for an objective, exclusive theology and apologetic always held it in sharp check. The tension between these two drives characterized the high church ministerial model during the early decades of the century. Thus when called upon to describe Hobart, who became among high churchmen the model of the ideal cleric, his biographer praised him for his "woman's warmth and gentleness—man's energetic will; [since] without the latter he would have been the creature of impulse and the slave of his affections, —without the former he would have been the stern ruler whom all would have feared and none loved."[59] It was this self-perceived tension between theology and piety, not the simple move toward feminization that Douglas suggests, that characterized the Hobartian understanding of the ministry.

Two practical ramifications, however, resulted from this model. Although these high churchmen put great stock in piety and doctrine, they placed surprisingly little emphasis upon learning. Although Hobart had from as early as 1813 advocated the founding of a theological seminary for the more regular education of the clergy, his understanding of the role of that education differed from that found in a contemporary evangelical seminary such as Andover. Seminarians were regularly warned about allowing their studies to infringe upon time that should have been devoted to growth in piety. Part of this suspicion of learning for learning's sake stemmed from Hobart's own impatience with high scholarship. Once in conversation he dismissed the importance of Herbert Marsh, translator of the great German biblical critic Johann David Michaelis, by simply noting, "Oh, he's nothing but a biblical critic."[60] Indeed, Hobart at one point even advocated the reduction of the course of preparation for the ministry from three years to one. But this attitude was not limited to Hobart. High church Episcopalians during these years found little place for the tradition of scholarship that characterized the American reformed churches. Except perhaps in the narrow question of the Episcopal apologetic,

58. See Ann Douglas, *The Feminization of American Culture* (New York, 1977), 17–139. For a summary of recent criticisms of her argument, see David S. Reynolds, "The Feminization Controversy: Sexual Stereotypes and the Paradoxes of Piety in Nineteenth-Century America," *New England Quarterly* 53 (1980): 96–105.

59. McVickar, *Hobart*, 432.

60. Samuel Turner, *Autobiography* (New York, 1863), 95.

almost no high church writer reached the scholarly stature of a Moses Stuart, Andrews Norton, Charles Hodge, Albert Barnes, or Nathaniel William Taylor. Piety and apologetical soundness were the mark of a good cleric, not intellectual curiosity.

A second result of this ministerial model was a subtle intellectual distancing of the clergy from the laity. Since ministers were seen not solely as teachers but also as nurturers, the minister inevitably assumed a role of intellectual superiority since he alone had the knowledge of the plan of nurture. In its reliance upon a devotional attraction that was nonrational in nature, high church piety always ran the risk of becoming only a technique, indeed as much a one as that of any revivalist. Particularly in missionary areas, where many of those who made up the new Episcopal congregations had been brought up in other denominations, clergy admitted that they took great care in determining how much of episcopal exclusivity could be revealed at a given point. As one missionary candidly acknowledged, "I am sure that one sermon in the high church tone would disperse my congregation."[61] This intellectual distancing clearly implied that the church's teachings were under the stewardship of its ministry, in whom professional responsibility and pastoral concern required that they reveal only those parts of the corpus which could be understood or accepted at any given time.

Perhaps the most controversial part of the high church view of the ministry was the place they allowed for "innocent amusements." The minister, as embodiment of the morality of the church, had the responsibility of reflecting the proper attitude toward recreation. "The purpose of necessary relaxation," Hobart explained, "the courtesies and innocent joys of life still further require that the student of theology should sometimes leave, which certainly should be the place in which he most delights, his study, to join the social and domestic circle."[62] By mixing with the world a minister might increase his effectiveness as well as avoid a dour, pharisaical piety. Yet for those who had a hard enough time tolerating Episcopal lay morality, this ministerial attitude was simply too much. Even Episcopal evangelicals considered the high church willingness to attend events such as parties

61. Henry U. Onderdonk to Hobart, 23 Jan. 1816, Hobart Correspondence. For other examples of this attitude, see the letters printed in Dix, *History of Trinity* 3:134–37. Hobart himself recognized this need for discretion: see *A Charge to the Clergy* . . . (New York, 1815), 18.
62. Hobart, *Address . . . General Theological Seminary* (New York, 1828), 18.

and dances "a little out of character for Divines."[63] Among high churchmen themselves, furthermore, while there was unanimity on the theological level concerning amusements, on the practical level it was never certain where in the spectrum between asceticism and over-indulgence the true line lay. The image of the pleasure-loving eighteenth-century English cleric was never really forgotten, and the concern for apostolic purity and discipline, even when it did not directly have an impact, often indirectly countered the permissive attitude toward innocent pleasures. Clergy were called at the same time to be at one with their flock, yet better, since it was imperative to avoid actual scandal. As a practical result, for example, a number of clergy publicly defended the use of alcoholic beverages while remaining abstinent themselves. The tension between a clergy at one with their congregation, yet at the same time superior to it, would erupt in a series of scandals during the 1840s.

III

No aspect of antebellum Protestantism has attracted so much interest as has its social ramifications, and in particular the attempt by evangelical Protestants to forge a truly Christian nation. To assert that the Evangelical United Front was the Whig party at prayer is perhaps an overstatement, yet the evangelical agenda during the antebellum years clearly had social implications.[64] We have already seen in the case of the Bible Society movement how one of the strong motivating forces behind the great evangelical effort was the millennial vision of America as God's new Israel. In the mind of a person like Lyman Beecher, society and Christianity were inextricably tied together by the fervent belief that "this nation is, in the providence of God, destined to lead the way in the moral and political emancipation of the world."[65] Much of

63. Pintard, *Letters*, 3:125.

64. See, for example, Robert T. Handy, *A Christian America: Protestant Hopes and Historical Realities* (New York, 1971); Foster, *Errand of Mercy*, and Griffin, *Their Brother's Keeper*. Since the publication of Alan Heimert's *Religion and the American Mind*, the debate has raged whether the thrust of this evangelical movement was toward Whiggery or Jacksonianism. For a recent discussion of this question, see Daniel Walker Howe, *The Political Culture of the American Whigs* (Chicago, 1979), 150–80.

65. Lyman Beecher, *A Plea for the West* (Cincinnati, 1835), 10–11.

what was best and worst in nineteenth-century American life stemmed from just such a hope. Yet we have also seen that high church Episcopalians did not as a rule share this millennial vision, and accordingly they sharply criticized the evangelical enterprises and began to offer an alternative vision of the relationship between religion and American society.

Underlying high church social thinking was a radical separation of the concerns of the church and those of the state. In large part this high church reticence about politics must be understood historically. The public reputation of the Episcopal clergy had been badly undermined by the American Revolution, since many of their contemporaries had seen them as the chief supporters of the British cause. As a result, there was a strong reaction among Episcopal clergy against allowing any political discussion within the confines of the church. In contrast to an individual such as Lyman Beecher, who took time to vote even during his heresy trial, many Episcopal clergy did not even vote.[66] Throughout the early years of the nineteenth century the charge that Episcopalians secretly strove to regain their church's former privileged status was never completely abandoned, and during the War of 1812 anti-British broadsides often included attacks on the monarchical affinity of episcopacy.[67]

For Episcopal clergy in the state of New York there was even a more immediate need to keep the church separate from politics. The Cave Jones controversy of 1812, which began with Hobart's attempt to force Jones off of the staff of Trinity Church, quickly snowballed into an attack on Trinity's charter and precipitated a lengthy debate in the state legislature. Hobart's authoritarianism had alienated many of the chief Episcopal families of New York, some of whom as Federalist legislators supported the attack against Trinity. In planning the church's strategy, Hobart emphasized the necessity of keeping the church politically neutral so as not to alienate its support among Republican legislators.[68] The only course of safety for the church was to carefully avoid all questions of politics. As he explained in a letter to a

66. Henry Caswall, *America and the American Church* (London, 1839), 302. Hobart, for example, did not vote. See John Henry Hobart to Nathaniel Williams, 9 June 1813, Williams Papers. On Beecher, see Charles Beecher, ed., *Autobiography, Correspondence, etc., of Lyman Beecher, D.D.*, 2 vols. (New York, 1865), 2:354.

67. See, for example, *Archives*, 6:122, 309. On the War of 1812, see William Gribbin, *The Churches Militant: The War of 1812 and American Religion* (New Haven, 1973), 110–20.

68. Hobart to Nathaniel Williams, 19 June 1813, Williams Papers.

true church

friend, "I think it to be in utmost consequence to the present and future prosperity of the Church, that she should not be identified with any political party. Certainly her clergy in this city and I believe elsewhere are particularly cautious on this subject."[69]

Yet even more important than these factors were those stemming from the high church emphasis on ecclesiology. The church, according to high church theory, was a sacred vessel—a priceless gem in, but not of, the world. It was eternal; all political, social, and economic issues were ultimately only transitory. Hence all societal issues were to be judged by the same criterion—did they hinder the work of the church or not?

From as early as 1814 Hobart began to systematically elaborate this vision of the role of the church in society that was so much at odds with the rest of religious America. In May of that year, as the War of 1812 reached its most crucial stage, Hobart addressed the General Convention of the Episcopal Church, and there he attempted to give meaning to the historical identity of the American church. In his address he emphasized its continuity with the primitive church, and that it was hence of divine and not of human origin. He praised the Church of England, mother of the American church, not on account of its political establishment but for its being "a *spiritual society* possessing the faith, the order, and the worship which were the characteristics and glory of the primitive ages of the Church."[70] Only in that it retained the qualities of the primitive church did the Church of England merit praise. Its political establishment contributed nothing to its essence but was simply an accident of history. The true church could happily exist under any number of political systems since the church was in the world but not of it. An extended visit to England nine years later only made him more critical of the political ties of the English church and more laudatory of the apostolic independence of the American communion. The true church should ideally be completely separate from the influences of the state. Ties to the state only lessened a church's purity, either by forcing a toleration of heresy and metaphysical speculation, as it did in Germany, or by leading to inter-

69. John Henry Hobart to Nathaniel Williams, 9 June 1813, Williams Papers. Perhaps following the suggestion made by Dixon Ryan Fox in his *Decline of Aristocracy,* Wertz in his study of Hobart views Hobart as a bulwark of Federalism. The evidence from Hobart's letters seems to suggest that he was a man of almost no political interest, except in those few instances where politics touched his church.

70. John Henry Hobart, *The Origin, The General Character . . . of the Protestant Episcopal Church . . .* (Philadelphia, 1814), 12. Emphasis in original.

ference with the internal affairs of the church, as was the case in England. In contrast to both of these the independence of the American church was to be preferred since, "thanks to that good Providence who hath watched over our Zion, no secular authority can interfere with, or control our high ecclesiastical assembly."[71]

Just as Hobart had based his theory of the church on the life of the primitive ecclesia so too did he base his understanding of the relationship of church and state on the very same model. By adopting this model to help define the relationship between the Episcopal Church and American society, as well as to set the relationship between the church and the other denominations, Hobart successfully answered the old charges of political intrigue and anglophilism. The true church had no business in the political world, since its beau ideal was the pre-Nicene church of the fathers. The long-standing political interests of the established Erastian Church of England were a mere accident of history. Americans need never fear prelatical political intrigue. This sense of apostolic exclusivity, when coupled with an absence of millennialism, led these spokesmen to emphasize the radical division on the social level between the secular and the sacred. They prided themselves in their devotion to the separation of church and state. Often they sharply criticized evangelical attempts to influence the political life of the nation and expressed serious reservations over campaigns such as the attack on Sunday mail delivery, so dear to the hearts of evangelical reformers. Yet they never grounded their criticism on the harm such attempts might bring to the state, but rather on the damage that might be inflicted on the church. "The genius of civil government is totally unlike the spirit of Christianity," one of them explained, "hence all attempts to assimilate them [civil government and Christianity] have proved subversive of the spirit of the latter."[72] Such was not the conservative voice of an Edmund Burke or a Jonathan Boucher, advocating the close interrelationship of sacral church and sacral state. Nor was it the conservative voice of a Timothy Dwight, viewing America as God's New Israel, with all of the moral responsibilities implicit in that burdensome appellation. It was instead of a different tradition.[73] The social aim for the Hobartians was neither

71. John Henry Hobart, *The United States of America Compared With some European Countries, Particularly England* . . . (New York, 1825), 32.

72. "Sunday Mails," *Christian Journal* 14 (1830): 120–22.

73. Jonathan Boucher was perhaps the leading loyalist voice coming out of the American Revolution. On his conservatism, see Anne Y. Zimmer, *Jonathan Boucher, Loyalist in Exile* (Detroit, 1978). For a discussion of the various trends within the

organic union of church and state nor millennial glory, but apostolic
purity. The social effect of the apostolic metaphor was to erect an un-
breachable wall between the church and the secular world of politics,
since the church alone was divine and the state merely mortal. Political
issues became taboo for high church clergy, and they often criticized
their Protestant contemporaries for their political activities. Indeed,
one evangelical writer, tired of this high church boast about having
avoided dragging politics into their church, sarcastically commented,

> If men will but frame iniquity by a law, and cry "politics!" the
> Episcopal Church will bear no testimony against that iniquity. If the
> people of New York should make a law to take the wives and chil-
> dren of Irishmen, and to sell them at auction for the benefit of the
> canal fund, the question of the right and wrong of such a selling
> would be a political question; and the Episcopal church would "scru-
> pulously abstain from meddling with it."[74]

Whereas the social model of much of antebellum evangelicalism (perhaps as an outgrowth of its views on millennialism and benevolence)
emphasized the Christian's role in transforming society, the high
church apostolic model led in the direction of disassociating the concerns of the church with those of the state. The clash between these
two visions would have great influence on how Episcopalians would
view the great reform movements of the 1830s.

The conscious identification with the primitive church would involve high church writers in a number of difficult problems. As modern patristic scholarship has shown, the Christian church of the third
century was in a period of transition, at times being churchlike and at
times being sectlike. This confusing ambiguity would also plague
nineteenth-century Hobartians. Even more, this social vision, forged
while the Roman Empire was still pagan, often flew in the face of
American sociological reality as well as three centuries of post-Refor-
mation Anglican traditions. The Episcopalians of Hobart's New York
were not an isolated group, as were the Christians in Cyprian's Carthage. They were active participants in their society and could adopt
the Hobartian position only by a severe compartmentalization of their
psyches. Finally this Hobartian apostolic vision would be continually

---

American conservative impulse and their religious roots, contrast Allen Guttmann,
The Conservative Tradition in America (New York, 1967), 78–99, and Russell Kirk,
The Roots of American Order, (LaSalle, Ill., 1974), 347–441.

74. [Leonard Bacon], "Colton's Reasons for Episcopacy," *Quarterly Christian
Spectator,* 2d ser., 8 (1836): 609.

challenged by a far different social vision coming out of the Anglican tradition—one that believed that the church itself should take the lead in the social sphere, almost in the spirit of noblesse oblige. The life and ministry of William White—chaplain to the Continental Congress and first president of the Philadelphia Bible Society—reflected this alternative. The tension between these two conflicting visions would continually reemerge during the first half of the century.

An early challenge of this distinct high church social outlook came about almost by chance. In 1828, De Witt Clinton, governor of New York and one of the state's most important political figures, suddenly died. By a resolution of the city council all of the New York clergy were requested to notice Clinton's death from their pulpits. In a letter to the mayor Hobart wrote that he could not comply with the request, explaining that it challenged the apostolic separation of the concerns of the church from those of the state by the attempt to influence the ministrations of the clergy.[75] For a clergyman to be asked to eulogize a political figure led to the risk of seemingly linking the church to the principles that the figure represented and of thus alienating his political opponents. All political figures divided the populace, and it was the responsibility of the church to be above such divisions.

Although this simply rendered into practice his earlier principles, Hobart's decision quickly ran aground upon the great popularity of Clinton. Perhaps two of the important Episcopal congregations in New York City, St. George's and St. Stephen's, both evangelical in their emphasis, chose to ignore Hobart's lead and did eulogize Clinton.[76] Within the context of antebellum society the rigorous application of apostolic exclusivity in practical cases such as this became perhaps the most controversial aspect of the Hobartian synthesis. Although it was regularly invoked by Episcopal clergy in the decades before the Civil War, it never gained unanimous lay acceptance, particularly when the question seemed more patriotic than political.[77] For

75. Hobart to William H. Price, 16 Feb. 1828, reprinted in *Works*, 1:377–79.
76. See Henry Anstice, *History of St. George's Church in the City of New York . . .* (New York, 1911), 106–08; and [Joshua Newton Perkins], *History of St. Stephen's Parish in the City of New York, 1805–1905* (New York, 1906), 66–67. The evidence in the case of St. Stephen's is only circumstantial.
77. See, for example Philip Hone's consternations about the refusal to allow St. Paul's chapel to be used for a celebration of the anniversary of the inauguration of Washington, in Bayard Tuckerman, ed., *The Diary of Philip Hone*, 2 vols. (New York, 1889), 1:351–52. However, contrast this with the letter printed in Dix, *History of Trinity*, 3:450.

many of the clerical supporters of the Hobartian synthesis, however, this exclusivity was lauded as the natural corollary of the apostolic metaphor and was prized for its preservation of the inner cohesiveness of the church.[78]

IV

The Episcopal Church during the years of the Hobart episcopate grew steadily in size and influence. During his episcopate the number of clergy grew fivefold, and congregations multiplied perhaps even faster.[79] Particularly upstate this growth was marked. In the fifteen years following the War of 1812, when the population of the region between Utica and Buffalo increased 150 percent, Episcopal church growth was three times more rapid than the growth of the general population.[80] Yet the attraction of the Episcopal Church during this period and its remarkable growth are not attributable primarily to the high churchmen, who, though the dominant faction in the diocese, were not the only group. A growing number of Episcopal evangelicals were becoming visible in the diocese, the most prominent of them being James Milnor, rector of St. George's Church in New York, and Charles McIlvaine, at the time chaplain at West Point. These men had far more in common with the moral and benevolent spirit of the rest of antebellum Protestantism than with the Hobartian call for rigid exclusivity.[81] Milnor, for example, was an officer in the Bible Society. Furthermore they tended to be critical of the high church schema of grace and whenever possible urged a conversion experience. For them,

78. See the comments of A. Cleveland Coxe in Wilson, ed., *Centennial History of the Diocese of New York,* 167–68.

79. The paucity of figures for the early years makes it difficult to give exact statistics. In 1811, the number of congregations listed in the *Journal of the Diocese of New York* was 24; in 1831 there were 182 congregations listed. These figures of course cannot take into account congregations existing in 1811 but not reporting to the diocesan convention.

80. Charles Wells Hayes, *The Diocese of Western New York,* 2d ed. (Rochester, 1904), 36.

81. It should be emphasized, however, that until the 1840s there was no formal theological disagreement between high church and evangelical clergy. See, for example, Alexander C. Zabriskie, "The Rise and Main Characteristics of the Anglican Evangelical Movement in England and America," *HMPEC* 12 (1943): 85–115; and E. Clowes Chorley, *Men and Movements in the American Episcopal Church* (New York, 1950), 59–83.

the high church movement that Hobart represented seemed antagonistic to the "pious," "devoted," and "liberal."[82] Some of these evangelicals claimed that they were stronger in New York than the Hobartians, but this was probably not the case.[83] The continuing Hobartian control of Trinity Church gave to them the preponderance of power in the diocese, and this, coupled with the fact that they controlled the episcopacy, the diocesan press, the missionary society, and the theological seminary, allowed them to shape the course of the diocese.

Furthermore much of the appeal of the Episcopal Church during this period had little to do with either the high church or the evangelical movements but rather involved the social and aesthetic attractiveness of the church. Good church architecture, fine music (paid choirs were introduced as early as 1818), and dignified worship were the aim particularly of the urban churches.[84] The appeal of such congregations was not always theological. As one gentleman recalled, "As to creeds [my father] knew nothing about them, and cared nothing either; yet he seemed to know which sect he belonged with. It had to be a sect with a minimum of nonsense about it; no immersion, no exhorters, no holy confession. Since he was a respectable New Yorker he belonged to the Episcopal Church."[85] The dignity and decorum of the Episcopal Church were an attraction that transcended party distinctions.

Yet this aesthetic aspect of antebellum Episcopal worship created a decided problem, since it meant that it was not inexpensive. Even in the first decade of the century a chapel could cost as much as $180,000, and by the 1820s and 1830s, with the introduction of more elaborate architectural styles, the cost of church construction continued to grow. How to finance these churches became a problem. The usual method was a combination of pew sales and rents. Churches would sell pews—often in fashionable parishes for a price as high as $500—and also assess annually a percent of the value of the pew as a rent. As

82. John S. Stone, *A Memoir of the Life of James Milnor*, D.D. . . . (New York, 1849), 256.

83. The claim was made by William Jay in *A Letter to the Rt. Rev. Bishop Hobart* . . . (New York, 1823), 65–69. However, contrast this boast with the admission made by Pintard in *Letters*, 3:27–28.

84. Charles Haswell, *Reminiscences of an Octogenarian* . . . (New York, 1896), 74.

85. Clarence Day, cited in E. Digby Baltzell, *Philadelphia Gentleman: The Making of a National Upper-Class*, 2d ed. (New York, 1964), 226. Although the senior Day was of a later generation, such an attitude was fairly common in this earlier period.

the cost of churches continued to escalate, and along with it the cost of pews, the result became, as one observer noted, that

> The word of God, as it comes down to us from fishermen and mechanics, will cost the quality who worship in this splendid temple about three dollars every Sunday. This may have a good effect for many of them, though rich, know how to calculate, and if they did not go regularly to church they will not get the worth of their money.[86]

Whatever "good effects" such a situation brought about, a bad effect was to limit the appeal of the Episcopal Church both geographically and socially to those who could afford such worship. Foreign visitors were constantly struck both by the concentration of the Episcopal Church in urban areas and by the comparative absence of any poor or even English immigrants who would have been attracted ethnically to it.[87] The mission church and free church movement of the 1830s were in part attempts to respond to an issue brought about by the high cost of Episcopal worship.

Trinity Church did what it could to help other congregations, and without its purse the church could clearly not have grown at the rate it did. Yet by the 1820s even Trinity was in a weakened financial situation: it was forced to sell off stock and even some property to meet current expenses. By the 1820s the vestry found it necessary to refuse requests for grants-in-aid until the church's financial position improved.[88]

All this having been said, the question remains, What was the attraction of the Hobartian synthesis during this period? The answer is problematical because the high church combination of theology, devotion, and social vision offered not one simple attraction but several, and in some ways these contrasted with one another. Part of its appeal was conservative and the other part liberal.

Hobart's emphasis upon the importance of valid authority and his continuing expression of fear of disorder and anarchy indubitably struck a responsive chord in many of his hearers. Although almost all

---

86. Tuckerman, *Diary of Philip Hone*, 2:269.

87. See, for example, Caswall, *America and the American Church*, 24, 264; and Edward Waylen, *Ecclesiastical Reminiscences of the United States* (London, 1846), 299–300. For the difficulty in appealing to English immigrants, see Evan M. Johnson, *Duty to the Church . . .* (Brooklyn, 1841).

88. Dix, *History of Trinity*, 3:28–46. This was emphasized to the diocese by Hobart's Convention Address of 1822.

religious figures, recalling the excesses of the French Revolution, emphasized the conservative nature of their churches, Hobart's emphasis on ecclesiastical order took this general argument a step further. His attempt to find solace in a universally accepted order rather than in the democratic uniqueness of American life shows certain parallels with the movement in the legal arena toward adopting common law.[89] Order in worship and order in ministry, both of which transcended the immediacy of the early national milieu, gave a sense of stability and continuity to the religious community. One of the interesting factors concerning the Episcopal Church in these years was the great attraction its ministry held for members of other denominations, and the best figures suggest that over one-fourth of the Episcopal clergy were converts from other denominations.[90] Ministerial converts in particular tended to applaud the greater surety and validity of the Episcopal ministry. Yet this attraction to the authority of the Episcopal ministry was not simply a theological attraction. Both the apostolic argument's grounding of ministerial authority on the external factors of continuity and succession and the liturgy's shifting of the minister's role from the subjective to the formal won favor with prospective ministerial candidates from other denominations who were troubled by the more subjective nature of evangelical ministry and worship.[91]

Yet for others the attraction lay in the liberality of the Episcopal devotional system. To be freed from the demand to subscribe to an elaborate creed, of the necessity of showing evidence of a conversion, or of the necessity of following evangelical social morality was a great boon for many. Episcopal devotion allowed them to simply respond to the evocative power of the liturgy and demanded from them no subscription to a rigorous group rule.[92] The liturgical worship of the Episcopal system provided for them the best of both worlds: a sense of group participation without group demands. Nor should one discount the importance of the openness of Episcopal sacramental prac-

89. See, for example, the contrast Perry Miller makes between the vision of the lawyer and that of the revivalist in *The Life of the Mind in America* (New York, 1965), 121–34.

90. Manross, *Episcopal Church,* 70–77. In some localities the percentages were even higher. See the figures concerning Philadelphia in "Thanksgiving—Progress in the Church," *Protestant Episcopalian and Church Register* 5 (1834): 468.

91. See the praise of "the 'Apology,' 'Bowden,' and 'Potter,'" in Samuel Johnson to Hobart, 21 Nov. 1815; and William Lacey to Hobart, 2 Sep. 1812, both in Hobart Correspondence.

92. For an example of this appeal, see the letter of Douglas Fraser to Hobart, 26 July 1813, Hobart Correspondence.

tices, particularly vis-à-vis baptism, in the growth of the Episcopal Church during those years. Episcopal clergy on the whole generally baptized far more individuals than other clergy since they did not (as did the Congregationalists at the time) require that at least one of the parents be a communicant.[93] Indeed in many other instances one sees similar hints of the appeal of the Episcopal ritual. Dorothy Ann Lipson, in her study of Connecticut Free Masonry in the Federalist era, has observed that one of the factors in the popularity of Masonry, was that, in an American society sorely lacking in public ritual, Masons alone could offer public ritual at events such as funerals and building dedications.[94] This was a major factor in the growth of the Episcopal Church as well. The Episcopal funeral service in particular was thought to be both comforting and appealing.[95] From baptisms to burials, Episcopal worship and piety nicely fitted the needs of individuals tired of the constraining group demands of traditional evangelical religious life.

Finally the power of the apostolic metaphor cannot be overlooked. The chance to be able to position oneself in an alternative to the prevailing American evangelical religious culture, while not actually physically withdrawing from it, and to use the church as a place of psychologial or emotional sanctuary was to become a strong aspect of Episcopal self-understanding. Yet of course, in its ideal the apostolic metaphor was more than an emotional sanctuary; in its own way it was to be a rule. Here, however, was the fundamental problem. When the metaphor was used to advocate exclusivity it often found itself in conflict with the liberating aspect of the devotion. The controversies arising from the Bible Society debate and the De Witt Clinton funeral oration suggest that after all factors were weighed many a layman was

93. [Flavel Scott Mines], *A Presbyterian Clergyman Looking for the Church* (New York, 1855), 52–53, claimed that by the 1840s the Congregational sacramental practice had become the general practice in large parts of Presbyterianism as well. As early as 1807 A. G. Baldwin, in a letter to Benjamin Moore (4 March 1807, Hobart Correspondence), noted that Congregational baptismal practices were beginning to affect Presbyterians. Thomas C. Brownell, later Episcopal bishop of Connecticut, was one such individual never baptized as a child since his parents were merely attenders. See Beardsley, *Church in Connecticut*, 2:196–200. On Episcopal reaction to this baptismal practice, see J. C. Rudd to Hobart, 8 Jan. 1807, *Archives*, 5:256.

94. Dorothy Ann Lipson, *Freemasonry in Federalist Connecticut* (Princeton, 1977), 163–76.

95. Indeed, many first came into contact with the liturgy in such cases. See "Memoir of the Rev. Cornelius R. Duffie," in *Sermons by the Late Rev. Cornelius R. Duffie . . .* (New York, 1829), viii–ix.

all too aware that the apostolic metaphor was better suited for third-century Carthage than nineteenth-century New York. Missionary reports often indicated that it was most prominent in the congregations who were least willing to accept the exclusivity called for by the apostolic metaphor. Such reticence was less true among the clergy, for whom the metaphor was far more important, both intellectually, since it undergirded their theology, and psychologically, by reinforcing their authority. Indeed, as early as the Cave Jones controversy, Hobart's supporters were characterized as the "younger clergy," for whom the radical position had greater appeal and less cost.[96]

The unsolved problems in the Hobartian synthesis of theology, devotion, and social vision would come back to haunt and eventually to destroy it in the succeeding decades. Yet until then it would continue to grow with increasing rapidity in the 1830s and would attract numerous and important converts. Its appeal as the only major Protestant nonevangelical religious body south of Unitarian Massachusetts gave it great advantage as a socially and theologically acceptable alternative to antebellum evangelicalism.

96. [William Irving], *A Word in Season, Touching the Present Misunderstanding in the Episcopal Church* (New York, 1811), 6. Irving also listed "worthy matrons" as Hobart's peculiar supporters, yet this was probably not so much from an attraction to his call for exclusivity but from an appeal to the emotional fervor that distinguished the high churchmen in this period.

THE HIGH CHURCH
ALTERNATIVE IN ACTION

4

An Ark of Refuge

IN AUGUST OF 1830 HOBART LEFT NEW YORK CITY TO BEGIN STILL AN-
other visitation of his diocese, only to suffer a severe attack of illness
and fever and to die on September 12 in Auburn, New York, at age
fifty-five. His corpse was brought by canal boat back to New York
City to be honored and laid to rest. Over seven hundred persons,
including the acting governor of the state, the mayor of the city, city
judges, and numerous other officials, took part in the funeral proces-
sion.[1] With the death of Hobart a chapter in the history of the high
church movement ended—a chapter shaped both by Hobart's dynamic personality and style and by the immediate needs of the church in
the postrevolutionary generation. The next few decades would manifest an attempt by Hobart's successors to work out the implications of
the Hobartian synthesis and to adapt it to the continuously changing
religious panorama of the period.

The death of Hobart marks a significant change in both the shape
and tempo of the American high church movement. During the first
three decades of the century the history of the movement could be told
largely from the perspective of one man, John Henry Hobart, and one
location, the diocese of New York.[2] After 1830, however, this became

1. For an account of Hobart's funeral, see J. F. Schroeder, ed., *Memorial of
Bishop Hobart* (New York, 1831), 247–50.
2. This is not to deny that there were high church leaders in other parts of the
Union. James Kemp in Maryland and John Stark Ravenscroft in North Carolina both
provided important local leadership. See, for example, the memoir in *The Works of the
Right Reverend John Stark Ravenscroft, . . .* 2 vols. (New York, 1830). Yet on the
national level the importance of Hobart and New York greatly overshadowed
them.

less and less possible. A whole group of high church leaders in different parts of the nation began making their presence felt, a fact which led to more diversity in opinion than had been the case earlier, while at the same time increasing greatly the intellectual vitality of the movement.

Almost all of this new generation were trained and influenced by Hobart and continued to voice his themes as they began to occupy positions of authority within the church. Henry Ustick Onderdonk (1789–1858), after having served as both a missionary and a parish priest in New York, was elected assistant bishop in Pennsylvania in 1827 after a hotly contested election. A medical doctor by profession, he had studied theology with Hobart and had very early on shown a flair for religious controversy.[3] Levi Silliman Ives (1797–1867) was elected bishop of North Carolina in 1831. A convert from Presbyterianism, he was not only Hobart's student but his son-in-law as well.[4] William R. Whittingham (1805–79), still another young cleric influenced by Hobart, was perhaps the most scholarly of the new group. Until his election to the episcopacy in 1840 he was associated with General Theological Seminary, serving first as librarian and later as professor of ecclesiastical history.[5] In 1827, along with Samuel Turner, professor of biblical interpretation at the seminary, he translated and published the *Introduction to the Old Testament* by John Jahn.[6] Trends in English theology interested Whittingham even more, however, and throughout the early 1830s he was involved in the production of American editions of standard English theological works. George Washington Doane (1799–1859), a man characterized by his

3. For an early example of Onderdonk's apologetical flair, see *An Appeal to the Religious Public . . .* (Canandaigua, N.Y., 1818). On the disputed episcopal election of 1827, see David L. Holmes, "The Making of the Bishop of Pennsylvania, 1826–1827" *HMPEC* 41 (1972): 225–62, and 42 (1973): 171–97.

4. On Ives, see Marshall DeLancey Haywood, *Lives of the Bishops of North Carolina . . .* (Raleigh, N.C., 1910); and John O'Grady, *Levi Silliman Ives, Pioneer Leader in Catholic Charities* (New York, 1933). Ives converted to Roman Catholicism in 1852 to the consternation of many of his friends.

5. On Whittingham, see William Brand, *The Life of William Rollinson Whittingham,* 2 vols. (New York, 1883).

6. Jahn (1750–1816) was professor of Oriental Languages and Old Testament at the University of Vienna. Both his *Introduction* and his *Biblical Archaeology* (E. T. Andover, 1823) were popular among English-speaking readers. Their appeal was their providing of a conservative alternative to the more radical position of Eichhorn, since they linked together canon, inspiration, and church authority. See Brevard Childs, *Introduction to the Old Testament as Scripture* (Philadelphia, 1979), 37.

biographer as both a bishop and a poet, likewise was a Hobart protégé.[7] Doane taught for three years at what is now Trinity College in Hartford and also edited a number of religious journals before being elected bishop of New Jersey in 1832. His poetic interest led him to introduce John Keble's book of devotional poetry, *The Christian Year,* to the American public in 1832 and provide an American edition of it in 1834. As a correspondent of William Wordsworth he furnished material for two of the latter's "Ecclesiastical Sonnets," which dealt with the American Episcopal Church, so impressing the poet that he described Doane as a man of "no ordinary powers of mind and attainment."[8]

Still another figure associated more intellectually than politically with this group was the prolific author and bishop John Henry Hopkins (1792–1868), another convert from Presbyterianism. From the 1830s onward Hopkins was perhaps the most consistent defender of the apostolic argument and of the myth of the pure church.[9] Indeed, writing in the comparative intellectual isolation of Vermont he would continue to evoke the rule of Vincent of Lerins long after other high churchmen had begun questioning its usefulness. Yet Hopkins was not simply a defender of the apostolic argument; he also sympathized with the sentimental stirrings in the church and wrote the first book in America on Gothic architecture. Nowhere is the tension implicit between the theological principles and devotional spirit of the high church movement more clearly manifested than in the life of Hopkins.

Perhaps the two most important figures of this second generation were Samuel Seabury (1801–72) and Benjamin Tredwell Onderdonk (1791–1861). Seabury, grandson of the famous bishop with the same name, came from a long line of clerics. Although he served for much of his career as both a parish priest and as a teacher in various institutions, Seabury's real forte lay in his gift as a religious journalist. In September of 1833 he became editor of the *Churchman,* by this time a

7. George W. Doane, *The Life and Writings of George Washington Doane, D.D., LL.D., . . . With a Memoir by his Son, William Croswell Doane,* 4 vols. (New York, 1860–61).

8. On the Doane–Wordsworth connection, see Kenneth Walter Cameron, "Wordsworth, Bishop Doane and the Sonnets of the American Church," *HMPEC* 11 (1942): 83–91.

9. On Hopkins, see John Henry Hopkins, Jr., *The Life of the Right Reverend John Henry Hopkins . . . by One of His Sons* (New York, 1875). On Hopkins's theology see, Robert Bruce Mullin, "Ritualism, Anti-Romanism, and the Law in John Henry Hopkins," *HMPEC* 50 (1981): 377–90.

weekly newspaper, and through his influence made it the most celebrated and influential weekly in the Episcopal Church. In it he combined sharp, critical commentary on American religious trends and a continuing interest in English events with the more mundane and usual fare found in church newspapers. Much of the most valuable and important Episcopal writing during this period can be found in this periodical. The *Churchman* always suffered from financial difficulties—since it was usually read more than it was bought—yet it served as a combination bully pulpit and sparring arena for the high church movement. The positions taken by Seabury were often controversial, and the wit, sarcasm, and vigor with which he defended them often provoked bitter debates, yet the newspaper remained the central periodical of the movement.[10]

Perhaps the most enigmatic figure in the group was Benjamin T. Onderdonk, successor to Hobart as bishop of the diocese. Younger brother of Henry Onderdonk, he shared little of his brother's sharpness of mind or ability to turn a phrase. Even a sympathetic writer had to confess, "He was far from being brilliant or eloquent; not specially attractive as a preacher, so far as I can learn or remember, nor of much depth or orginality."[11] The unfortunate scandal, combining Tractarian theology and sexual indelicacies, that terminated his episcopate has not made an assessment of his influence any easier. A martyr to the Oxford Movement for some, for others he remains the "Apostolical Ram" described by his opponents.[12] Yet even more so than Hobart, Onderdonk's contribution lay not in what he said or wrote but in the vigor with which he attacked his episcopal duties. In the first eight years of his episcopate he ordained almost as many individuals as Hobart had in his entire nineteen years of service and consecrated even more church buildings. The diocese during this period grew so quick-

10. There is unfortunately no biography of Seabury nor a study of his thought. There is, however, a fragment of a manuscript autobiography in the Seabury Family Papers, New-York Historical Society, New York, New York. For a contemporary assessment of his personality see Brand, *Life of Whittingham*, 1:114–15.

11. Hayes, *Diocese of Western New York*, 84.

12. For two widely differing assessments of Onderdonk, see E. Clowes Chorley, "Benjamin Tredwell Onderdonk, Fourth Bishop of New York," *HMPEC* 9 (1940): 1–51; and Brickley, "The Episcopal Church in Protestant America," 212 ff. The title "Apostolical Ram" was coined in Spectator, *Bishop Onderdonk's Trial: The Verdict Sustained at the Bar of Public Opinion; . . .* (New York, 1845), 3.

ly that it had to be divided, and a separate diocese of western New York was erected in 1838.[13]

Two institutional innovations aided this acceleration of growth and reflect an increased willingness to adapt the church to some of the social realities that the Episcopal Church faced. The first was an increased emphasis upon the importance of the city in contrast to the frontier mission of the church, and in particular the mission to the city's unchurched. Unlike Hobart, who never really felt at home with city living, Onderdonk was a native New Yorker with a strong appreciation for its peculiar needs. The tremendous increase in the city's population aided by the opening of the Erie Canal called for immediate action, yet the traditional parish system with its often prohibitively high pew rents excluded much of the new population from Episcopal worship. As early as 1818 Onderdonk had argued for a free church (or a church without pew rents) to meet the needs of this group, and in 1822 plans were actually drawn up to form such a church—only to be shelved for lack of funds.[14] Practical accomplishments had to wait until 1831, when in September the Protestant Episcopal City Missionary Society was founded. From the high church perspective the City Missionary Society was the model of a benevolence society. It was headed by the bishop of the diocese, all the city Episcopal clergy were ex officio members, and the charitable aim was firmly linked to the vision of the church. As one of its supporters proudly noted, it reflected "the apostolic character of the church itself."[15] At its height the society supported three mission churches, a missionary at large, who served the needs of the unchurched, and several Sunday schools. Yet an uncertainty about its own mission always plagued the society. Should its concern be simply with those who could not afford to attend regular parish worship (such as many of the immigrants from the sur-

13. The comparative figures can be found in the *Journal of the Protestant Episcopal Church in the Diocese of New York* (1839), 21.

14. *Churchman* 6 (May 7, 1836): 1070. On the 1822 plan, see Christian Bergh to John Henry Hobart, 12 April 1822, Hobart Correspondence. One should quickly emphasize that this shift to the city was, throughout the 1830s, more a shift of perception than of materials. Even as late as 1842 there were eight missionaries supported by the diocese laboring outside of the city for every one working within.

15. *Sixth Annual Report of . . . the New-York Protestant Episcopal City Mission Society* (New York, 1837), 19. In fact, clergy support for the society was far higher than lay. Over 40 percent of the city clergy were patrons of the society, which required a hundred dollar contribution, although in at least one or two cases laymen contributed the money for the clergy. See *Second Annual Report,* 9.

rounding countryside and from Britain) or with the truly poor, the bulk of whom had almost no predisposition to the Episcopal Church?[16] Yet although the City Missionary Society would all but collapse by the mid-1840s, its efforts to eradicate the economic exclusiveness of the city churches was continued in the free church movement of William A. Muhlenberg, with its often-voiced concern in turning "drawing rooms" for a "select circle of genteel Episcopalians" into "parish churches."[17]

The second institutional innovation attempted to increase the level of lay financial support for the church. The Hobartian years had seen most of the backing for Episcopal benevolent endeavors coming from the coffers of Trinity Church, helped by only a minimal amount of lay support. During these years the same technique for fund raising employed by the evangelical societies was used by the Episcopalians. Usually a sermon or address would be delivered annually for a given cause and a collection would then be taken. Such a method reflected the rhythm of evangelical worship of judgment, call, and commitment, yet never really adapted well to the flow of Episcopal piety, with its emphasis upon gradual commitment over time. Hence in 1833 George Washington Doane began to advocate a return to what he called the "apostolic" form of charity, or the laying aside of a small amount of money and weekly offering of it at Sunday worship.[18] Although at first adopted only for missionary funding, Doane's plan of systematic charity became increasingly popular since it both practically and intellectually integrated itself into Episcopal church life and resulted in a marked increase in giving.[19]

II

By the 1830s the institutionally reinvigorated and intellectually pugnacious Episcopal Church was ready to challenge its Protestant neigh-

16. On this problem in particular and for a more extended discussion of the City Missionary Society, see Carol Smith Rosenberg, *Religion and the Rise of the American City: The New York City Mission Movement 1812–1870* (Ithaca, 1971), 125–59.

17. Waylen, *Ecclesiastical Reminiscences,* 423. On Muhlenberg's role in the free church movement, see Alvin W. Skardon, *Church Leader in the Cities: William Augustus Muhlenberg* (Philadelphia, 1971), 100–24.

18. Doane, "Ancient Charity," in *Works,* 4:472–88.

19. *Churchman* 5 (November 21, 1835): 974; Caswall, *America and the American Church,* 262; *PECMS Eighth Annual Report,* 5–8.

bors over who was to direct the American religious scene. A new vitality emboldened the church. As one observer recalled, "During the decade between the years 1830 and 1840 the Episcopal Church made such an advance as it had never known before. The number of clergy doubled during this period, and for the first time in its existence its influence began to be felt somewhat generally in the community."[20] To understand the background to this remarkable growth, however, the state of the evangelical churches must be sketched, since the 1830s witnessed both the high point and the crisis of the great antebellum evangelical crusade.

By the late 1820s the evangelical dream of creating a truly Christian America was going neither unnoticed nor unanswered. Many interpreted Ezra Stiles Ely's call during the election of 1828 for "a new sort of union . . . a *Christian party in politics*" as a blatant example of the churches trying to interfere in political concerns.[21] After this, if only by coincidence, evangelicals found themselves increasingly opposed in their attempts to gain government support for their endeavors. In 1828 the American Sunday School Union applied to the Pennsylvania legislature for a charter. Perhaps as a result of tensions heightened by the sermon by Ely, who was closely associated with the Sunday School Union, the request was refused twenty-one to nine.[22] Yet the great cause célèbre was the controversy over Sunday mail, mentioned in the previous chapter. In 1810, Congress, through *An Act Regulating the Post Office Establishment,* had ordered federal post offices to open on Sunday, and from at least 1814 petitions began to appear urging the abolition of this affront to Sabbatarian sensibilities. By 1828 the campaign had become a national movement bombarding Congress with hundreds of petitions. The Senate refused to bow to this pressure. Indeed, the sentiment expressed by Senator Richard M. Johnson of Kentucky became a classic statement of the American ideal of the separation of church and state:

> Our government is a civil and not a religious institution. . . . The petitioners for [the discontinuance of Sunday mail] appear to be

20. Thomas March Clark, *Reminiscences,* 2d ed. (New York, 1895), 32.
21. "The Duty of a Christian Freeman to Elect Christian Rulers," in John F. Wilson, ed., *Church and State in American History* (Boston, 1965), 96. Emphasis in original. The sermon had first been delivered the previous year. As later commentators have usually noted, however, Ely was directing his critique not against Andrew Jackson, usually viewed as the chief opponent of American evangelical hegemony, but against the Unitarian John Quincy Adams.
22. Hood, *Reformed America,* 139.

actuated by a religious zeal, which may be commendable if confined to its proper sphere; but they assume a position better suited to an ecclesiastical than to a civil institution. . . . Extensive religious combinations to effect a political object are, in the opinion of the committee, always dangerous.[23]

Johnson's report, later published as a tract, achieved wide circulation and served as a manifesto for many individuals who were uneasy about the evangelical political agenda. Yet even among evangelicals there was from the 1830s onward increasing debate over the propriety of directly influencing public policy.[24]

Nor was evangelical theology having an easy time of it. As we have already observed, much of the excitement energizing evangelicalism in the decade and a half following the War of 1812 was the sense of transdenominational unity. The successful crushing of Deism and containing of Unitarianism as well as the achievements of organizations such as the Bible Society gave to the evangelical cause a millennial glow. The stellar example of this spirit of cooperation, the Plan of Union of 1801, linked in common fellowship the three great intellectual citadels of antebellum evangelicalism: Andover, Princeton, and Yale. By the 1820s, however, rifts were beginning to develop that threatened this cooperation. In 1822 Samuel Miller of Princeton publicly challenged the teachings of the great Andover scholar Moses Stuart on the eternal generation of the second person of the trinity. The almost quizzical response by Stuart reflected the growing theological separation within the reformed community:

> During all my theological life, I ha[ve] never once heard the doctrine of the eternal generation seriously avowed and defended. Nearly all the ministers in New England, since I have been on the stage, have, so far as I know their sentiments, united in rejecting it, or at least as regarding it as unimportant.[25]

23. "Senate Report on Sunday Mails," *American State Papers on Freedom in Religion,* 3d ed. rev. (Washington, D.C., 1943), 191–92. For the two best accounts of the Sunday mail campaign, see John R. Bodo, *The Protestant Clergy and Public Issues, 1812–1848* (Princeton, 1954), 39–43, and Anson Phelps Stokes, *Church and State in the United States,* 3 vols. (New York, 1950), 2:12–20.

24. Hood, *Reformed America,* 141. The collapse of the first phase of the evangelical endeavor left to its successors the continually debated question: to what extent was America actually a Christian nation?

25. Moses Stuart, *Letters on the Eternal Generation of the Son of God, Addressed to the Rev. Samuel Miller, D.D.* (Andover, 1822), 4–5.

Far greater controversy emerged from the modifications of New England theology emanating from Yale College, inspired by its professor of theology Nathaniel William Taylor. In his attempt at modifying the inherited Calvinism so as to find room for a more active and revivalistic faith, Taylor had been pecking away at the doctrines of depravity and predestination during his entire tenure at Yale. His famous *Concio ad Clerum* of 1828 brought all of these issues out in public.[26] In it he argued that sin and guilt pertained exclusively to voluntary actions and that sin was inevitable but never necessary. Bennett Tyler, another Congregationalist minister, immediately leapt to the defense of the traditional formulations. The result was not simply the famous Tyler–Taylor debate, but also the casting into suspicion, at least among the sons of Princeton, of the whole edifice of New England theology. The decade following Taylor's *Concio* would record an increasing number of heresy trials, involving such well-known figures as Lyman Beecher and Albert Barnes, the eventual splitting of Old and New School Presbyterians, and the collapse of the Plan of Union.

This growing breakdown of consensus must not be seen as an isolated argument over grace. Scholars have noted that much of antebellum evangelicalism can best be understood as an uneasy tension between pietism and confessionalism. The movement toward evangelical consensus and active moralistic reform that characterized the voluntary societies was usually counterbalanced by other movements desiring to defend ecclesiastical and confessional autonomy.[27] We have already noted that as early as 1824 Samuel Miller had found it necessary to defend the use of creeds, and by the beginning of the 1830s these rumblings were becoming louder. Within Old School Presbyterianism there developed a movement away from interdenominational voluntary societies in favor of a heightened ecclesiology which saw the denomination itself as the true missionary society.[28] During the years after 1830 a number of other denominations began to experience the emergence of an "old school," or confessionalist, party anxious both to distinguish their churches from the overarching theological and moral principles of transdenominational evangelicalism

26. On Taylor, see the general works of Foster and Haroutunian; Mead, *Taylor;* and Sydney E. Ahlstrom, "Theology in America, An Historical Survey," in *Religion and American Life,* ed. James Ward Smith and A. Loland Jamison, 4 vols. (Princeton, 1961), 1:254–60; and his *Theology in America: The Major Protestant Voices from Puritanism to Neo-Orthodoxy* (Indianapolis, 1967), 41–45, 211–49.

27. Howe, *The Political Culture of the American Whigs,* 162–63.

28. Hood, *Reformed America,* 193–95.

and perhaps indirectly to thwart a perceived New England hegemony flowing from the voluntary society movement.[29]

If these two factors were not enough to upset the uneasy theological coexistence of the evangelical united front, by the 1820s European and particularly German ideas were beginning to be heard on this side of the Atlantic. For many, German theology was a vague threat more than an intellectual system, and the works of the Neologians or the Rationalists were haphazardly lumped with the new ideas of Kant and the early Romantics, and both were linked to Deism. Indeed, one of the early interpreters of German thought for Americans could write, "It is curious to observe that the common principle of rejecting everything above reason, has conducted the learning of the German and the gross ignorance of the English schools to the same point of absurdity."[30] Yet along with a continuing suspicion of German ideas there also was an increasing openness. Even at conservative Princeton Charles Hodge found Friedrich Tholuck's combination of evangelical theology and warmhearted piety immensely attractive and published numerous translations of German writers in the first series of the *Princeton Review*.[31] George Ticknor (1791–1871), Edward Everett (1794–1865), Joseph Cogswell (1786–1871), and George Bancroft (1800–91) were but the first of a long string of bright American students to study in Germany. In evangelical theological circles the stock of German scholarship also began to rise, as it was slowly learned that German scholarship had more to offer than Rationalism and Neology. With Moses Stuart at Andover leading the way, American scholars increasingly turned their attention to German theological works.[32] Yet the new ideas of Kant and Schelling, when popularized in English

---

29. The Baptists, Presbyterians, Dutch Reformed, and German Reformed all experienced such movements toward either confessionalism or heightened denominational identity, though they were called by different names and emphasized different issues. For the factor of anti-New England motivation, see Dixon Ryan Fox, *Yankees and Yorkers* (New York, 1940), 199–206; and James F. Maclear, " 'The True American Union' of Church and State: The Reconstruction of the Theocratic Tradition," *Church History* 28 (1959): 41–59.

30. Hugh James Rose, *The State of Protestantism in Germany Described* . . . , 2d ed. (London, 1829), 167. In 1827 Rose's work was excerpted and published in the *Biblical Repertory and Princeton Review*.

31. A. A. Hodge, *The Life of Charles Hodge, D.D., LL.D.* (New York, 1880), 116.

32. On the effect of this German culture, see Henry A. Pochman, *German Culture in America: Philosophical and Literary Influences, 1600–1900* (Madison, Wisc., 1952), 128–30.

by Samuel Taylor Coleridge and given a boost in America by James Marsh's edition of Coleridge's *Aids to Reflection,* proved a serious challenge to the underlying assumptions of evangelical theology and the cause of even more division. All of these factors—the growth of divisions among the major seminaries, a growing confessional rather than evangelical understanding of denominational reality, and the radical implications of the new German theology and philosophy—contributed toward the erosion of the unity and concord that had characterized evangelical thought in the previous two decades. One minister could only lament,

> There is . . . a continual increase in the number of theological systems, which present views of truth of which we cannot approve. . . . The old authors are thought to have lived in times of comparative ignorance; and a recommendation of them as guides in a course of theological study, is regarded as a proof positive of a deplorable *behindedness* in reference to the march of the mind. In the meanwhile we have a flood of German books, partly neological, and partly exegetical. . . . We have metaphysico [*sic*] theology from other sources; and true, old-fashioned orthodoxy produces nothing but now and then a valuable little thing on practical religion.[33]

Confusion and complexity seemed to challenge the theretofore buoyant evangelical self-confidence.

An even more divisive issue emerging during these years was the development of a new emphasis on the revivalistic impulse, usually associated with the name of Charles Grandison Finney (1792–1875). Finney's family joined the great migration of New England, leaving Connecticut for Oneida County in New York when the boy was only two. Although originally intending to go to Yale College for his education, he was dissuaded by his tutor, "who told him he was bright enough to educate himself in less time and at less expense."[34] While practicing law he underwent a conversion and, in his famous phrase, accepted "a retainer from the Lord Jesus Christ to plead his cause." Avoiding any formal theological education he began his famous career as a revivalist. The importance of Finney's subsequent career is difficult to assess, since its importance lies in at least three areas. On one

33. John Holt Rice to Archibald Alexander, 9 March 1830, in William Maxwell, *A Memoir of the Rev. John Holt Rice, D.D.* (Philadelphia, 1835), 369. Emphasis in original.

34. William McLoughlin, *Modern Revivalism: Charles Grandison Finney to Billy Graham* (New York, 1959), 15.

level he popularized trends already present in New Haven theology. His emphasis upon human ability and the active call for repentance led one commentator to write, "Mr. Finney of all others has taught the New Haven Theology in its greatest purity and has ventured to push its principles to their legitimate results."[35] Second, Finney also changed the shape and tenor of revivalism and merits the title Father of Modern Revivalism. Perhaps in an effort to avoid the emotional excesses of the First Great Awakening, subsequent revivals in the East tended to be emotionally restrained and parochially based. When revivals such as the famous one at Cane Ridge in 1801 did break out in shouting, crying, and barking, they often became schismatic. Finney, however, by a forceful, colloquial preaching style, by praying for sinners publicly by name, by the instituting of an anxious bench for sinners wrestling with conversion, and by other such innovations known collectively as the New Measures dramatically increased the emotional power of his revivals. Although these measures were opposed by some as innovations and by others as unscriptural, they gave to his revivals great success. Through them Finney also broke with the older understanding of the revival stemming from Jonathan Edwards. Revivals were not a miraculous occurrence but rather the result of constituted means. Yet third, Finney greatly shaped the evangelical tradition that came from Edwards and was modified during the Second Great Awakening. By his reevaluating of human ability (which eventually evolved into perfectionism), by his shifting of conversion from the private to the public mode, and by his increased emphasis upon a social zeal and a new activism Finney radically affected much of American Protestantism. The two central features of antebellum evangelicalism—the conversion experience and the benevolent society— were bound more closely together than ever before. Whether this was a fundamental change or merely a change in degree is difficult to assess, yet it is clear that Finney's form of revivalism was a source of serious division within the evangelical ranks.[36]

35. *Literary and Theological Review* (December, 1835), cited in McLoughlin, *Modern Revivalism*, 14.

36. Two of the more recent studies dealing with Finney, Paul Johnson, *A Shopkeeper's Millennium: Society and Revivals in Rochester, New York, 1815–1837* (New York, 1978), and Hood, *Reformed America*, argue for the radically new nature of Finney's brand of revivalism, and both suggest that before him revivalism and benevolence were two distinct movements. This may well be the case with regard to the great reforms of the 1830s, total abstinence and abolition, yet one should be wary about generalizing. The career of a person such as Lyman Beecher, whose ministry

The most explosive threat to evangelical unity, however, did not directly involve either theology or Finney's New Measures but rather the intensification of the moral reform movements in the 1830s, which alienated both political and religious conservatives. From women's rights to food reform, a surfeit of programs posited by "ultraists" seemed to be undermining religion and destroying order. Nowhere were the risks higher than in the volatile issues of temperance and slavery. The shift in the question of temperance from the eschewal of spirits to the total abstinence advocated by Lyman Beecher in his *Six Sermons on Intemperance* (1826) to the teachings of Finney and Theodore Dwight Weld, in which total abstinence became the badge of the new birth, has been told in detail elsewhere.[37] For the religious conservative, two aspects of the temperance controversy were particularly disturbing: the elevating of total abstinence to a prerequisite for holy communion and the substituting of grape syrup for wine in holy communion. Practices such as these appeared to substitute some independent rule for the plain teaching of scripture. When even the moderate biblical critic Moses Stuart could publicly defend the switch to grape syrup, conservative voices refused to be silent. As the noted Old School Presbyterian William Sprague observed, "Another way in which men make themselves overwise is by *modifying the ordinances* to suit their own views; especially in inculcating the doctrine or adopting the practice, of dispensing with the appropriate elements, or substituting something in place of them, which the Scriptures does not warrant."[38] It appeared increasingly to many that the Bible and the spirit

closely combined both revivalism and benevolence, suggests that even before the time of Finney evangelical piety was connected with evangelical reform.

37. Useful studies of the temperance movement are John Allen Krout, *The Origins of Prohibition* (New York, 1925), and Joseph R. Gusfield, *Symbolic Crusade: Status Politics and the American Temperance Movement* (Urbana, 1963). Two recent studies, Donald Scott, *From Office to Profession: The New England Ministry, 1750–1850* (Philadelphia, 1978), and Barbara Leslie Epstein, *The Politics of Domesticity: Women, Evangelism, and Temperance in Nineteenth-Century America* (Middletown, Ct., 1981), have suggested ways in which the antebellum concern for temperance had far-reaching implications for the way American Protestants understood the nature of both sin and piety. The most complete discussion of drinking patterns in antebellum America is W. J. Rorabaugh, *The Alcoholic Republic: An American Tradition* (New York, 1979).

38. Quoted in *Churchmen* 5 (July 18, 1835): 901. Emphasis in original. See too "Bacchus and Anti-Bacchus," *Biblical Repertory and Princeton Review*, 2d ser., 13 (1841): 267–306. Moses Stuart raised this issue in a tract originally written for the Religious Tract Society in 1834 and later published in *Methodist Magazine and Quarterly Review* 17 (1835): 411–39. Interestingly, not even the Methodists were willing

of reform, which earlier had been at one, were now beginning to part company.

Even more volatile was the question of slavery, the ever-dangerous powder keg of the antebellum period. The long struggle for emancipation—beginning with such solitary figures as Samuel Sewall, inspired by such diverse impulses as the enlightenment view of natural rights, Quaker moral perfectionism, and a general spirit of benevolence, yet constantly in conflict with the growing institutional acceptance of slavery by many of the churches—has similarly been told in great detail.[39] Up through the 1820s the antislavery movement was characterized by a gradualist mentality that hoped for the ending of slavery as a result of the gradual working out of natural law and the enlightening of the consciences of the slaveholders themselves. No institution better reflected this hope than the American Colonization Society, founded in 1817, through which it was believed that America might be freed of the burden of slavery with a minimum of disturbance to its society and culture.[40] Yet by the late 1820s activists such as Benjamin Lundy and William Lloyd Garrison began to take a different tack, criticizing gradualism in general and the Colonization Society in particular. The abandonment of gradualism in favor of immediate emancipation gave to the antislavery movement a new intensity. Slavery was no longer viewed simply as either a political or social evil but as a sin in itself (*malum in se*), and the antislavery cause often became connected to the religious intensity of Finney's followers. For the opponents of slavery the moral intensification caused by the *malum in se* argument was a great boon since "at one stroke it cut through the dilemma of immediatism, for as the South itself admitted, 'if slavery be adjudged, if it be condemned by the revealed word of God, then in

to accept the substitution of grape syrup for wine in 1835. See the note on page 431 of the *Review*.

39. In the great mass of literature on the question of slavery, the pathbreaking study of Gilbert Barnes, *The Anti-Slavery Impulse, 1830–1844* (New York, 1933); Louis Filler, *The Crusade Against Slavery, 1830–1860* (New York, 1960); and the magisterial works of David Brion Davis, *The Problem of Slavery in Western Culture* (Ithaca, 1966) and *The Problem of Slavery in the Age of Revolution, 1770–1823* (Ithaca, 1975), stand out. On the question of the churches and slavery, see Donald G. Mathews, *Slavery and Methodism: A Chapter in American Morality, 1780–1845* (Princeton, 1965); Andrew E. Murray, *Presbyterians and the Negro: A History* (Philadelphia, 1966); and Douglas C. Stange, *Patterns of Antislavery Among American Unitarians* (Rutherford, N.J., 1977).

40. On the Colonization Society, see P. J. Staudenraus, *The African Colonization Movement, 1816–1865* (New York, 1961).

Christendom it cannot exist.' "[41] The "if" however was the catch. By linking the slavery question to the Bible, related issues such as the rules for scriptural interpretation and the authority of the text, dear to the hearts of religious conservatives, became entangled in the debate over slavery. As one writer noted, "If we are wiser, better, more courageous than Christ and his apostles, let us say so; but it will do no good, under a paroxysm of benevolence, to attempt to tear the Bible to pieces, or to extort, by violent exegesis, a meaning foreign to its obvious sense."[42] The reaction to the shift to immediatism was swift and decisive in the North as well as the South and ranged from elaborate treatises to riots in the streets.[43]

Thus many of the very same factors that had contributed to the evangelical successes in the two previous decades had become more points of division than of consensus by the 1830s. The long-standing high church ambivalence to the direction of evangelical thought and action left them in an excellent position to launch an even more fundamental critique of American Protestantism.

III

During the decade of the 1830s, due in part to a decline in the internal debates over churchmanship, high church writers began seriously to address the problems facing both evangelical religion and American society generally. From their perspective all of the problems pointed to the same conclusion, that American Protestantism was in sad array, divided and confused. Their old antagonists the Calvinists seemed to be falling apart, as seen by the theological and political debates wracking Presbyterianism and Congregationalism. Nor, from their perspective, was the state of Protestantism any healthier in Europe. On

41. Barnes, *Anti-Slavery Impulse,* 103.

42. Charles Hodge, "Slavery," *Biblical Repertory and Princeton Review,* 2d ser., 8 (1836): 276. For a more extended discussion of the exegetical problem of antislavery, see Robert Bruce Mullin, "Biblical Critics and the Battle over Slavery," *JPH* 61 (1983): 210–26.

43. For studies of the northern reaction to abolition, see Adelaide Avery Lyons, "The Religious Defense of Slavery in the North," in Trinity College Historical Society, ser. 13, *Historical Papers* (Durham, N.C., 1919), 1–34; Lorman Ratner, *Powder Keg: Northern Opposition to the Anti-Slavery Movement* (New York, 1968); and Leonard L. Richards, *"Gentlemen of Property and Standing": Anti-Abolition Mobs in Jacksonian America* (New York, 1970).

the Continent "the sun of the Reformation sunk beneath the horizon, and left Germany involved in the darkness, mazes, and labyrinths of a new school of philosophy, from which they have not yet to emerge."[44] Except in England and in the Episcopal Church in America the evidence of what one cleric called "a failure of tremendous import, in the protestant enterprise" seemed all too apparent.[45]

The high church observers did not need to search long to find what they believed to be the cause of this disarray. A lack of authority, both intellectual and institutional, lay behind the declension. Part of the traditional high church critique of Presbyterianism had been for its artificial distinction between essential truth and unessential order. The increasingly acrid theological debates within the Presbyterian General Assembly, which pitted Old School confessionalists against New School defenders of a more liberal interpretation of the creeds, demonstrated to them the failure of the Presbyterian distinction between truth and order. Unorthodoxy had apparently entered the hyperorthodox Presbyterian communion only through its union with the less ecclesiological Congregationlists.[46] Yet this Protestant error only reached a crisis with the ministry of Finney. His willingness to employ his innovating New Measures suggested that the question of truth, in any formal or objective way which acknowledged the authority of the witness of scripture and the primitive church, had been abandoned and all that remained was a concern for successful means:

> We should say that the characteristic of the present time is to elevate *practice* above TRUTH, and to cry up *measures*, at the expense of *principles*. The importance of solid learning, of patient intellectual discipline and of sound doctrine, is most sadly depreciated, and a man's usefulness is estimated in proportion to the bustling activity and declamatory eloquence that qualify him to produce an *immediate* effect.[47]

44. [Calvin Colton], *Protestant Jesuitism: By a Protestant* (New York, 1836), 128.

45. Benjamin T. Onderdonk, "Episcopal Address," *Journal of . . . the Diocese of New York* (New York, 1841), 80 (hereafter referred to as *JDNY*).

46. Modern commentators such as George Marsden in *The Evangelical Mind and the New School Presbyterian Experience* (New Haven, 1970) have suggested that the Old School/New School debate was far more complicated than a simple liberal/conservative split. High church writers, however, not only inevitably took the side of the Old School (whom they believed to be the conservative party), but also generally used Old School newspapers for their source of information on the debate. See *Churchman* 1 (July 23, 1831): 72.

47. "The Practical Spirit of the Nineteenth Century," *Churchman* 5 (July 18, 1835): 902. Emphasis in original.

Much of this type of criticism became tied to a more general criticism of the "spirit of the age" and a marked hostility toward any attempt to apply the social and intellectual principles of the nineteenth century to the life of the church. As one cleric, despairing of the "new spirit," noted, "I shall die of it as Busby did of bad Latin."[48] In part this flurry of criticism of the modern spirit was an outgrowth of trends discussed earlier. The intellectual/theological world of the high church apologists, with its apologetical and theological anchor in the witness of the primitive church, left little space for any ideas that smacked of innovation. Even a movement such as the City Missionary Society was justified as being a return to apostolic practice. Likewise the high church rejection of the millennial hopefulness that characterized much of the rest of Protestant thought made them even less open to any innovations that seemed to be based on the modern spirit. To them, many of the problems confronting American Protestantism stemmed from a willingness to modify their teachings to fit the modern temper. Finney's apparent preference for the practical over the theoretical, for example, was traced back to his adapting of certain social attitudes such as a confidence in practical science and a tendency to dismiss all that was stable in theology as antirepublican—all of which were all too common to American society as a whole. So far-reaching was this critique of the innovating spirit that among some even Protestantism itself began to be criticized as being the "offspring of innovation."[49]

One practical manifestation of this critique was the elevation of the apostolical argument as a solution to the problem of doctrinal authority. The scripture as it was interpreted by the witness of the pure church could serve as an intellectual ark of safety in the turbulent waters of the time. Such was the theme of John Henry Hopkins's *The Primitive Church* (1835), in which he argued that only through a return to the apostolical rule could Protestantism escape continuing decline. The truth once delivered and preserved in the witness of the primitive church must provide the certainty on which Christians could rely:

> A wiseman, receiving medicine for the body from the hands of his physician, keeps close to all the directions of the prescriptions. . . . The bodily medicine may cure, it is true, even when many of the directions are disregarded; but would any man of prudence venture

48. T. W. Coit to Samuel Seabury, 24 July 1835, Seabury Correspondence. Richard Busby (1606–95) was one of the famous headmasters of Westminster School.

49. William R. Whittingham, *Count the Cost* (New York, 1836), 24.

upon such an experiment, if it could be helped? So the doctrine of the Gospel may save, when many of the Apostolic rules are overlooked, but who would trifle with a question of such moment, or exchange a sure promise for a probability?[50]

The usefulness of the apostolic witness in counteracting the apparent decline of American evangelicalism became an extremely popular theme among high church writers.[51]

Yet the concern with authority was not limited to the theological or intellectual arenas. Arising out of the apostolic argument was a new claim, that the veracity of the episcopal system could be proved not simply from the witness of the early church but also by the negative witness of contemporary America. Whereas earlier champions of the apostolic argument had emphasized the independence of the law of the church from the law of the world, by the 1830s some were pressing further and claiming that church principles were the only solution to the problems plaguing both the churches and the society at large. The social ramifications of the high church teaching were at times boldly set forth:

> It is the glory of our Church that she maintains and seeks to perpetu-
> ate a reverence for order. The reality and nature of her divine con-
> stitution is, theoretically, a question of theology; and must be decid-
> ed in the polemical arena. Practically, however, it is a question of
> social order; and every individual may judge for himself, whether
> her system is not the most conducive to the interests of society. The
> great practical feature of that system is subordination,—a subordina-
> tion based on principle and not convenience,—existing in virtue and
> divine command, and not of human suggestion. . . . This subor-
> dination involving *right,* or authority, as its conservative principle, is
> the grand characteristic of heaven, and to the violation of it may be
> traced the origin and all the subsequent developments of evil.[52]

Although never doing so in any completely systematic way, Episcopal apologists in the 1830s for the first time began to break the bounds of a

50. *The Primitive Church Compared with the Protestant Episcopal Church of the Present Day: Being an Examination of the Ordinary Objections Against the Church in Doctrine, Worship, and Government,* 2d ed. (Burlington, Vt., 1836), 7.

51. See, for example, E. M. Johnson, *The Decline of Religion and its Causes . . .* (Brooklyn, 1836); B. T. Onderdonk's introduction to *Works on Episcopacy;* H. U. Onderdonk, *Episcopacy Examined and Reexamined* (New York, 1835); and Thomas Brittan, *An Apology for Conforming to the Protestant Episcopal Church* (New York, 1833).

52. *Churchman* 1 (November 26, 1831): 142. Emphasis in original.

purely ecclesiological argument and at times began to join hands with other conservative proponents of order and subordination. The crisis in evangelicalism raised anew the need for a sure and certain authority to prevent splintering and fanaticism, and the political crisis of the same period enlarged the audience anxious to hear such a message. For the first time in the history of the Episcopal high church movement the apologetical thrust centered on the Episcopal Church as a refuge of peace and order rather than primarily as the preserver of apostolic truth.[53]

The errors that high church critics condemned as reflective of the innovative spirit of the nineteenth century were not of course visible only to them. Perry Miller has observed that the legal profession occupied a parallel role in the same society in that "they stood for the Head against the Heart" and in doing so served as a bulwark against the overwhelming vigor and occasional irrationality of millennialism, revivalism, and democracy.[54] Numerous observers of American society, both native and European, spoke critically of the American tendency to prefer the practical over the theoretical, of their granting of near-demagogical power to public opinion, of their religious tendency toward sectarianism, and of their need for greater social order. Indeed, James Fenimore Cooper in *The American Democrat* could defend the propriety of social station, when based on a natural aristocracy, as part of the law of society.[55] Yet, as has been noted, even in *The American*

53. One should be careful about pressing this association too far. Even during the 1830s this apologetic based on the present crisis in society was still less frequently invoked than the older forms of apologetic, and they never elevated their immediate criticisms of the course of the society into a general questioning of the legal underpinnings of the society. Furthermore one finds almost no high church invocation of the idea of natural law, even though it was an integral part of the Anglican classic, Richard Hooker's *Laws of Ecclesiastical Polity*. Two factors might help explain this absence. Hobartians had a long-standing suspicion of the political realm, and second, high church writers tended, as has been shown, to shy away from speculation. Resting their arguments on an a posteriori examination of the facts of revelation as manifested in scripture and the primitive church, they had little sympathy for the more speculative questions that intrigued legal theorists and other Protestant writers.

54. Miller, *Life of the Mind*, 118–21. Miller here attempted to refine Tocqueville's famous observation that in Jacksonian America the legal profession acted as a counterpoise to the excesses of democracy. See *Democracy in America*, edited and abridged by Richard D. Heffner (Mentor ed., New York, 1956), 123–27.

55. James F. Cooper, *The American Democrat* (Penguin ed.: Baltimore, 1969), 150–54.

Democrat Cooper, although critical of American social practices of the 1830s, had not abandoned his Jeffersonian faith, confirming Louis Hartz's well-known observation that in America even tradition was liberal.[56] The uniqueness of the high church critics lay in their combining of a social criticism of excesses with a fundamental intellectual critique that was based upon a distinct theological tradition and held a different criterion for determining valid and invalid argument than other critics possessed. Their combining of appeals for both intellectual and social authority left the high church writers out of step even with other conservative critics of Jacksonian America.

The actual relationship between high church social critics and the more general conservative impulse of the time was accordingly ambiguous. High church writers often attempted simultaneously to appeal to the broader cultural movement while refraining from sanctioning it fully. Hence when they proclaimed the stability of the Episcopal Church (due, it was argued, to its liturgy and polity) they usually acknowledged that the question of stability and order was also becoming a political issue as well. Politicians, one editorialist noted, were beginning to reassess their confidence in democracy, and some, such as John C. Calhoun, went so far as to claim that "the majority were likely to go wrong, and that the object of the statesman . . . [has] been to exclude a preponderating influence of the majority." While gingerly passing over whether this sentiment was always true in the political realm, the editorialist concluded by adamantly noting: "In regard to Church polity we receive the observation as sound. If the polity and doctrine of the Church were matters to be regulated by the will of the majority, the Church would gradually dwindle away to a state of annihilation."[57]

The concerns for intellectual and social authority were of course not mutually exclusive, and many of those attracted to the Episcopal Church as an oasis of peace, a "refuge from the storms of sectarian party and folly," also came to accept its theological vision. Of this group none was more famous than Calvin Colton (1789–1857). Edu-

56. Louis Hartz, *The Liberal Tradition in America* (New York, 1955), 50. On Cooper's political thought, see John P. McWilliams, Jr., *Political Justice in a Republic: James Fenimore Cooper's America* (Berkeley, 1972), 197–216 in particular. For other conservative voices during this period, see Russell Kirk, *The Conservative Mind: From Burke to Santayana* (Chicago, 1953), albeit Kirk's definition is sometimes slippery.

57. "The Protestant Episcopal Church," *Churchman* 4 (September 13, 1834); 725.

cated for the Presbyterian ministry at both Yale College and Andover Seminary, he left the active ministry in 1829 for both health and personal reasons and served as English correspondent for the *New York Observer* from 1831 to 1835. He spiritedly defended American customs and mores while abroad against critical English observers. The more he observed, however, the intensification of both the religious and political life of the young republic, the more he became convinced that its roots lay in a spirit of fanaticism. Before returning to America, he left Presbyterianism for the Episcopal Church.[58] He lamented for his former church and its succumbing to the new religious spirit:

> [T]he Presbyterian and Congregational denominations of Christians, . . . seemed to me, to a very great extent, lying under the blighting desolation of the new and extravagant measures, by which religious excitement, had been attempted and managed on one hand, and on endless and bitter controversy on the other.[59]

Although Colton did become ordained and even served for a while in an Episcopal parish, he eventually found his real forte in journalism and political pamphleteering. Colton's significance lay not in his theological speculations but in his uniting of a conservative social critique of Jacksonian America with a plea for the Episcopal Church. As a religiosocial commentator, he was concerned with three issues: the apparent proliferation of extravagance and controversy as a result of the introduction of Finney's New Measures, the decline of ministerial authority within Presbyterian and Congregational churches, and the social disruption often associated with the new modes of piety. He criticized in particular the presbygational practice of publicly examining candidates for church membership, a practice he considered offensive to cultivated individuals. Much of the presbygational discipline in addition to its demand for "mutual watch and care" seemed to have little to do with the true purposes of religion, which for Colton were individual uplift and public peace. Indeed, for Colton the great appeal of the Episcopal Church was that it made the fewest demands on the social structure of society. He praised the church in particular for its refusal to meddle in political questions:

58. On the life and thought of Colton, see Alfred Cave, *An American Conservative in the Age of Jackson: The Political and Social Thought of Calvin Colton* (Fort Worth, 1969).

59. Calvin Colton, *Thoughts on the Religious State of the Country with Reasons for Preferring Episcopacy* (New York, 1836), 25.

This uniform and conscientious abstinence from politics is a most important feature, and a practically salutary element of the American Episcopal Church. It is meddling with politics that has for centuries been most injurious to Christian churches—injurious and destructive to their appropriate character and spiritual influence.[60]

In Colton one can see to what degree the new pragmatic apologetic for the Episcopal Church could be taken. In his concern for a stable public order with the function of religion integrated with but subservient to that of the state, he sounds more like an Edmund Burke than a Hobart. Indeed, many of the latter's principles are put on their head. Whereas for Hobart ecclesiology—or the vision of the holy church, in continuity throughout time—was the motivating metaphor that informed his call for apostolic exclusivity, which in turn undergirded his social vision, in Colton it was the reverse. His thought moves from the pragmatic and social to the theological. The existence of extravagance and excitement confirmed for him the need for order. Furthermore, where in Hobart the individualizing of the religious experience and the tendency to separate piety from social action was always counterbalanced by his rigorous and individually demanding ecclesiology, in Colton this is no longer the case. Hobart and his circle had striven to preserve what for them was the essence of religious truth from all lesser considerations, in the same manner in which Tertullian had driven a wedge between Jerusalem and Athens. Colton, on the other hand, saw the religious peace of the Episcopal Church as the best evidence for its truthfulness. The crisis within evangelicalism in the 1830s had brought together these two contrasting positions, yet, as we shall see, the intraepiscopal conflicts of the 1840s would tear them asunder.

Yet this is to get ahead of the story. Both the apostolic and the pragmatic apologists could unite in a critique of the new claims of the temperance movement. Indeed, throughout the 1830s high church critics achieved notoriety in their opposition to temperance agitation. From its very outset the call for total abstinence did not fall on receptive ears among Episcopalians. Even in the 1820s Hobart, in his *Church Catechism,* had urged only moderation concerning drink, not total abstinence, and wine at ecclesiastical affairs was still common among New York Episcopalians long after the practice had lost favor in New England.[61] The call for moderation of course meant different

60. Ibid., 97.
61. Hobart, *The Church Catechism* (New York, 1826), 26. Powel Mills Dawley, *The Story of the General Theological Seminary* (New York, 1969), 65.

things for different people. In his diary, Philip Hone, a vestryman at Trinity Church, New York, observed that his wine cellar contained 2,180 quarts and 254 half-gallons of Madeira and sherry![62]

Despite, however, the often repeated claim that the high church party opposed the temperance movement from its inception, a survey of the editorial positions taken on this issue by the *Churchman* suggests that such a generalization should be qualified.[63] Instead of direct opposition, the editorial position reflected a shifting viewpoint that only after a number of years solidified into complete opposition.

In the early 1830s the editorial page of the *Churchman* reflected a decided ambivalence—support for the objectives of the society, caution over some of its tactics, yet a quickness always to add, "God forbid that we should *oppose* them or their measures as yet developed."[64] Not until Moses Stuart began to suggest that wine might be excluded from holy communion did the editorial policy begin to change, and even then it was hoped that Stuart's speculations would not affect temperance policy. Not until the spring of 1835 were the editorial guns of the *Churchman* squarely directed against the temperance movement and only when it was perceived that the fundamental issue had become the question of limiting communion to total abstainers. This aggressive intrusion into the realm of church discipline opened the temperance advocates up to attack:

> The imposition of arbitrary terms of communion not sanctioned by the Gospel, but made in compliance with popular opinion, is only another exhibition—taking a different complexion from the character of the age—of the spirit of ecclesiastical tyranny and priestcraft, which have degraded the church of Rome.[65]

Not temperance, nor even abstinence, but the combination of the calling for the excommunication of imbibers and the removal of wine from communion enraged the editors of the *Churchman*. What could have been accepted as a dietary rule was unacceptable as a rule for sacramental practice. Thus by 1836 the editorial position had retreated to a dogmatic defensiveness and, in commenting on the plan to rewrite older temperance tracts to support total abstinence, could pronounce,

62. Tuckerman, *Diary of Philip Hone*, 1:208.
63. See, for example, W. W. Manross, "The Episcopal Church and Reform," *HMPEC* 12 (1943): 355–56.
64. *Churchman* 3 (April 13, 1833): 431.
65. *Churchman* 4 (January 31, 1835): 806.

> The experience of the last two years has proved, that the same spirit which demands the alteration of the tract may in perfect consistency demand the alteration of our communion office, and the virtual suppression of parts of our Bible, and therefore any concession to such a spirit may tend to impair the authority of the sacred oracles.[66]

What had begun as a disagreement over the most effective way of dealing with the social problem of intemperance had become transmuted in high church eyes into a defense of the truthfulness of revelation.

Two other Episcopal voices also leveling criticism on the temperance movement were John Henry Hopkins and Calvin Colton. Though often at the time lumped together both by friend and foe on account of their common rejection of the fanaticism that seemed to emanate from the movement, their criticisms reflect the differing perspectives of the apostolic and pragmatic approaches.

In addition to defending Episcopal theology and practice, Hopkins in his *Primitive Church* offered an extended critique of both the philosophy and effects of the modern temperance movement.[67] At first glance Hopkins's argument seemed quite unusual. He had no objections to any of the practical political goals of the Temperance Society, such as restrictions on the manufacture and use of alcoholic beverages, but only to its quasi-religious goals. The fundamental error of the Temperance Society lay in its converting a practical question into a moral one and hence in confusing a change in behavior with a change in heart. Hopkins suggested that the idea of a temperance pledge presupposed the belief that the will could change itself. The Temperance Society, as a social and not a religious society, could reform actions but it could never reform morals. The church alone could be the only true *moral* reform society, since it alone held the sacred records upon which moral rules should be based. Indeed, in his implication that true moral reform could be found only within the confines of the divinely instituted church, Hopkins raised the *prima ecclesia* even higher than Hobart had, since the latter had left some room for individual moral sentiment so long as it did not make any doctrinal demands. For Hopkins, the moral schema of the Temperance Society directly challenged the prerogatives of the church, and no amount of temporal good could meliorate this fact. In its

66. *Churchman* 6 (July 2, 1836): 1102.
67. Krout, *Origin of Prohibition*, 120; David M. Ludlum, *Social Ferment in Vermont* (Montpelier, Vt., 1948), 75–78.

elevating of an independent morality over the revealed record, which nowhere demanded total abstinence, the Temperance Society reflected the modern spirit of innovation. Hence, along with the editor of the *Churchman,* Hopkins could write,

> We protest against improvements made upon the Gospel or the Church, in the nineteenth century of the Christian era. We protest against the claims of new inventions in Christian morals, and especially against that morality, which the infidel set up by itself, without any reference to Christ, or any acknowledgement of his divine authority. In a word, we adhere in this, as in every point, to the Scriptures, and to the Church which the Apostles planted.[68]

Clearly for Hopkins the issue was far larger than that of temperance; it involved the very authority of the apostolic promise. In setting up its own moral good the Temperance Society implicitly threatened the primacy of the church, just as for Hobart the Bible Society had threatened it twenty years before. Both of these reactions suggest a mind set little in tune with the millennial hopes of other antebellum Protestants. Critics of Hopkins treated this rejection of millennial confidence as a near blasphemy and challenged him to point out another period of history so blessed by divine favor. Rather than castigating the spirit of the age, they could claim, "The Christian philosophers see in this enlightened spirit of the age, one of the greatest promises, after the promises of the bible, of the perpetuity and advancement of these good works, until Christ shall finally triumph."[69] Just as had Hobart's opponent William Jay two decades before, sharers of the millennial hope could see in the apostolic metaphor only obscurantism and defeat.

Colton faulted the temperance movement on far different grounds. His chief broadside against the movement was *Protestant Jesuitism,* published anonymously in 1836. Though critical of much of the reforming zeal of Jacksonian America, Colton found the temperance movement particularly obnoxious because it had been pushed by a radical fringe far beyond the bounds of common sense. Colton, like Hopkins, dismissed the call for total abstinence as a novelty, and "novel views and novel measures relating to Christianity, growing up in a night, are, on that very account, suspicious."[70] Yet what con-

---

68. *Primitive Church,* 151.

69. *A Reply to Bishop Hopkins' Attack on the Temperance Society* . . . (Philadelphia, 1836), 6.

70. Colton, *Protestant Jesuitism,* 212.

cerned Colton was not so much the theory upon which the reforms were based but their practical effects. The fanaticism of the reform zeal threatened the common sense and common uprightness of the society. In contrast with Hopkins, who found the temperance movement erring in granting too much power to the will to change itself, Colton found the demand for a public pledge an affront to both individual and group virtue, since it presupposed that without such a pledge individuals could not control their own appetites and wills.[71] As a solution for such fanaticism, Colton, like Hopkins, saw the importance of the role of the church, yet even in his praise of the church Colton showed his preference for political over theological virtue. The church was not praised as the vessel of apostolic truth, but as the arena of the broad Christian public: "In the present state of society, it is not a few, but the community at large, who are most competent to determine the expedient modes of maintaining and advancing the interests of Christianity."[72] The church as bulwark against the fanaticism of the temperance movement had two different meanings in Hopkins and Colton.

Contemporaries found these approaches to be complementary rather than conflicting, and no commentator pointed out what strange bedfellows they made. Yet they suggest that in the broadening of the appeal of the high church criticism of evangelical culture, conflicting principles began to appear that would bode ill for the movement in the 1840s.

Many of the trends and attitudes that emerged in the discussion over temperance may help shed light on a question that has puzzled historians for a century—why the Episcopal Church was so strangely free from agitation over the question of slavery. While the Presbyterians, Methodists, and Baptists were dividing, Episcopalians avoided almost all public discussion of the question. Social and economic factors undoubtedly played an important role, since slavery was far from solely a religious question. As Philip Foner has observed, much of the enormous prosperity of New York City was based upon the cotton trade.[73] Many an Episcopal vestryman whose livelihood depended upon the city's bustling commerce was loath to stir up the

71. Ibid., 69.
72. Ibid., 212.
73. Philip S. Foner, *Business and Slavery* . . . (Chapel Hill, 1941), passim. On the role of economic concerns in affecting the church's response to slavery, see the comments of William Jay recorded in Tuckerman, *William Jay,* 144.

question of slavery. The ambivalence expressed by Philip Hone was perhaps typical of many:

> The abolitionists, Arthur Tappan and his fanatical coadjutors, are certainly engaged in a most mischievous undertaking, which may bring destruction on their own heads and civil war into the bosom of our heretofore happy country; but the remedy is worse than the disease. . . . [Yet] I do not choose to surrender the power of executing justice into the hands of the slaveowners of South Carolina.[74]

Other factors, however, cannot be ignored. For many Episcopalians abolition seemed to be but the culmination of the New England attempt to impose its fanaticism upon the whole life of the country. James Fenimore Cooper's thrice damning, in *Wing-and-Wing*, of his New England villain Ithuel Bolt—by making him deacon of a sectarian church, a patron of the temperance society, and an abolitionist—reflected a common tendency throughout the period of lumping abolition together with the rest of the rejected evangelical enterprise.[75] Nor did the fact that the chief Episcopal antislavery voice in New York belonged to William Jay, long the proponent of evangelical causes and opponent of high church prerogatives, endear the abolitionist cause to New York high churchmen.[76]

On a deeper level, the entire Hobartian synthesis, in its ecclesiology and theology and piety, proved a grave stumbling block to any high church sympathy with the antislavery movement. The high church emphasis upon the sacred nature of the church, its fear of schism, and its concern with unity as a mark of the spirit of God retarded any radical action on the question of slavery. From the days of Hobart the message had been carefully taught that the church was the sacred body of Christ and that it was a duty of all its members to "preserve its peace and unity."[77] Furthermore, no greater sacrilege could be imagined than the breaking of this body. This fear of schism permeated much of northern high church thinking; as early as 1825 southern sensibilities were manifesting themselves even in tasks such

74. Tuckerman, *Diary of Philip Hone,* 1:156.

75. See William M. Hogue, "The Novel as a Religious Tract: James Fenimore Cooper—Apologist for the Episcopal Church," *HMPEC* 40 (1971): 10.

76. On the role of the Jay family in the antislavery crusade, see Robert Trendel, "William Jay, Churchman, Public Servant, and Reformer" (Ph.D. diss., Southern Illinois University, 1972).

77. Hobart, *Church Catechism,* 13.

as hymnal reform.[78] Nor did the events happening outside the church calm their anxieties. If the murder of the abolitionist publisher Elijah Lovejoy in Alton, Illinois, in 1837 by an angry mob sent an electrifying tremor all across the North, the splitting of the Presbyterian Church that same year sent a similar shock wave for quite different reasons. If the important and powerful Presbyterian communion could succumb to schism, no institution was safe.[79] Such fears, when linked with the traditional Episcopal avoidance of political issues, effectively segregated the question of slavery from the proper concerns of the church. "Abolition and anti-slavery societies are more political institutions than otherwise," observed one cleric, "and therefore, I have not meddled with them, and do not see that I am likely to do so."[80] Episcopal avoidance of the question of slavery went to such lengths that in 1823 the General Convention refused, over the objections of some southern members, to send a delegate to an intended meeting of the Colonization Society since, as William White observed, it was "rather of a political than a religious nature."[81]

Similarly the theological framework of the Hobartian synthesis provided poor soil for abolition. Unlike their English cousins, for many of whom the conflict with the Deists had led to a positing of the idea of a divinely guided moral progress, American high church Episcopalians had acquired their theological habits through two generations of defending the office of the episcopacy.[82] By the 1830s the

78. Henry U. Onderdonk to Bird Wilson, 6 June 1825, Bishops Collection, General Theological Seminary Library, New York, New York.

79. See, for example, Henry U. Onderdonk to Samuel Seabury, 24 May 1837, Seabury Correspondence. The great fear of schism was always stronger among American Episcopalians than it was with their cousins in the Church of England, as was the self-identification with the apostolic church, for reasons we have explained earlier. This difference in perspective may perhaps explain some of the differences between English and American Episcopalians on the question of slavery. English clerical visitors often castigated American Episcopalians for their silence on slavery, and the first major history of the American Episcopal Church, written by the English bishop Samuel Wilberforce, was largely shunned in America because of its critical comments on racial issues. See William Jay, "Introductory Remarks on the Reproof of the American Church . . . in . . . 'History of the Protestant Episcopal Church in America,'" *Miscellaneous Writings on Slavery* (Boston, 1853), 409–52.

80. Henry U. Onderdonk to Samuel Seabury, 23 December 1833, Seabury Correspondence.

81. White, *Memoirs of the Protestant Episcopal Church,* 51.

82. On English developments in this regard, see Davis, *Problem of Slavery in Western Culture,* 333–64. On pages 348 ff. Davis includes an important discussion on the various roots of the origin of the sense of benevolence in Western thought, and

apostolical argument and the myth of the pure church reigned un-challenged within high church circles. The rule of Vincent of Lerins was a procrustean bed for all theological discourse, and the religious argument against slavery did not fit well into it. From the high church perspective the modern antislavery movement had to be rejected since it was "opposed by the unanimous voice of the Universal Church [and was] at war with the manifest sense of Scripture," being "a notion so recent, that we all can bear testimony to its rise and progress within our own day."[83] The religious antislavery movement of the eighteenth and nineteenth centuries rested upon principles such as a belief in moral progress and an appeal to religious feeling that high church theological writers had explicitly excluded from the realm of proper theological discourse. Just as with an individual like Charles Hodge, in whom the rejection of abolition was integrally connected with a concern for a defense of the plain reading of scripture, among high churchmen antiabolition quickly became linked with a defense of the apostolic argument.

Finally not even the piety of the high church movement was particularly conducive to abolition. Scholars have recently traced the religious roots of immediatism to the new evangelical spirit of the 1820s and 1830s, and the gradual identification of abolition with a true Christian commitment.[84] The converse, however obvious, bears mentioning. The high church rejection of the new evangelicalism made it not only less conducive to abolitionist rhetoric, but tempera-mentally out of touch with the call for immediatism. The entire rhythm of Episcopal piety favored a gradualist approach since nothing in Episcopal piety or devotion happened immediately; all presup-posed a pattern of God working over time in cooperation with human endeavor.

One sees all of these factors cropping up in the *Churchman*'s edi-torial stance on the slavery question. It is striking for both the paucity

---

also the interrelatedness of the rise of the "man of feeling" and opposition to slavery. It must be reemphasized, however, that the theological world of English lati-tudinarians was a far cry from that of American Hobartians, and that these dif-ferences in theological outlook help explain their differing responses to the problem of slavery.

83. John Henry Hopkins, *Slavery: Its Religious Sanction, Its Political Dangers, and the Best Mode of Doing it Away* (Buffalo, 1851), 9. Colton was an even more famous Episcopal critic of abolition, yet the great bulk of his antiabolition argument is legal rather than religious in nature, simply classifying the abolitionists as religious fanatics. For this reason it will not be discussed here.

84. Scott, *Office to Profession*, 91–94.

of the discussion and by its pattern, which, as in the case of the temperance movement, shows outright opposition emerging only eventually. In December of 1831, far from condemning the antislavery movement, the *Churchman* contented itself with emphasizing both the evils of slavery and yet the difficulty of coming to any simple solution for its eradication. On one point, however, the editors were certain: "We do not, however, wish to insinuate, because Christianity has not condemned slavery by express precept, it is, therefore, a condition, the principle of which is sanctioned and approved by the Gospel."[85] Throughout the first half of the 1830s this ambivalent attitude remained the editorial position. Hence when reporting on the emancipation of the slaves in the West Indies the journal's enthusiasm was hard to contain. The event was not simply a triumph for Britain: "It is a triumph of MAN, it is a triumph of Truth and Justice, it is the triumph of Jesus Christ. . . . *Things* have been turned into *persons*."[86]

Not even the New York antiabolitionist riot of 1834 made the *Churchman* take a definite stand against abolition, although events such as this, and the indirect Episcopal involvement in it, convinced the editors of the value of the Episcopal emphasis on ecclesiastical discipline. Peter Williams, a protégé of Hobart, was at the time rector of St. Philip's Church, the only black Episcopal congregation in New York City.[87] During a riot in the summer of 1834 an angry crowd surrounded St. Philip's, incited by Williams's membership in the Anti-Slavery Society. Williams's willingness, at the request of Bishop Onderdonk, to publicly resign his membership in the Anti-Slavery Society in the interest of the peace of the church was interpreted as the triumph of church unity over misplaced individualism. As one writer noted, "We aim as Episcopalians to direct the current of Christian feeling in the channels marked out for it by collective wisdom and guard against its being diverted by wayward impulse and wasted on worldly and ephemeral projects."[88]

Not until two years later, in 1836, was the antislavery movement finally rejected and lumped along with the temperance movement as

85. *Churchman* 1 (December 10, 1831): 150.

86. *Churchman* 4 (August 23, 1834); 714. Emphasis in original.

87. George F. Bragg, *History of the Afro-American Group of the Episcopal Church* (Baltimore, 1922), 81–89.

88. "St. Philip's Church," *Churchman* 4 (July 19, 1834): 695. This example of clerical submission was also praised by other Protestant papers of the city.

"inebriated by too copious draughts of the spirit of the age." Both reflected the modern tendency toward ultraism.[89]

The editorial reaction of the *Churchman* and to a certain extent the response of many of the high church commentators to the issues of temperance and slavery display much the same pattern: an early moderate and hopeful tone, challenged by a perceived threat to the well-being of the church, that finally ended in a complete rejection of the reform as an innovation and reflective of the spirit of the times. Far more high church concern was exercised over the validity of abolitionist argument than over the question of slavery itself. Why such a path ended up being followed and why certain connections were invariably drawn, however, is not completely obvious. Perhaps at least part of the answer lies in the apologetical dynamic out of which most of these writers operated, since they were by profession defenders of the church and not social analysts. Decades of apologetical disputation had willed to the contestants certain rhetorical "triggers" and certain conditioned responses. An appeal to the spirit of the Bible invariably provoked a defense of the witness of the primitive church, while an appeal to the independence of human conscience usually evoked a defense of subordination and tradition. The apologetical rhetoric had been carefully crafted to defend the vital centers of the Episcopal system, and granting the presuppositions of the high church commentators, it defended them well. Yet it did so by retranslating, as it were, any perceived threat to the church into the religious categories of the apologetic. It was not the external logic of events alone, but also the internal logic of rhetoric that led to the identification of the temperance movement with infidelity. When social questions such as abolition or temperance stayed outside of the defensive perimeter of the church they could be treated simply as social questions, yet as soon as they breached an ecclesiastical prerogative, they became translated, as we have seen, into very peculiar religious categories. Loyalty to the apologetical framework upon which the high church enterprise rested led these writers to venture forth, like modern day Tertullians, and follow the implications of their argument wherever they might lead. Yet Ronald Knox's observation concerning Tertullian, "To me he is the born arguer, who talks himself, rather than thinks himself, into extreme positions, and is too dazzled by his own eloquence to recede

89. "Infidelity," *Churchman* 6 (May 14, 1836): 1074.

from them," is aptly descriptive of the high church response to the intensified social reforms of the 1830s.[90]

Furthermore this position struck at a precarious seam in the Hobartian synthesis. Hobart never rejected the usefulness or importance of sentiment but rather its applicability in theological discourse. Indeed, if the "man of feeling," upon whom reforms such as antislavery were predicated, was rejected theologically, he was encouraged in Hobartian piety. The implicit conflict between the objective theology and sentimental piety of the high church system would only be aggravated by a question such as slavery. As antislavery sentiment grew during the following decades it was unable to be integrated into the theological presuppositions of high church thought, even within a given individual. Slavery was an issue that the Hobartian system was simply incapable of dealing with, without abandoning some of its most cherished assumptions.

IV

Issues such as temperance and slavery, though important to modern historians, were not the central concerns of high church writers in the decade of the 1830s. Treatises in defense of episcopacy and studies of the apostolic church continued to be their main literary concerns. But also during this decade at least a few individuals attempted to patch up a number of troublesome holes in the Hobartian synthesis, and their endeavors resulted in a flurry of theological speculation interesting not only in its own right, but also indicative of the direction of Episcopal concerns during this period.

Two figures stand out: Samuel Seabury, editor of the *Churchman*, and Henry U. Onderdonk, bishop of Pennsylvania and chief voice of the *Protestant Episcopalian and Church Register*. The immediate problems confronting them were the doctrines of justification and regeneration. They were of course not alone in these concerns. In almost all of the nations of the English-speaking world church writers were grappling with the question of justification and in particular looking for an ethical and internal solution to the problem.[91] Yet

90. Ronald Knox, *Enthusiasm: A Chapter in the History of Religion with Special Reference to the XVII and XVIII Centuries* (Oxford, 1950), 45.

91. Peter Toon, *Evangelical Theology, 1833–1856* (London, 1979), 169. Toon cited as his examples Alexander Knox in Ireland, J. McLeod Campbell in Scotland, and F. D. Maurice and John Henry Newman in England.

these questions were particularly pressing on American Episcopalians for two reasons. First, the Hobartian heritage had left them with the problem of uncovenanted mercies, which seemingly largely restricted the love and mercy of God to church members, and the regeneration/renovation distinction, which seemingly put greater weight on right (that is, apostolical) order than on holiness. Second, in the continuing context of revivalism, justification was usually understood as being instantaneous and usually in practice tied to an emotional experience.

To answer these problems Onderdonk in 1832 proposed a major revision in the Waterland–Hobart distinction between regeneration and renovation that while holding on to baptismal regeneration created more room for moral action.[92] He began by distinguishing between two modes of regeneration—the change in state and the change in character—and suggested that not one but two regenerations had to occur.[93] Through the regeneration of baptism the individual made the transition from being outside of the church to being within it. Yet each individual was also called to a second, moral regeneration in which the person was actually recovered from the dominion of sin. Though both regenerations were works of the holy spirit, the work differed in that with the former both the minister and the spirit were coagents, while with the latter the spirit acted alone, and that the first was an ecclesiastical gift and the second a moral one.[94] This formulation of Onderdonk's corrected two of the most flagrant problem areas in the old Waterland–Hobart formulation. Rather than having to consign those outside of the apostolic church to the slim hope of benefiting from the uncovenanted mercy of God, even in those cases when their lives showed evidence of regeneration, it could now be claimed that they were beneficiaries of moral regeneration, yet still awaited ecclesiastical regeneration. Second, to those within the church the doctrine was a call not to rest upon the regeneration of baptism but to strive for holy change. Sacrament and holy living were brought more closely together since both were necessary: "the pious ought to be baptized and the baptized ought to be pious, and . . . there is an inconsistency in separating the two requisites—it is not the plan of

92. Onderdonk's thoughts on the question went back to 1818. The work was published in the *Protestant Episcopalian and Church Register* in 1832, and in the *Churchman* in 1834. It was later expanded and published separately as *An Essay on Regeneration* (Philadelphia, 1835). All succeeding citations are from the 1835 edition.
93. Ibid., 7.
94. Ibid., 13.

God but the perverseness of man, that his sons in either one sense are not his sons in the other."[95]

Perhaps the most provocative part of Onderdonk's argument was that this second regeneration was both gradual and progressive and involved increase or decay and renewal or repetition depending upon the will and action of each person.[96] Far from being an instantaneous change, it proceeded slowly, and the only true evidence of the regeneration was a holy life. In his formulating of a progressive regeneration Onderdonk went further and coupled this with a new view of the atonement. Protestant theologians, in his view, had erred in linking the atonement to the justice of God, which in turn necessitated a juridical view of the work of Christ, or one in which Christ paid the legal debt of sinners.[97] Such a view presented a twofold problem: just as a paid debt was immediately eradicated, so implicitly in the juridical view must justification also be instantaneous. Furthermore since such a debt repayment was complete and final it had to lead to either predestination (if Christ died only for the elect) or universalism (if Christ died for all). In lieu of the juridical approach Onderdonk proposed a view of the atonement that linked it to the holiness rather than to the justice of God: "Sin does not resemble a pecuniary debt, which may be discharged by a substitute: when it takes that name, its punishment, like that of a criminal offence, is a debt that the individual himself must pay; or else he must be forgiven, and the debt never paid."[98] God, having forgiven humanity freely out of his love rather than through the payment of a debt, could still freely impose conditions on that forgiveness. The necessity of a moral change was the essence of this condition. Onderdonk naturally attempted to distinguish this formulation from the condemned teachings of Pelagianism, which held that individuals could earn their salvation. The divine holiness, vindicated by the atonement, demanded these conditions not to cause salvation but to be the sine qua non of it. "Holiness exclude[s] all human merit, yet exact[s] all possible human obedience."[99]

These themes were taken up by Seabury in numerous *Churchman*

95. Henry U. Onderdonk to Samuel Seabury, 6 December 1833, Seabury Correspondence.

96. *Essay on Regeneration,* 9.

97. Henry U. Onderdonk, "The Atonement," [Episcopal Charge of 1838] *Sermons and Episcopal Charges,* 2:310.

98. Ibid., 2:313.

99. Ibid., 2:330.

editorials, where he too attempted to define an Episcopal approach to justification and regeneration that was both progressive and freed from any reliance upon juridical understandings. Like Onderdonk, he contrasted the popular Calvinist approach, which saw justification as a covenant between God and Jesus and which resulted in perfect right-eousness being imputed to true believers, with the conditional An-glican approach, in which God tendered pardon through the ministry, on condition that the terms of the gospel were complied with.[100] Justification took place not at the beginning of the Christian life but was the goal, intricately connected with the life itself.

This speculation and its apparent challenge to the notion of justifi-cation by faith alone—a formulation that was sacrosanct for evan-gelicals—stirred up a great deal of controversy. Yet if a spirited dis-cussion resulted from the speculation concerning a progressive and moral view of justification and regeneration, it was minor in relation to the controversy surrounding Seabury's bolder theological sug-gestion. In the spring of 1838, in an editorial entitled "Salvability of the Heathen," Seabury pushed the Episcopal critiques of Calvinist theories of grace to their logical conclusion. Since Christ was incar-nated as a man and not merely as a Christian, the glory of the gospel lay in the fact that the work of Christ benefited all, the heathen as well as the Christian. The work of Christ reconciled God to all mankind and offered to all a relationship with the Father. All people and not simply the elect were restored. Christ's redemptive power was in all humanity as a spark of life. From this perspective just as an individual might have his being in God without any knowledge of what this means, so too might he partake of the blessings of Christ's atonement while still being ignorant of it. To explain how this might be, Seabury made use of a distinction borrowed from the seventeenth-century Anglican theologian Henry Hammond between legal and evangelical obedience. Individuals were justified not by sinless obedience but by sincere obedience.[101] The heathen could hence hope that God would accept their humble and sincere obedience to the law of nature. "The God of their hearts," he assured his readers, "manifesting himself by a light of the mind, by instincts of goodness, by a sensibility of guilt, by awakening and warnings of the conscience," was their hope, since Christ "suffered death universally for all men, in consequence of which, the Holy Ghost is in the most liberal largeness dealt upon all

100. See *Churchman* 7 (April 15, 1837): n.p.
101. On this point in Hammond, see Allison, *Rise of Moralism,* 97–102.

the world."[102] Christ, having died for all, asked only for that obedience that they might be able to offer.

Seabury's speculations were the logical extension of the Episcopal rejection of limited atonement as well as of the tendency to extend the net of grace. Indeed, Thomas Yardley How had hinted at much the same position almost twenty-four years earlier. The demand to integrate a moral vision into the theological understanding of the nature of salvation had been a trend present in Episcopal thinking for decades. Yet Seabury's solution, which appeared to challenge the doctrine of justification by faith even more than progressive justification had, seemed to many to have gone too far. Such an uproar occurred that the trustees of General Theological Seminary, at which Seabury was a professor, felt it necessary to publicly distance themselves from his views.[103] The controversy raged among various journals on this subject, and it soon became entangled in the question of support for foreign missions. For Seabury, however, the advantage of his approach was quite practical: "Universal redemption holds up to all society a law to which, through the preventing and assisting grace of God, they can render an acceptable obedience. It is thus conservative, and leavens society with a wholesome, even minded, consoling and conservative influence."[104] The fundamental social problem with partial redemption lay in its presenting of a law that some could not obey. In these cases the law merely convicted them of their sin and showed them of their need for some overpowering act of divine omnipotence. As a result, virtuous subordination and obedience lost all theological support.

The issues of moral responsibility, the duty of the individual in the society, and the idea of gradual growth all came together in the theological writings of the 1830s. Troubled by the problems that were endemic to the Hobartian synthesis and by the evangelical tendency toward seeing justification as both immediate and overwhelming, both Onderdonk and Seabury attempted to set forth new categories of analysis.

---

102. *Churchman* 8 (September 8, 1838): 101.

103. See the letter by Thomas H. Taylor printed in the *Churchman* 8 (June 16, 1838): 53; and also the discussion of the incident in Brand, *Life of Whittingham*, 1:190.

104. *Churchman* 8 (June 2, 1838): 47.

V

The struggle by high church writers to maintain a conscious identity in the midst of a strongly evangelical religious environment did not stop, however, with the questions of theology and society. Their struggle included a wrestling with the broader questions of the meaning of the American past and the fundamental nature of American society.

Numerous historians over the past few decades have emphasized the importance of the memory of the Puritan past in the shaping of the ideology of both the revolutionary generation and of the young republic.[105] In large part the works of the eighteenth-century historians Daniel Neal and Edmund Calamy facilitated this, since in their histories the Puritans were transformed from creators of a godly commonwealth to defenders of liberty and popular sovereignty. This became the predominant understanding of the Puritans, and as one of their sons, George Bancroft, in his famous history noted, "It was Religion struggling in, with, and for the People; a war against tyranny and superstition. . . . It was its office to engraft the new institution of popular energy upon the old European assumption of feudal aristocracy and popular servitude."[106] The importance of the Pilgrims and of the Puritan fathers during the early national period is hard to overestimate. At annual Plymouth Rock orations, Forefathers Day celebrations, thanksgiving sermons, and other such events, "the celebrity of the Plymouth Rock heroes is exploited year by year, with most unflagging perseverance."[107] This veneration, however, stemmed not only from the fact that the writing of American history during this period remained something of a New England cottage industry, but also from the importance of this history in giving a sense of national self-definition.[108] The Pilgrims' values were the American values,

105. Hatch, *The Sacred Cause of Liberty;* Bernard Bailyn, *The Ideological Origins of the American Revolution* (New York, 1967); Heimert, *Religion and the American Mind;* and Edmund Morgan, "The Puritan Ethic and the American Revolution," *William and Mary Quarterly* 24 (1967): 3–43.

106. George Bancroft, *History of the United States of America,* 6 vols. (New York, 1887), 1:317.

107. Thomas W. Coit, *Puritanism* (New York, 1845), 15. As is obvious from the above citation, Coit was not happy about such veneration.

108. On this point, see Wesley Frank Craven, *The Legend of the Founding Fathers* (New York, 1956). Craven also has some illuminating suggestions as to why *the* founding fathers were seen as coming from New England rather than from the older colony of Virginia.

their hopes were the nation's hopes, and no more so than in their staunch opposition to both political and religious tyranny. Religion and nationhood were held in tandem in the image of the Pilgrim, and Samuel F. Smith, penning his national hymn in 1831 while studying at Andover Seminary, could find no higher praise than to christen this the "land of the Pilgrims' pride."

The memory of the founding fathers also served a practical religious purpose. For an evangelical alliance that was slowly breaking up into squabbling factions, the memory of the Pilgrims, particularly in New England, served as an important source of unity, a historical myth covering a multitude of divisions. However divided, all the children of the Puritans were heirs to a common blessing and common story: "We open another seal in the apocalypse of history. The Puritans, failing to accomplish their object in England, fled from the fires of persecution to the wilds of America. The church in the wilderness was clothed in the sun. Her light and her freedom were greatly increased."[109]

Episcopalians, however, had a fundamental difficulty accepting this story. If America were indeed the land of the Pilgrims' pride, what place in the national story could be found for the heirs of those who harried the Pilgrims out of England? A figure such as William Laud, the bete noire of New England historians, could not simply be excised from the Episcopal story, since to him belonged the honor of freeing Anglicanism from the bondage of Calvinism. Nor were high church writers oblivious to the fact that much of the panegyric to the Puritans contained a veiled critique of their church. Works such as Leonard Bacon's *Historical Discourses* (1839) loved to extol the piety and liberality of the New England settlers while sharply contrasting them with the pomp and despotism of Charles and Laud.[110] At times this theme became more explicit, and Joel Hawes in *A Tribute to the Memory of the Pilgrims* used his address to attack the growing popularity of the Episcopal Church and claimed for the Puritans the honor of originating the New England traditions of both civil liberty and public morality.[111] One correspondent to Samuel Miller even suggested that a new Sunday School history of the Puritans be issued to

109. "The Comparative Influence of Calvinism and Arminianism on Civil Liberty," *New Englander* 3 (1845): 517.

110. Leonard Bacon, *Thirteen Historical Discourses* . . . (New Haven, 1839), 11–16.

111. Joel Hawes, *A Tribute to the Memory of the Pilgrims and a Vindication of the Congregational Churches of New England* (Hartford, 1830), 61–72.

keep their memory alive against "Hume," "the devil," and "Prelates."[112]

Hence throughout the 1830s numerous Episcopal writers took up this gauntlet and attempted to wrest control of the national past from the sons of the Puritans. Some, such as James Fenimore Cooper, did this via the instrument of the novel. As one writer has noted, "[He] was a Yorker through and through. But in this character it was not enough to celebrate the majesty of the New York forest and the nobility of its denizens, red and white. It was necessary to contrast them with the shrewd, ill-favored, hypocritical sons of the Puritans to the eastward."[113] We have already seen how Cooper often chose as his villains New Englanders—penurious yet moralistic descendents of the Puritans. Others chose the more mundane arenas of articles and books. In a review, for example, of Leonard Bacon's work the writer chided Bacon for his ancestor worship, going on to suggest that along with other eulogists of the Puritans he "may have personal, political, or sectarian interests to be advanced by it."[114] In their answers to the defenders of the Puritans these writers tended to emphasize four points. First, in contrast to the claim that the Puritan party was the pious party in seventeenth-century England and was forced out of the country on account of the religious views of its members, high church writers argued that the real contest at the time was political and not religious. "It was the question of whether *Puritanism* or *Prelacy* should be the religion of the State, that divided the parties," as political a question as a presidential election.[115] Second, only after they had been defeated politically did the Puritans venture to America and then not for religious reasons but for economic ones, or the hope of gaining "exclusive trade in fur and fisheries."[116] Profit and not the prophets led them to abandon their homes in Holland for the American shore, a characteristic that had been inherited all too well by their Yankee descendents. Third, far from being the founders of American liberty they harshly persecuted all who would not hold their creed. High church writers took great relish in relating all the stories of the persecutions of Anglicans, Quakers, and Baptists, and then contrasting the memory of the Puritans with their historical reality. "We regard

112. John Alden to Samuel Miller, 28 November 1845, Miller Correspondence.

113. Fox, *Yankees and Yorkers,* 200.

114. "Politics of Puritans," *New York Review* 6 (1840): 51.

115. [Alonzo B. Chapin], *Review of the "Tribute to the Memory of the Pilgrims"* . . . (Hartford, 1836), 19.

116. Coit, *Puritanism,* 18.

our Puritan ancestors as pious, good, upright, but, in many respects, deluded men," one Episcopal writer observed; "we yield to the Puritans all they claimed for themselves, but we cannot grant all that the eulogies of their descendents have attributed to them."[117] Finally, the real origin of American freedom did not lie with the Puritans, but with the long historical rise of popular freedom and the moral and physical environment of the new nation.

Implicit in all of these criticisms was a vision of America far different from that offered by Plymouth Rock orators. America was indeed blessed, though whether it was uniquely blessed these high church critics never made explicit. Yet these blessings were of a general nature and hence mediated through such factors as the physical environment and the English common law tradition and not simply by a narrow religious tradition. Furthemore the strength of American society lay in its balance. The Episcopal Church served the well-being of American society by counterbalancing the centrifugal tendency of other aspects of American life. In a society marked by individualism and change the church offered continuity and order.[118] Although neither society nor church explicitly influenced the other they worked in common to create a psychic equilibrium necessary for the well-being of the nation.

The Anglican invocation of a Puritan "black legend" had a long history in England and had earlier occurred in America in the decade before the Revolution, as a counter to the Presbyterian campaign against the colonial bishopric. Yet its reappearance in the 1830s seems to have served at least two other purposes. It first of all defined a place for high church Episcopalians in the new society. Just as in their opposition to the millennial consciousness high church writers rejected any overly narrow definition of American destiny, their rejection of the Pilgrim panegyric was a rejection of any overly limiting notion of the American past. On a second level, however, their writings suggested to their audience that the true heritage of Puritanism was not liberty but the problems plaguing America in the 1830s. Both in the fanaticism of the evangelical reform endeavors and in their tendency to splinter one could see the "sincere filial veneration" of the

117. "Origin and Progress of Popular Liberty," *New York Review* 2 (1838): 96. See too "The Pilgrims," *Protestant Episcopalian and Church Register* 2 (1831): 7–9.

118. See "Extension of the Church," *Churchman* 9 (August 10, 1839): 86. This continued to be an important theme in high church social thinking. See "The National Fast," *Churchman* 30 (December 20, 1860): 344.

Separatist tradition.[119] Furthermore the final fruit of Puritanism was to be seen in

> the levelling and revolving system in politics—the system of depressing the rich and elevating the poor—of turning out the skilful and putting in the uninitiated, for the sake of change—of making the clergy, who tell us more religious truth, to say the least than anybody else does—of making them hirelings by the year, or month; and the judge, who speaks the voice of justice, dependent on a partisan vote.[120]

The problems of a surfeit of individualism and the breakdown of order were both firmly placed on the memory of the Puritan fathers. The debate over the national past ineluctably glided into the question of the national future.

VI

Perhaps the best way to understand all of the various ideas and trends discussed in this chapter is to see how they surfaced in the life of a single layman, George Templeton Strong (1820–75), who left a very complete and thoughtful private diary. Strong might be taken as typical of many of those coming of age in the 1830s who found themselves attracted to the alternative the Episcopal Church provided. Brought up a Presbyterian in New York City, Strong was sent by his father to Columbia College rather than to Yale because of some qualms concerning the theology of Nathaniel William Taylor.[121] At Columbia he fell under the influence of John McVickar, professor of moral philosophy and biographer of John Henry Hobart. In 1838 he converted to the Episcopal Church and quickly became a vigorous high church layman. For him, high churchmen were nothing less than the "restorers of apostolic usage."[122] The true church could have nothing to do with the prejudices of the nineteenth century and had to abjure "everything that appertained to enlightened Protestantism." The stale, flat, and sad state of the Protestant churches convinced him

119. Coit, *Puritanism*, 103.

120. Ibid., 235.

121. Allan Nevins and M. H. Thomas, eds., *The Diary of George Templeton Strong*, 4 vols. (New York, 1952), 1:xix–xx.

122. Ibid. (1839), 1:112.

that only by separating itself from them could the Episcopal Church escape their fate. Enraptured by the Gothic style, he daydreamed of being incredibly wealthy so as to rebuild Columbia in the model of an English university, outside of the city and connected to a cathedral and a theological college, and then of appointing Samuel Seabury as president over it.[123] He applauded the *New York Review* for its attacks on the Pilgrim fathers, whom he found politically "bad" and religiously "vile," and he disliked linking in common cause with heretics and infidels, which was the heart of his objection to the Temperance Society. In manners and mores his world view reflected the issues dear to the high church writers. Even concerning the question of slavery he shared their common ambivalence. Slavery was wrong,

> a national sin, and the future parent of national curses and calamity. But the Bible and the Church are silent—and unquestionably were there such moral guilt in slaveholding as its opponents insist on, the primitive church would have entered its protest against it and overthrown it with the overt corruptions of the old world. Let it be shown that there are any indications even of such a feeling in the remains of that period, and I will call myself an abolitionist most gladly. But I'm suspicious of all the religious improvements of the nineteenth century.[124]

The alternative to evangelical theology and culture which the high church movement offered gained a hearty convert in Strong. Evangelicalism, Puritanism, and temperance all came under his critical eye. Yet even in the layman Strong there are hints that the high church synthesis would be sorely tested in the crisis over slavery.

Thus the decade of the 1830s saw the Episcopal Church in general and the high church wing in particular cast into a far more prominent role than at any point in the preceding two decades. The alternative it offered to the crisis in the evangelical enterprise proved immensely appealing to many during the decade.

123. Ibid. (1842), 1:182–83.
124. Ibid. (1842), 1:195.

5

New Challenges and Controversies

In the summer of 1838 a lay convert to the episcopal church wrote to the *Churchman* and praised both the newspaper and the Episcopal Church in general for its success in avoiding both "novelty" and "division."[1] From the perspective of many a disinterested observer it did seem as if the church had managed to avoid the woes that had befallen American evangelicalism. Prophecy, however, was not this *funny* unknown layman's strong point. Even while this letter was being confidently penned, forces were already at work that would not only disturb the peace of the church and severely challenge the framework of the Hobartian system, but also resurrect evangelical concerns over the compatibility of episcopacy and American democratic culture.

The first thirty years of the new century had not been uneventful ones in the intellectual annuals of Europe. In fields as diverse as science and poetry new ideas and understandings had arisen and were overthrowing the remains of Augustan and Enlightenment civilization and culture. American Episcopalians had not been oblivious to these rumblings from Europe. Throughout the 1830s Samuel Turner, the professor of biblical literature at General Seminary, together with a small group of associates had attempted to kindle interest in some of the more moderate German scholarship. Works of G. C. Storr, Johann Gottfried Eichhorn, H. F. W. Gesenius, and Johann David Michaelis were carefully translated and published, yet they created little popular interest within the church. Indeed, Turner's translation and abridgment of G. J. Planck's *Introduction to Theological Knowledge* sold a scant thirty-five copies.[2]

---

1. *Churchman* 8 (August 4, 1838): 82.
2. Turner, *Autobiography,* 167–71. As a group these German authors (partic-

Of far greater attraction were the stirrings of romanticism coming out of England, which is not surprising since more than a common language bound Episcopalians more closely to England than to Germany. Always on the lookout for English trends, American high church journals faithfully monitored their English counterparts such as the *British Critic* and the *London Quarterly Review.* Nor did changing sensibilities in art, literature, and philosophy go unnoticed. Episcopal interest in Gothic architecture has already been noted, and particularly the usefulness of the style for evoking awe and reverence. Similarly, during Hobart's extended visit to Europe (1822–25) he made it a point to visit William Wordsworth, Robert Southey, and the nephew of Samuel Taylor Coleridge.[3] As the clerical tour of England became more common, either for reasons of health or for raising money among wealthy Englishmen for American Episcopal projects, the awareness of English cultural trends grew even more dominant. The case of John McVickar, biographer of Hobart, may not be atypical. During his visit of 1830 he made it a point to converse with Coleridge, Wordsworth, Southey, and Sir Walter Scott, and the impression they made upon the Columbia professor was marked.[4] A major appeal of the romantic generation of Wordsworth, Scott, and the others for American high church visitors was that all of these writers, to one degree or another, professed loyalty to some branch of the Anglican communion and hence could be viewed by extension as the property of American Episcopalians. Like poor country cousins, American churchmen basked in the pride and status reflected upon them through the accomplishments of their English ecclesiastical relatives.

Yet what to do with this inheritance was a question that remained to be answered. As Anglican as Wordsworth and others might have been, the Hobartian system had made little room for a positive role for any art not immediately ecclesiastical. The proper relationship of the church to this secular culture was in no way clear; for if on the one

---

ularly Storr and Planck) tended to buttress the older eighteenth-century belief in supernatural-rationalism. Because of this, as Turner himself admitted, they were liable to attack from both conservative, ecclesiological critics such as writers in the *Churchman,* who objected to the making of scriptural interpretation independent of the authority of the church fathers, and more liberal critics, who found their approach anachronistic. Ibid., 182.

    3. *Works,* 1:299–300.

    4. See John Brett Langstaff, *The Enterprising Life: John McVickar, 1787–1868* (New York, 1961), 127–60; and William A. McVickar, *The Life of the Rev. John McVickar, S.T.D.* . . (New York, 1872), 138–47, 157–72.

hand it benefited from the medieval sensitivity permeating the literature, the literature nonetheless still represented a secular form of culture. Thus when an appeal signed by both the archbishops of Canterbury and of Dublin was circulated on behalf of Walter Scott, who had suffered grave financial reverses, the propriety of church periodicals supporting it became a source of controversy. For many, even though Scott belonged to the small Scottish Episcopal Church and his novels exuded medieval flavor, the long-standing suspicion regarding secular literature could not be assuaged. Scott's novels were "too often employed as palliatives, lulling into a stupor those moral sensibilities which should be awakened and directed with sacred diligence to their proper objects."[5] But in the view of others such an opinion smacked more of excessive Puritan rigorism than of traditional Anglican openness to the innocent enjoyments of the world.[6]

An even greater problem confronted American high churchmen in their attempt to domesticate the thought of Samuel Taylor Coleridge (1772–1834), perhaps the greatest religious genius produced in nineteenth-century England. The main outlines of Coleridge's life and thought are well known: his early fascination with the French Revolution and mechanistic philosophy, his absorption of the German philosophy of Kant and Schelling, and his later interests in literary criticism and religion. His religious ideas in particular attracted great interest and excitement throughout much of the nineteenth century.[7] Broadly speaking, Coleridge's religious writings attempted to liberate Christianity from the restrictive confines of both older, hardened orthodoxy and eighteenth-century rationalism. He had little tolerance for a religion constantly searching in the manner of a William Paley for external evidences. By philosophically distinguishing between reason and understanding he could suggest that religion was not ultimately a concern of the understanding, which would have grounded it in the

5. "Romances," *Churchman* 2 (January 26, 1833): 386.

6. On this squabble, see *Churchman* 2 (January 19, 1833): 381; 2 (February 2, 1833): 390; and 2 (February 16, 1833): 398.

7. Coleridge's two most important religious works were *Aids to Reflection* (1825) and *Confessions of an Inquiring Spirit,* published posthumously in 1840. For secondary studies of Coleridge's influence on religious thought, see James Denis Boulger, *Coleridge as Religious Thinker* (New Haven, 1961); Charles R. Sanders, *Coleridge and the Broad Church Movement* (Durham, N.C., 1942); J. R. Barth, *Coleridge and Christian Doctrine* (Cambridge, Mass., 1969); Stephen Prickett, *Romanticism and Religion: The Tradition of Coleridge and Wordsworth in the Victorian Church* (New York, 1976); and Basil Willey, *Nineteenth-Century Studies: Coleridge to Matthew Arnold* (New York, Harper Torchbook ed., 1966), 10–45.

science of phenomenon, but stemmed instead from that intuitive immediate beholding which he called reason. In this he claimed to return
to the spirit of the seventeenth century, yet not to the century of Laud
and Pearson but to that of the Cambridge Platonists. Religion was
viewed as the highest activity of the human spirit and Christianity was
the highest of religions since it centered on both sin—or the worthlessness of a life given over to the senses—and redemption, which was
understood as the true meaning and vocation of the human soul.
Furthermore the Bible also took on a new meaning, being no longer
simply a book of infallible utterances but now the arena in which God
illuminated the believer through the holy spirit. In Coleridge both
religion and culture and church and state became more organically
bound together than in either the older orthodoxy or the rational
religion of the eighteenth century.[8]

Any simple integration of these ideas into the Hobartian system
was no easy task. The Coleridgean distaste for a religion based on
external and historical evidence severely undermined the Hobartian
theological method. Although it had shown comparatively little interest in the evidences of Christianity, high church theology (with its
foundation on the myth of the pure church) was firmly committed to
the presentation of the evidences of the church. The patristic record
was to them what watch-laden beaches were to Paley, a sign of divine
providence and direction. Furthermore Hobartians had long taken
pride that their theology rested empirically (or so they believed) on the
primitive witness, and hence largely free from the metaphysics and
metaphysico-theology of both Calvinism and German theological
speculation. In light of this long-standing suspicion of "metaphysics,"
Coleridge's religious teachings, with their basis in his idea of reason
rather than in the witness of the pure church, proved no easy obstacle
to overcome. Finally, the very spirit of Coleridge seemed to clash with
Hobartianism. If the metaphorical vision of the latter was that of the
apostolic church, surrounded by opponents yet remaining pure, in
Coleridge the vision was that of a transcendental catholicity. Religion
as part of humanity was coterminous with it. Rather than the vision of
the pre-Constantinian church, Coleridge offered the vision of a truly
national church encompassing all.

Coleridge's *Aids to Reflection* had been known to American Episcopalians as early as 1827, yet throughout the 1830s there emerged little
consensus concerning its applicability to the American religious

8. Willey, *Nineteenth-Century Studies,* 10–45.

scene. To some he seemed to offer the long-feared but little-known German philosophy of Kant and Schelling and was hence suspected of undermining traditional high church teachings. To others, however, he seemed to bear not heresy but a new breath of spiritual sensitivity, the roots of which lay not primarily in German philosophy but in the Neoplatonist tradition of the Cambridge Platonists.[9] As the importance of Coleridge's thought increased in England, however, and as he became too big a prize not to try to lay claim to, at least some Hobartians began to try publicly to associate his teachings with their church. This desire became particularly acute in the late 1830s, when Coleridge's name and reputation began being linked with the Transcendentalism of Ralph Waldo Emerson and Margaret Fuller.[10] Thus when in 1839 John McVickar was invited to write the preface for a second American edition of the *Aids* he used it as an opportunity to try to accomplish just that. In 1829 James Marsh, a Congregationalist minister and president of the University of Vermont, had published the first American edition of the *Aids* and prefaced it with his now famous "Preliminary Essay," which suggested that Coleridge's categories might serve as a possible solution to the then current theological turmoil over free will and moral obligation.[11] In his essay Marsh praised Coleridge for emphasizing reflection over speculative doctrine and for his suggestion that the Christian faith was the perfection of human reason, which in effect united theology and philosophy.

To McVickar, Marsh's essay failed by presenting a Congregational rather than an Anglican reading of Coleridge, a reading which did not interpret him as a member of the Church of England. Indeed, when justifying his new introduction he admitted,

> In entering upon [the task] he [McVickar] would fain avoid all idea of competition with his predecessor, as being well aware that his own chief fitness for the task, and certainly his only vantage-ground in it,

9. For this debate, see the *Churchman* 3 (May 18, 1833): 449; 3 (June 8, 1833): 462; 3 (June 22, 1833): 470, etc.

10. On the appeal of Coleridge to New England Transcendentalists, see Octavius Brooks Frothingham, *Transcendentalism in New England* (New York, Harper Torchbook ed., 1959), 76–92.

11. On Marsh and his interest in Coleridge, see *The Remains of the Rev. James Marsh D.D. . .* (Boston, 1843); John J. Duffy, ed., *Coleridge's American Disciples: The Selected Correspondence of James Marsh* (Amherst, 1973); and Ronald Vale Wells, *Three Christian Transcendentalists: James Marsh, Caleb Sprague Henry, Frederick Henry Hedge*, rev. ed. (New York, 1972).

arises from being of "kin" in church and doctrine with the author whose philosophy of both he presumes to comment upon.[12]

However, this kinship, implied McVickar, was no mean advantage. Marsh's essay erred in that it addressed issues such as free will and metaphysical divinity, which were the concerns of Calvinists rather than Anglicans. McVickar on the other hand downplayed the philosophical aspects of Coleridge's thought, calling them simply "occasional touches of transcendental metaphysics," and chose rather to emphasize the *Aids'* devotional usefulness.[13] He also ignored the German roots of Coleridge's ideas and emphasized instead their English precursors. McVickar linked Coleridge with the Irish high church layman Alexander Knox because of their common uniting of reason, revelation, learning, and orthodoxy to a spiritual creed. McVickar, however, was not content to simply identify Coleridge with Anglicanism in general but proceeded to link the poet's thoughts with the revival of high church theology then going on in England:

> If it be further asked, what aspects the teaching of Coleridge bears towards the theology which under the title of the "Oxford Tracts" has recently awakened so much misplaced alarm among well-meaning churchmen both in England and America, the answer is, that of friendly travellers, on roads different indeed, but not diverse, setting out in their journey from distant points, but guided by the same compass, and tending to the same haven. . . . Both are warring against the same modern errors, both fighting for the same deep, despised, ancient truths, and both exposing and refuting the same logical fallacies—the one in the Church, the other in philosophy, and thus both labouring in a common cause, to bring back an unreflecting, arrogant, all things understanding age to the docile, reflecting, mystery-admitting spirit of earlier and better times.[14]

To McVickar, Coleridge was ultimately just one more Anglican critic of the spirit of the age.

Rarely has Coleridge been so misread as he was by McVickar. Almost all of the important themes in Coleridge's work—his new view of the function of poetic language, his distinction between reason and understanding, and his ideas on the relationship of philosophy and religion—were either ignored or overlooked by McVickar, who possessed so little philosophical background and sensitivity that his essay

12. *Aids to Reflection . . . to Which is Prefixed a Preliminary Essay by John McVickar, D.D. . .* (New York, 1872), ix–x.
13. Ibid., xviii.
14. Ibid., xxxiv.

is at times akin to a Joyce Kilmer lecture on Shakespeare.[15] Several writers leapt to the defense of Marsh's essay and challenged any high church absconding with Coleridge. McVickar's essay was dismissed as "but a leaf plucked out of an ecclesiastical romance."[16] Even Henry Nelson Coleridge, executor of his uncle's literary estate, felt compelled to write to Marsh, "My uncle was born and bred, and passed all his later life, and died an affectionate member of the church of England; but the fact of church membership would not have influenced one of his conclusions."[17] Yet McVickar's misreading is perhaps as significant for its error as others were for their accuracy. Henry Coleridge's observation "In America they have now *two* schools of Coleridge" implicitly acknowledged that two very different approaches to the same material did indeed exist. A narrowly Anglican, devotional, and high church interpretation challenged a general, metaphysical, and linguistic interpretation. The former interpretation served, according to McVickar, to free Coleridge from association with Transcendentalism, a movement which in high church eyes simply showed the logical degree to which the Protestant lack of authority could be taken. Indeed, Transcendentalism was even occasionally referred to as New School Unitarianism to link it explicitly to the more common failure of American Protestantism.[18] The Anglican Coleridge could never succumb to such errors as "the utterly wild irreligious speculations that of late have become so rife in our land."[19] For McVickar, Coleridge was the proponent of neither "ultra-Protestantism" nor "impious rationalism" but instead of a personal God and a visible church.

15. Not even McVickar's son (and biographer) could defend his interpretation of Coleridge. See McVickar, *Life of McVickar,* 295–97.

16. [George Allen], "Dr. McVickar's Coleridge," *Churchman* 10 (March 14, 1840): 2.

17. H. N. Coleridge to James Marsh, 1 April 1840, in Duffy, *Coleridge's American Disciples,* 230. In a private letter to McVickar, Coleridge was even more pointed in his criticism, concluding, "And really if the contrary of Dr. Marsh's position quoted by you . . . be true, I am at a loss to know what object Mr. Coleridge could have had in writing the Aids to Reflection or any person in reprinting it." H. N. Coleridge to John McVickar, 18 April 1840, typescript copy, McVickar Family Papers, St. Mark's Library, General Theological Seminary, New York, New York.

18. See, for example, *Churchman* 6 (March 4, 1837): 1244.

19. [John McVickar], "Coleridge's Literary Remains," *New York Review* (1840): 410. For the ascribing of this article to McVickar, see the letters printed in Duffy, *Coleridge's Amercan Disciples,* 250.

What one sees in McVickar is the attempt to fit Coleridge into the preexisting Hobartian categories. On many nontheological levels Coleridge's new vision proved attractive. Many a Hobartian appreciated greatly the spiritual sensitivity and the enhanced cultural status the teachings involved. Yet on the level of theology and philosophy the two systems could be merged only by bending one or the other woefully out of shape. The intellectual categories of Hobartianism, forged by a century of disputation, were drastically ill-equipped to understand, much less adapt, the uniqueness of Coleridge's thought.

The compelling attractiveness of Coleridge, however, can best be seen in the willingness of some younger high church writers to jettison the apostolic argument in favor of Coleridgean sensitivity. For them Coleridge seemed to offer a new spiritual basis for their views by freeing them from the crabbed and narrow confines of the appeal to the primitive church. The *New York Review*, edited by Caleb S. Henry from 1837 to 1840, attempted to defend in its pages both high church ideals and the new philosophy and in doing so to loosen the high church apologetic from its moorings to the apostolic argument, which was the hallmark of Hobartianism. For Henry the great appeal of the Episcopal Church was not epistemological but spiritual, since for them the fundamental problem of the modern age was its lack of spiritual sensitivity. "We believe," he explained, "that . . . the religion of the present day, while more widely extended, is not as deeply seated as formerly." The attraction of Coleridge was that in him prayer, poetry, music, and architecture could be seen as part of a common unity. Henry implicitly faulted the older apologists for reducing ecclesiastical ritual to "bits of Greek out of Gregory or bits of Latin out of Jerome" rather than seeing it as dynamically related to the culture itself.[20] The older high church attitude had often devolved into mere negativism and legalism, seeing the function of ritual as simply the keeping out of error or insuring faithfulness to the primitive tradition. Coleridge, however, broke the bounds of this stultifying ritualism by showing that the real purpose of ritual was in the end poetical: "The denizens of Eden were and must have been *all* poets:—*all* must have been alive to the beauty that was poured out around them and for them."[21] In Henry and other younger high churchmen one sees the first movements toward a transformation of high church thought that,

20. "Rituals," *New York Review* 4 (1839): 146.
21. Ibid., 118. Emphasis in original.

while keeping and even deepening its piety, shifted its intellectual presuppositions away from the apostolic argument.

II

Of far greater impact on the lives of American Episcopalians was the movement for ecclesiastical and spiritual regeneration flowing forth from the common room of Oriel College, Oxford, and known as the Oxford Movement. From that July day in 1833 when John Keble delivered his sermon "National Apostasy" the movement rapidly grew throughout the 1830s and became perhaps the most important influence on the Church of England in the nineteenth century and central to the development of what Yngve Brilioth has called Neo-Anglicanism.[22] The lives and characters of the main participants have been poignantly etched in the annals of the history of the church and require little introduction: John Keble, the poet and pastoral model; Hurrell Froude, the young firebrand so aptly described by Hugh James Rose as a man "not afraid of inferences"; E. B. Pusey, the donnish scholar of oriental languages, who gave to the movement both its name and his concern for devotion and asceticism; and finally, John Henry Newman, the brilliant and haunting preacher and writer.[23] Likewise the history of the movement is well known: with its first phase, which witnessed the beginning of the *Tracts for the Times,* and the call for the English church to reclaim its religious heritage and

22. Yngve Brilioth, *The Anglican Revival: Studies in the Oxford Movement* (London, 1925), passim.

23. On the subject of the Oxford Movement there is such a plethora of literature, both primary and secondary, concerning all of its phases and implications, that any short list of sources must be serendipitous. On the movement itself, in addition to Brilioth see, Owen Chadwick, *The Mind of the Oxford Movement* (Stanford, 1960); Richard Church, *The Oxford Movement,* ed. and with an introduction by Geoffrey Best (Chicago, 1970); Marvin R. O'Connell, *The Oxford Conspirators: A History of the Oxford Movement* (New York, 1969); and Geoffrey Faber, *Oxford Apostles: A Character Study of the Oxford Movement* (London, Faber Paper Covered Ed., 1974). For both historical context and various aspects of the movement, see C. C. J. Webb, *Religious Thought in the Oxford Movement* (London, 1928); William George Peck, *The Social Implications of the Oxford Movement* (New York, 1933); Bernard M. G. Reardon, *From Coleridge to Gore: A Century of Religious Thought in Britain* (London, 1971), 90–157; and Desmond Bowen, *The Idea of the Victorian Church: A Study of the Church of England, 1833–1889* (Montreal, 1968), 41–138.

perhaps culminated in the condemnation by the convocation of Oxford of R. D. Hampden, Regius Professor of Divinity, for suspected heresy; its second phase, which experienced the growing estrangement between Tractarians and Evangelicals over questions such as baptism and justification and the larger fear of the "romeward" tendency of the movement, that culminated in the condemnation of *Tract 90* in 1841 and with it the attempt to reconcile the Articles of Religion with catholic teaching; and the final phase, when Newman was on his "death bed" as an Anglican, which saw not only the condemnation of Pusey in 1843 for his views on the real presence but also culminated in Newman's entrance into the Roman Catholic Church in 1845. Although no brief sketch can do the movement justice, some awareness of the distinct teachings of the Tractarians, both in theology and devotion, is necessary in order to understand the nature of the impact of the Tracts in America.

Like American Hobartians, Tractarian writers constantly warned against the "modern spirit," yet in the British religious scene it had a far different connotation than it had in America. American high church writers usually understood the "modern spirit" to be connected with the exuberance of democratic evangelicalism that would devolve ultimately into ecclesiastical anarchy. In England, however, the modern spirit signified not democratic evangelicalism but "liberalism" that tended toward rationalism. To combat this liberalism Tractarians began by defending the traditional high church understanding of the nature of the church. Like the older generation of Jones of Nayland and Daubeny, they adamantly defended the doctrine of apostolic succession, claiming "every bishop of the Church whom we behold, is a lineal descendent of St. Peter and St. Paul after the order of a spiritual birth," and their writings bristle with citations from the apostolic fathers.[24] Yet tradition took on for them a new meaning. It was viewed not simply as the conserver and preserver of the past that justified in a Tory like manner the status quo, but had a restorative function and offered the church a vision of what it might be. Thus Newman admitted that the via media, in which Anglicans had always taken so much pride, had never existed except in the minds of some theorists. It was a goal yet to be achieved. This different appreciation for tradition bespoke a distinction of some importance, which Brilioth has called a difference between a static and a progressive view

24. Chadwick, *Mind*, 143.

of the nature of the church.[25] In contrast to Daubeny's concentration on ecclesiastical institutionalism, among some Tractarians there began to arise an understanding of the church as the extension of the incarnation, or as the true body of Christ.[26] This dynamic element of the church may also perhaps be seen in the shift from a concern for apostolic evidence to a concern for dogma. Hobart, following William Reeves, had argued that it was the facts attested to and not the theology presupposed that was the normative value of the apostolic fathers—a distinction that was particularly useful in debates with Presbyterians over the doctrine of apostolic succession. The Tractarian preoccupation with dogma as the answer to liberalism carried with it an added function for the apostolic witness; the early church did not simply give evidence of practice but actively defined true teaching.

A second hallmark of Tractarianism was its concern for piety. Where the earlier generation of English high churchmen had striven primarily to defend apostolic order and authority, much of the thrust of the Tract writers was for an increased holiness. The text of Newman's first *Parochial and Plain Sermon,* "Holiness, without which no man can see the Lord," might be taken as the motto of the entire movement. The concern for moral and pietistic fervor was so strong that one historian has noted, "Like its predecessor the Evangelical Movement, it was more a movement of the heart than of the head."[27] The piety of the older high church tradition had all too often been tinged with the balanced rational spirit of the eighteenth century. To see the Oxford Movement as a religious corollary to the Romantic Revolution—because of its emphasis on feeling, awe, and mystery—is perhaps an overstatement, yet the Tractarian piety did show certain parallels to romantic sensitivity.[28] Yet there was always a strongly rigoristic element in Tractarian piety. Holiness involved no simple or

25. Brilioth, *Anglican Revival,* 180 ff.

26. Reardon, *From Coleridge to Gore,* 99. On this theme, see the excerpt from Robert Wilberforce, *The Doctrine of the Incarnation,* in *The Oxford Movement,* ed. Eugene R. Fairweather (New York, 1964), 283–362.

27. Chadwick, *Mind,* 11.

28. Pusey in particular was influenced by Friedrich Schleiermacher, the great German romantic theologian. See Faber, *Oxford Apostles,* 134–35. On the interrelation of Tractarian theology and romantic theories of aesthetics, see G. B. Tennyson, *Victorian Devotional Poetry: The Tractarian Mode* (Cambridge, Mass., 1981), 12–71. The Tractarians, however, were often hesitant to identify outright their movement with other cultural trends. See Keble's essay "The Life of Sir Walter Scott," in *Occasional Papers and Reviews . . .* (London, 1877), 1–80.

quick change. The road to salvation was narrow and hard and required discipline and desire. The call to holiness was further strengthened by linking it to a new concept of faith. Rather than viewing faith as intellectual assent (as even Hobart had done), faith was seen as the acting on hope. Not external evidences but the harmony of the Christian truth with the inner feelings was the ground of faith and hence it could not be divorced from action. "Our doubts if we have any," Newman explained, "will be found to arise after *disobedience*. . . . And if we but obey God strictly, in time (through His blessing) faith will become like sight."[29]

Nowhere can the new Tractarian emphasis be seen more clearly than in the questions of justification and baptism. Newman's *Lectures on Justification* have been called the "chief theological document of the Oxford Movement," and they provide an important insight into the practical ramifications of the trends heretofore discussed. Newman's aim was to find a via media between the teachings of the Continental reformers and the position of the Council of Trent on the question of justification. He began by suggesting that justification by faith and justification by obedience were not antithetical. Ever since the Restoration many Anglican theologians had steered away from any strict position of solafideism, since it seemed to undermine any demand for obedience. Continuing in this line, Newman argued that justification involved both being accounted righteous *and* being made righteous, usually reflected in the traditional distinction between justification and sanctification. Newman, however, taking his lead from teachings found in the early church, suggested that justification came first neither from faith nor from works but rather through the righteousness of Christ indwelling in the individual through the holy spirit, and that the sacraments were the channels of this indwelling. All things came together as a whole in this new life:

> It seems, then, that whereas Faith on our part fitly answers or is the correlative, as it is called, to grace on God's part, Sacraments are but God's acts of grace, and good works are but our acts of faith; so that whether we say we are justified by faith, or by works, or by Sacraments, all these but mean one doctrine, that we are justified by grace, given through Sacraments, impetrated by faith, manifested in works.[30]

29. Newman, "Saving Knowledge," cited in Brilioth, *Anglican Revival,* 236.
30. John Henry Newman, *Lectures on Justification* (London, 1838), 348.

One sees that although Newman used the same locution of baptismal regeneration as American high church writers, the term took on a new and deeper meaning. In the Waterland–Hobart understanding, baptismal regeneration had a largely objective significance, which H. U. Onderdonk only intensified by suggesting that in baptism an individual received regeneration only *titularly* but not *actually*. Baptism placed the individual in the body of the church. For the Tractarians, however, baptism was ethically and religiously deepened by interpreting it as the true birth of the inward life, and hence the gift of God.[31] Holiness and piety became far more closely tied to baptism than in any of the earlier teachings.

At first glance it would seem that American high churchmen would have had numerous difficulties with the new Tractarian mood. They had invested so much time and energy in developing the apostolical argument, with its grounding in the static view of the church, that defending it should have been a major priority. Furthermore the swirling temper of Jacksonian America seemed to be far more in need of the static, objective, institutionally oriented Hobartian synthesis than the newer Tractarian one.

To explain the American high church response to the Tracts, we must keep two points in mind. The first is that the Tracts were far more a symbol than a source among American Episcopalians. Although excerpts from the Tracts had been published sporadically from as early as 1835, no complete American edition appeared before 1839–40.[32] To a surprising degree, even the alleged supporters of the Tracts did not read them in any systematic way. According to one witness not even such a proponent of them as the editor of the *New York Review* (probably Caleb S. Henry) was really familiar with them: "Some time since I dined in his company; and the subject of the Oxford tracts was brought upon the carpet. At that time he had evidently made himself but little acquainted; yet with very imperfect and second hand information, he undertook to become their defender."[33] Indeed as late as

---

31. That such a reinterpretation of baptism also created an enormous problem regarding the question of postbaptismal sins, the later history of Anglo-Catholicism would of course attest to.

32. On the introduction of the Tracts into America, see the letter from Charles S. Henry printed in H. P. Liddon, *Life of Edward Bouverie Pusey*, 4 vols. (London, 1893), 2:124–26.

33. John S. Stone, *A Memoir of the Life of James Milnor, D.D. . . . Abridged by the Author* (New York, [1849]), 447. Most historians have usually emphasized the

1843 William Berrian, rector of Trinity Church and one of the pillar high church clergy in New York, admitted that he had not recently read much of the Tracts, and even a year later another high church leader admitted, "Many indeed who have been mentioned at the very head and front of Puseyism, have never read one page of the Tracts."[34] Most American Hobartians, at least up to the appearance of *Tract 90*, generally believed that the Tracts simply continued the defense of the appeal to the primitive church. As the *Churchman* humorously noted, "People almost fancied they saw living skeletons, flitting up and down Oxford, terrible in Greek, and sackcloth; and calling upon men neither to repent nor believe but to fast and read the fathers."[35] The seeming continuity in language with the older high church tradition usually caused American Hobartians to underestimate Tractarian theology both positively and negatively. Furthermore it also led them to assume that the real contribution of the Tract writers was not theological but devotional. The Tractarian writers helped excite an increased reverence for holy things that the church already possessed, such as the liturgy and the historic ministry. High church writers viewed the deepening of the spiritual sense as the chief contribution of the Tracts, and in applauding the decision to publish an American edition of them, the *Churchman* lauded them primarily not for their theological worth but for their practical value in promoting piety.[36] When the Tract writers defended traditional theology or strengthened the devotional sense they received praise, but whenever they overstepped this role by either speculating in theology (as Newman had done

popularity of the Tracts in America, generally basing their argument on Bishop Stewart of Quebec's often quoted observation that he had heard more about the Tracts in a three-day sojourn in New York than in a year's residence in London (first cited in Stone, *Life of Milnor*, 1848 ed., 554). For such an interpretation, see Chorley, *Men and Movements*, 194–227; Margaret Norheim O'Connell, "'A Spirit Afloat': The Impact of the Oxford Movement in America," (Ph.D. diss., University of Chicago, 1962); and Kenneth M. Peck, "The Oxford Controversy in America: 1839," *HMPEC* 33 (1964): 49–63. My reading of the literature, particularly the private correspondence of the time, suggests that this belief should be reexamined. There was undoubtedly much discussion over the Tracts, yet there seem to be few acknowledgments, even in private correspondence, of people having read them. The American perception of them was accordingly often at variance with the Tracts themselves.

34. William Berrian to William F. Morgan, 27 July 1843, William Berrian Correspondence, copy in St. Mark's Library, General Theological Seminary, New York, New York; Edward Higbee cited in *Churchman* 14 (October 19, 1844): 129.

35. *Churchman* 9 (March 30, 1839): 9.

36. *Churchman* 9 (June 29, 1839): 62.

on the question of justification) or by innovating in ritual in a way that threatened the peace of the church, the *Churchman* quickly disassociated itself from them.[37]

Second, it is important to emphasize that the Hobartians responded to the Tracts with decided ambiguity until late autumn of 1839. What caused the change in opinion was not the Tracts themselves but the appearance of an American edition of E. B. Pusey's *Letter to the . . . Lord Bishop of Oxford,* which quickly became the most important Tractarian work for American Hobartians. The *Churchman* called it "a summary of the real views of the Oxford divines," and the *New York Review* was even more profuse in its praise: "[It is] one of the most admirable theological productions of its class that the world has ever seen."[38] Pusey's *Letter* became the lens through which the Tracts were read. The praise heaped on the *Letter* strikes the modern reader as surprising since it is now little read even by scholars, having long ago been eclipsed by *Tract 90* and Newman's *Essay on the Development of Doctrine.* Yet Pusey's systematic and plodding endeavor to free the Tracts from the charge of "romanizing" appealed to the American audience both in substance and tone and made the Tracts seem continuous with the older high church tradition. His appeal to a via media between Rome and the "ultra Protestants" who "would cast aside all but Scriptural terms" echoed decades of American high church apologetic.[39] On most of the main points of contention Pusey quietly and dispassionately explained the teachings of the Tractarians.

Via Pusey, however, a new category entered the American high church theological vocabulary which would have major ramifications. In his *Letter* Pusey popularized the idea of "indefectibility," a concept Newman had broached in his *Lectures on the Prophetical Office of the Church,* which claimed that when the church was truly one it did not err. As Newman explained,

> If this view of the subject be in the main correct, it would follow that the Ancient Church will be our model in all matters of doctrine, until it broke up into portions, and for Catholic agreement substituted

37. See "Innovations," *Churchman* 7 (October 14, 1837): n.p.; and "Oxford Tracts," 8 (March 2, 1839): 202.

38. *Churchman* 9 (November 23, 1839): 146; "Oxford Theology," *New York Review* 6 (1840): 237.

39. E. B. Pusey, *A Letter to the Right Rev. Father in God, Richard Lord Bishop of Oxford . . .* (New York, 1839), 15 ff.

peculiar local opinions; but since that time the Church has possessed no fuller measure of the truth than we see it has at this day, *viz.* merely the fundamental faith.[40]

At first glance the Tractarian argument for indefectibility seems like a simple restatement of the apostolic argument dear to the hearts of American Hobartians. Yet the apostolic argument had always had two sides, each with a subtle difference in emphasis. The myth of the pure church suggested that the reliability of the apostolic witness lay in the fact that it was a *primitive* witness and was hence closest to the apostles. Accordingly, the fundamental use of the witness had been to interpret scripture and, as an example, help define the *episcopos* referred to in I Timothy in light of the practice reflected in Ignatius of Antioch. The rule of St. Vincent of Lerins, however (*quod semper, quod ubique, quod ab omnibus*), could also imply that the reliability of the witness was derived not from the fact that it was primitive, but that it was a *united* witness. Newman's category of indefectibility provided the groundwork for such an interpretation by positing a more positive role for tradition in the church, beyond that of simply providing a context to interpret the scripture: "[The Church] is indefectible in [the truth of the Christian faith], and not only has authority to enforce, but is of authority in declaiming it. . . . [T]hat doctrine which is true, considered as an historical fact, is true also because she teaches it."[41] Indefectibility created a rift between the Vincentian strain and the primitive church strain of the argument from antiquity. The change may have been subtle but its importance was marked. The traditional confession of "one holy, catholic, and apostolic church" had largely theretofore been taken as a unity, yet after the end of the 1830s catholic and apostolic were no longer necessarily synonymous.

Seabury and the *Churchman* found Pusey's presentation of Newman's idea of indefectibility immensely appealing and singled it out for particular praise. It seemed to provide a solution to a problem endemic to the apostolic argument as it had developed, a problem that was gradually being recognized by some American high churchmen. As H. U. Onderdonk put it, "Tradition needs an interpreter, as well as scripture, and the abuse of private judgement is as great with the one as the other."[42] As the knowledge of the ancient history became more detailed and complex, the basis of surety shifted from the historical

40. John Henry Newman, *Lectures on the Prophetical Office of the Church* (London, 1837), 241.

41. Ibid., 226.

42. H. U. Onderdonk to Samuel Seabury, 8 March 1841, Seabury Correspon-

record per se to the indefectibility of the church. One sees this shift in a *Churchman* editorial entitled "Private Judgement and Infallibility." Seabury attempted to use indefectibility to establish a more positive role for church authority. While denying any infallibility to the church's testimony, he emphasized its certainty and went on to laud the propriety of accepting the decisions of the "Catholic Church" from "reliance on her authority and not on her testimony."[43] The believer could have so much confidence in the church that infallibility was not even necessary, since "the Church, being the appointed vehicle for transmitting the knowledge of God, may be reasonably and firmly believed to deliver her faith on scriptural grounds."[44] The desirability of establishing a new ground of surety for the evidence from antiquity came increasingly to be recognized. As William R. Whittingham, bishop of Maryland, in emphasizing the importance of Catholic tradition, admitted, "The next thing to establishing the *fact* of being a Church is to settle the *authority* of *the* church as the interpreter of the written word. That question lies beneath all *others* that are in such fierce discussion, not even excepting the form and mission of the ministry."[45]

The shift in the argument from antiquity, however, provoked a theological "civil war" among American Hobartians, and no individual defended the older understanding with as much vigor as John Henry Hopkins. The reasons behind Hopkins's sharp attack on the Tractarians from 1844 on are various. On one level he rejected the attempt to push the teachings of the church beyond the bounds set by the "Course of Ecclesiastical Study" (long ago drawn up by William White) and the eclectic tradition that the list represented.[46] Further-

---

dence. Onderdonk, however, was privately critical of the solution that Seabury proposed to this problem.

43. *Churchman* 10 (July 4, 1840): 66.

44. Ibid. In making this point, Seabury claims the authority of William Palmer's *Treatise on the Church of Christ,* the American edition of which was edited by William R. Whittingham. See vol. 2:81–82.

45. William R. Whittingham to Benjamin Haight, 17 April 1844, Protestant Episcopal Bishops Papers, Sterling Memorial Library, Yale University, New Haven, Connecticut.

46. Indeed, throughout much of Hopkins's writings one can see the attempt to hold together the high church and the eclectic theological traditions. See his letter to Samuel Seabury, 29 November 1837, Seabury Correspondence. The task became increasingly more difficult as the issues of debate shifted away from the older questions of Calvinism and the apostolic nature of episcopacy and toward the questions raised by the later tracts.

more he feared the apparent willingness of some Tractarians to lessen the theological divisions separating Anglicans and Rome. Yet perhaps most important, he rebelled against accepting any modification in the apostolic argument that seemed to threaten its traditional basis of certainty.[47] In his most extreme defense of the apostolic argument (not formulated until 1855), he suggested that unity in and of itself could provide no surety of truth but only reflected the degree of ecclesiastical discipline. Rather than simply showing the presence of unity it was necessary "to prove the unity of [the] Church, not simply among themselves, but *with the primitive Church of the Apostles in faith, worship and government.*"[48] Unity in error could just as easily occur as unity in truth, and only agreement with the teaching of the pure church could guarantee the latter to be the case. Furthermore for unity and catholicity to be truly the marks of the church that the creeds saw them to be, they must imply a unity and catholicity with the primitive church.[49] The doctrinal innovations of the Tractarians and their American supporters were "novelties," as alien to the true nature of the church as the temperance movement had been.

Hopkins was extremely critical of the theological views of the Tractarians since for him they destroyed the ground of certainty that the appeal to the primitive record seemed to provide. Yet even he willingly admitted his attraction to the movement in all areas except theology. Writing at the height of the controversy, he acknowledged,

> [W]hen has the world beheld such a band of intellects, combined in such an enterprise? The startling energy of Froude, the lovely poetry of Keble, the learned mysticism of Pusey, the profound yet simple eloquence of Newman, . . . to say nothing of a host of auxiliaries in every form of taste and feeling and operating in . . . church music, church painting, church architecture, church history, church ritual, and unhappily church doctrine—in tales for the young, and arguments for the old, in grave truth and amusing fiction, while the whole tended to the same end with marvelous strength and harmony.[50]

47. For three different phases in Hopkins's opinions on the Tracts see *The Missionary Constitution, The Oxford Tracts, and Nestorianism* . . . (Burlington, 1842); his opinion in the extended pamphlet debate with Francis Patrick Kenrick, Roman Catholic archbishop of Philadelphia; and *The Novelties Which Disturb Our Peace* . . . (Philadelphia, 1844).

48. John Henry Hopkins, *"The End of Controversy" Controverted* . . . , 2 vols., 3d ed. (New York, 1855), 1:355. Emphasis in original.

49. Ibid., 1:353–56.

50. Hopkins, *Novelties Which Disturb Our Peace,* Letter IV, 5–6.

Even to a theological critic like Hopkins the devotional and aesthetical spirit of the movement seemed strangely alluring. The dilemma of the Tracts for the Hobartians lay in the fact that they aroused the sense of piety and appreciation for the church that had characterized the older tradition while undermining the theological superstructure.

III

The Oxford Movement of course resulted in far more than an internal theological debate within the Hobartian camp: it also precipitated a decade of turmoil within the Episcopal Church. Although this conflict is well known and has been the subject of numerous books and articles, a brief review of the major events is necessary in order to provide a context for understanding the challenge which the Oxford Movement posed to the rest of American Protestantism.[51]

The thirty years following John Henry Hobart's consecration to the episcopate in 1811 witnessed the growth not only of a high church party but also of a strong evangelical movement within the Episcopal Church.[52] Indeed, as historians have often noted, the occasion of the consecration of Hobart also saw the consecration of another bishop, Alexander V. Griswold, who is often considered to be the guiding light of American Episcopal evangelicalism. Evangelicals within the Episcopal Church were not so much a different group theologically as they were a group possessing a different vision from that of the Hobartians. They rarely formally disagreed with such claims as that the office of the episcopate was a divine institution which was necessary

51. All of the standard histories of the Episcopal Church—such as those by S. D. McConnell, C. Tiffany, W. W. Manross, J. Addison, and R. Albright—contain long chapters on the high church/low church clash caused by the issue of the Oxford Movement in America. Two other useful studies on the question are Chorley, *Men and Movements,* and DeMille, *Catholic Movement.* The following account will not attempt to repeat the narrative in any detail but rather to integrate it in the categories outlined in the previous chapters.

52. The literature on the Episcopal evangelical movement is sparse. In addition to the general sources mentioned above (and in particular Chorley), see Alexander Zabriskie, ed., *Anglican Evangelicalism* (Philadelphia, 1943), and W. A. R. Goodwin, ed., *A History of the Theological Seminary in Virginia and Its Historical Background,* 2 vols. (New York, 1923), as well as any of the mass of contemporary biographies of the leading figures of the movement. The literature is far better on the evangelical movement in England. See in particular John Overton, *The Evangelical Revival of the Eighteenth Century* (London, 1891), and Toon, *Evangelical Theology.*

for the perfection of the church, yet they differed on the emphasis that such theological statements should have. Whenever possible they preferred to emphasize the congruity of the church with the broader evangelical consensus rather than harp upon points of discontinuity. Themes such as justification by faith, the importance of a conversion, and evangelical piety and social morality sound throughout their preaching rather than the elaborate defenses of the peculiar claims of the Episcopal Church that all too often concerned high church homilists. For three decades their opposition to Hobartian exclusivity had waxed and waned. Their English cousins had early awakened them to the threats the Tracts posed, and this knowledge led American Episcopal Evangelicals to begin challenging Tractarian doctrines well before they had attracted any significant high church attention.

Another factor in the high church/low church debate over the Tracts, as Margaret O'Connell has shown, was the role played by the increasing presence of Roman Catholicism in America from the 1830s onward.[53] The Roman Catholic challenge was not simply social but also intellectual, with Catholic writers often attacking the high church claim of being an alternative to evangelicalism by republishing works such as Nicholas Wiseman's *Dublin Review* essays, which challenged the theological justifications of Anglicanism. As the intraepiscopal debate increased, journals such as the *Catholic Herald,* founded in 1833, seemed to take pleasure in pouring oil on the fires of contention within the Episcopal Church, to the consternation of high churchmen and the alarm of evangelicals.

Although to a certain extent the debate over Tractarianism can be seen as an extension of the longer debate over Episcopal exclusivity, it may better be divided into four phases. The first concerned the question of the doctrine of justification. Seabury had already provoked alarm concerning the doctrine of justification by faith in his "Salvability of the Heathen," and Newman's more extreme ideas on the question (which not even Seabury could accept) created still more concern. Charles P. McIlvaine, bishop of Ohio and one of the best theologians in the evangelical camp, leapt to the defense of the doctrine of justification. First in his episcopal charge of 1839, "Justification by Faith," and the next year in his massive work *Oxford Divinity,* he went to ponderous lengths attempting to link Tractarian views with Triden-

53. O'Connell, "A Spirit Afloat," 53–69, and passim. The reader interested in a study of the Roman Catholic response to the Oxford Movement in America should consult this work.

tine doctrine. Oxford divinity was "the systematic abandonment of the vital and distinguishing principles of the Protestant faith, and a systematic adoption of the very root and heart of Romanism, whence has issued the life of all its ramified corruptions and deformities."[54] Seabury's answer to these two works was less than tactful. He claimed that the first, which seemed to defend instantaneous justification, was so heretical that it kept him from even attempting to read the second volume, which he blithely dismissed as a "Romance of Gambier."[55]

A more important question arose over the ordination of Arthur Carey, a student at General Seminary. A young man weak in body but keen in mind, Carey attended General Seminary in the early 1840s and became deeply enamored of Tractarian teaching and devotion then flourishing, particularly among the student body.[56] Too young to be ordained when he graduated, he served as a layman in St. Peter's Church in New York. When the time came for his ordination, however, his rector, Hugh Smith, refused to sign the canonical testimonials, having doubts about Carey's orthodoxy. A committee of eight headed by Bishop Onderdonk met to examine Carey. What became clear from the examination was that Carey, although not a Roman Catholic, evidently sympathized with the sentiments expressed in Newman's *Tract 90*. Six of the eight examiners judged him acceptable for ordination.[57] At the time of the ordination the two dissenting ministers, Smith and Henry Anthon, made a public protest and published the reasons for their action, which became the first of a flurry of pamphlets on the question.[58] Since Carey, after a short ministry, died in 1844, the continuation of the controversy suggests that the issues in-

54. Charles McIlvaine, *Oxford Divinity Compared with the Romish and Anglican Churches* . . . (Philadelphia, 1841), 14. For a recent discussion of McIlvaine's book, see Toon, *Evangelical Theology*, 158–59, and passim.

55. "The Romance of Gambier," *Churchman* 10 (February 27, 1841): 202.

56. On Carey, see the memoir included in Sprague, *Annals of the American Pulpit*, 5:799–807, as well as Chorley, *Men and Movements*, 207–09, and DeMille, *Catholic Movement*, 87–91. For two accounts of life at General Seminary during these years, see Clarence A. Walworth, *The Oxford Movement in America: or Glimpses of Life in an Anglican Seminary* (New York, [1895]); and Walworth, *Reminiscences of Edgar P. Wadhams* . . . (New York, [1893]).

57. The six examiners were Samuel Seabury, John McVickar, Benjamin Haight of General Seminary, Joseph Price, rector of St. Stephen's Church, and William Berrian and Edward Higbee, both of Trinity Church. Significantly, the last two named by their own admission had only scant knowledge of the Tracts.

58. For an abridged list of the pamplets involved, see Sprague, *Annals of the American Pulpit*, 5:801.

volved were larger than the ordination of one individual, but concerned the apparent legitimization of the controversial teachings of
Tract 90. Onderdonk's action became a red flag of warning, arousing
Episcopal fears of Rome. In July of 1843 Philander Chase, then presiding bishop, sent a circular letter to his episcopal colleagues calling for
action on the case.[59] Although some bishops defended Onderdonk's
action, the majority believed it essential to make some stand against
the perceived "creeping Romanism" the case seemed to suggest.

Action was taken on a number of fronts. Bishops Chase, McIlvaine, and Hopkins all wrote public letters protesting the ordination,
but to little avail. Of slightly greater success was a challenge to General
Seminary, long considered to be a hotbed of Tractarian teaching.
There was at the seminary more than enough questionable practice to
arouse evangelical fears. As one student later described it, "We had in
truth a little Oxford on this side of the Atlantic. It was located in a little
suburban appendix to New York City, known as Chelsea. Its name
was the General Theological Seminary of the Protestant Episcopal
Church."[60] At some points it is still difficult to determine exactly
where issues of serious churchmanship ended and where endemic
student precocity began, such as when students stole into the chapel
one Christmas eve and refurbished it (to the exasperation of Dean
Samuel Turner) with crosses, flowers, and greens.[61] Yet enough suspicion abounded that through the prompting of the diocese of South
Carolina the board of trustees of the seminary in the summer of 1844
established a committee of inquiry to investigate the institution. The
task eventually fell upon the House of Bishops, who dispatched a list
of forty-three questions for the faculty concerning their teaching of
Tractarian, Calvinistic, or German Rationalist errors.[62] The question
of Tractarianism also emerged as an issue of debate at the General
Convention of 1844, highlighted by a two-hour homily by one delegate "against the Tracts, Carey, and the *Churchman*."[63] For days the
debate raged until finally on the thirteenth day of the convention a

59. See Richard Saloman, "The Episcopate and the Carey Case . . . ,"
HMPEC 18 (1949): 240–81.
60. Walworth, *Oxford Movement in America,* 119.
61. For two different perceptions of this event, see Walworth, *Oxford Movement in America,* 28, and Turner, *Autobiography,* 198–99.
62. For the list of questions, see *JGC,* 1844, appendix F.
63. For a contemporary account, see Charles Burroughs to Samuel Seabury, 7
October 1844, Seabury Family Papers, New-York Historical Society, New York,
New York.

resolution was accepted that declined to pass judgment on the question and simply affirmed that "the Liturgy, Offices, and Articles of the Church [are] sufficient exponents of her sense of the essential doctrines of Holy Scripture, and that the Canons of the Church afford ample means of discipline."[64]

One point of great importance that the General Convention did agree on, however, was the finalization of a canon changing the rules for the trial of bishops. Up to 1835 judicial arrangements had been up to the discretion of each diocese. To correct this a canon was formulated in the early 1840s, largely through the influence of John Henry Hopkins, that made each bishop accountable first to his peers, by providing that a bishop could be tried when charged by three other bishops. Whether this change was made expressly to weed out obnoxious bishops is still not clear, yet the change in canon did coincide with an increased attack on the leading pro-Tractarian bishops.[65] The General Convention of 1844 accepted the resignation of Henry U. Onderdonk as bishop of Pennsylvania and suspended him from the exercise of his ministry on moral grounds. Onderdonk had never particularly enjoyed the rigorous and strenuous travel required of a bishop, and from early in his episcopate he began using brandy to ease his physical discomfort. The habit of brandy and water led to occasional instances of public intoxication and even indecorous actions toward some of the female members of the diocese.[66] The situation was complicated by the high church/low church dissension plaguing the Episcopal Church in Pennsylvania, but as one layman confessed, "How far faction is at the bottom of this affair I cannot say, but brandy and women, are said to be the common basis."[67]

Of far greater importance for this study was the problem con-

64. *JGC*, 1844, 64.

65. Hopkins's son in the biography of his father argued that the change in canon had nothing to do with the trials of the 1840s. See Hopkins, Jr., *Life of Hopkins*, 265–66. Chorley, however, in a study of the case argued the opposite. See "Benjamin Tredwell Onderdonk," 17–18. Although (because of the limitations of this chapter) only the cases of the two Onderdonks are to be discussed, George Washington Doane, bishop of New Jersey, also was tried, Whittingham of Maryland was to have been a target (see Hopkins, Jr., *Life of Hopkins*, 233), and Levi S. Ives was under continual attack from the diocesan convention of North Carolina.

66. For a contemporary confidential account of Onderdonk's reputation, see Philander Chase to [?], 5 October 1850, Protestant Episcopal Bishops Papers.

67. James Fenimore Cooper to Susan Cooper, 27 May 1844, in James Franklin Beard, ed., *Letters and Journals of James Fenimore Cooper*, 4 vols. (Cambridge, Mass., 1960–64), 4:457–58.

fronting Onderdonk's younger brother, Benjamin, of New York. Rumors abounded in the church that he too suffered from an all-too-common use of the cup and the occasional unapostolic laying on of hands. Rumors of the bishop's moral lapses had circulated as early as 1838. At this late date it is virutally impossible to separate a general concern for morality from a displeasure over Onderdonk's churchmanship, particularly since the case is cloaked by the Victorian proclivity toward obfuscation and titillation. It is undoubtedly true that the charges against Onderdonk arose only after the attempts to bring him to trial on theological grounds had failed. Furthermore, since he was tried by the House of Bishops, the three bishops publicly on record against him on account of the Carey ordination were also among his judges. Yet from the best reading of the contemporary evidence it is fairly clear that certain improprieties had taken place. The strategy of Onderdonk's defense counsel of challenging the testimony of chief accusers proved far from persuasive, for as one critic noted, when it came to "thrusting [a] hand into the naked bosom . . . about such a fact can any woman, modest or immodest be mistaken?"[68] Even the supporters of the bishop could not deny some of the charges, but only the evil intent of them, and lay letters of the period are often filled with acknowledgments of disgust as the case evolved.

The details of the trial unfortunately fall outside of the scope of this study. It suffices to say that in January of 1845 Onderdonk was found guilty by a vote of eleven to six and was later saved from deposition only by his episcopal supporters' accepting the compromise sentence of indefinite suspension from office.[69] Yet what is of more importance

68. Charles King, *A Review of the Trial of the Rt. Rev. Benjamin T. Onderdonk* . . . (New York, 1845), 10.

69. The vote on Onderdonk reflects the division within the high church camp caused by the Tracts. One of his three accusers, James Otey of Tennessee, was until the early 1840s considered a high church bishop. Of the six bishops originally supporting the sentence of admonition all were of the high church school (Ives, Doane, Whittingham, C. E. Gadsden of South Carolina, William De Lancey of western New York, and Jackson Kemper, missionary bishop of the northwest). Ives, Doane, and Whittingham, the three strongest episcopal supporters of the Tracts, added that the admonition should be "as slight . . . as the canon will admit." Of the three bishops voting for suspension, two, T. C. Brownell of Connecticut and George Freeman, missionary bishop of the southwest, were usually considered high church. Indeed, Brownell had recently published an important tract, *The Errors of the Times,* which had defended the apostolic argument and attacked the declension rampant among the descendents of the Puritans. Hopkins was the sole high church supporter of deposition. For a defense of his reasons, see Hopkins, Jr., *Life of Hopkins,* 229–45.

was the effect the Onderdonk trial had on the diocese in general and the high church movement in particular. In the internal history of the high church movement the episcopal trials marked the end of an era. From the days of Hobart the high church movement had been predicated upon the rigorous leadership of an apostolic-like bishop. After the 1840s, however, this was no longer the case for a variety of reasons. On the practical level the suspension of the bishop left New York high churchmen in a painful situation, for the issue quickly became whether or not to replace the suspended Onderdonk. Their loyalty to the *person* of the bishop made them desire to stand with him, but their view of the importance of the *office* of the bishop convinced many that without an active bishop the diocese could not properly function. Both in the debate at the diocesan convention of 1845 and in the private correspondence surrounding it, the issue raged over whether to replace Onderdonk or not.[70] Just as it had among their Nonjuror forbearers, the question of loyalty to person versus loyalty to church bedeviled the high church cause. There was a certain amount of poetic irony when in 1861 the *Churchman* in its very last issue published a long and emotional obituary of Onderdonk. The bishop and his chief journalistic supporter were to expire at the same time.

Furthermore the B. T. Onderdonk case also hinted at an underlying tension between a desire for a clerical morality that was not antagonistic to the innocent pleasures of the world and a desire for apostolic holiness and purity. Indeed, one of Onderdonk's sharpest critics was not a low churchman at all but a friend of the Oxford Movement. In recalling his meeting of Newman, he pointedly noted, "He bears no resemblance to a New-York Puseyite. He walked (with me) seven miles to read prayers before fifteen people, or less, and is a hard student, a self denying man, who takes up the cross."[71] Rather than fasting and prayer, New York high churchmen prefer "fat dinners and good wine in Lent." At least part of the furor over the Onderdonk case

70. The diocese had no bishop until the election of Jonathan M. Wainwright in 1851, and until the death of Onderdonk all bishops of New York were referred to as provisional bishops as a sign of continuing loyalty. On the dilemma the case provoked, see the large body of correspondence addressed to Samuel Seabury, not only editor of the *Churchman* but also chief supporter of Onderdonk, collected in the Seabury Family Papers, 1 January 1845 to March 1845 (NYHS). See too John Williams to Samuel Seabury, 10 March 1845, and 25 April 1845, Seabury Correspondence (GTS)

71. James C. Richmond, *The Conspiracy Against the Late Bishop of New York Unravelled . . .* (New York, 1845), 2.

THE HIGH CHURCH ALTERNATIVE IN ACTION

stemmed perhaps from an uncertainty over whether a clergyman was to be an individual not averse to the world or instead to be a saint. It has earlier been suggested that there was a subtle paradox imbedded in the idea of Episcopal clerical morality. The clergy were encouraged not to hold themselves aloof from innocent worldly amusements, yet it was an unstated recognition that any overstepping of the bounds of propriety was to be treated not as a peccadillo but as a serious offense. The cases of the two Onderdonk brothers perhaps reflect this ambiguity.

IV

The controversy that the issue of the Tracts created within the Episcopal Church has been well documented, but surprisingly little has been written on the equally important question of the reaction the Tracts provoked within the other Protestant communities of the period. As much ink, however, was spilled outside of the Episcopal Church as within over the question of the Oxford Movement, since the issue became the existential culmination of forty years of high church/evangelical debate. Almost all the other religious communions took an interest in the question. One Episcopal minister acidly observed as much in the opinions of his neighbors:

> [They believe that] at some bad place called Oxford, one Pusey . . .
> and some others, his accomplices, in connexion with the Evil one,
> who is supposed to have had his headquarters in the Church of
> England, have been uttering something that Presbyterians, Anabap-
> tists, Unitarians, Universalists, and probably Mormons and other
> "evangelical Christians," find great difficulty, in their stomachs, in
> digesting: and that certain abettors of the respectable firm just men-
> tioned, hereabouts, have formed a wicked conspiracy to overthrow
> and destroy . . . all the religion and liberty of "this our most free,
> most enlightened, most religious, and most glorious of all nations
> under heaven."[72]

The Tracts raised Episcopal claims to a higher and more visible plane than at any time during the antebellum period, and in doing so threatened the other American denominations. Yet the exact nature of the threat was perceived far differently in each of the different communions, and an examination of the responses of the different denomina-

72. [?] Phillips to Samuel Seabury, 21 May 1842, Seabury Family Papers.

tions to the Oxford challenge not only illuminates the Protestant concerns over the Tracts and provides a perceptive insight into the complex theological world of American Protestantism in the 1840s, but also clearly shows the degree to which Protestant objections to high church ideas had changed since the days of Hobart.

Methodism during the antebellum period had largely avoided the theological controversy that had befallen other evangelical denominations in the 1820s and 1830s. Hence when the issue of the Oxford Tracts first surfaced at the end of the 1830s little theological soul-searching was necessary in order to formulate a response to them. The Tracts—by voicing the exclusive claim that there was but one true church—revived a "Cyprianical divinity" that threatened the mutual toleration that existed among American denominations. As the Tracts continued, American Methodists became even more critical of their attempt to "unprotestantize" both the Church of England and the Episcopal Church. Increasingly, Methodist writers provided defenses of what for them were the key points of the Protestant creed, such as the rule of faith grounded on the Bible and justification by faith.[73] Yet of particular concern for them was the issue of baptismal regeneration, the "Thermopylae of Protestantism."[74] The belief that baptism and not the converted heart was the key to the kingdom of heaven lay at the root of the Tractarian error, since it both opened up the churches to the unconverted and increased the authority of the ministry who administered the sacrament. Nor did the new piety that accompanied these changes in theology, reflected in such works as Keble's *The Christian Year,* provide any attraction. It was a fashionable folly for upper-middle-class dilettantes and completely unsuitable to the truly pious:

> The mysteries it contains suit not the vulgar ear; the instruction it conveys—the consolation it imparts—are for those who wear fine linen, and fare sumptuously every day; its appropriate place is the centre-table of the richly furnished room; and its office is to beguile the tedium of the sabbath evening, to such as have some vague idea that it should not be spent either in reading novels or visiting.[75]

The upper-class sentimentality that Keble's work apparently repre-

73. Interestingly, Methodist writers showed at least some sympathy with the Tractarian concern for justification, since in their view it was a response to the common reformed view of justification and sanctification, which divorced the former from morality. See "Justification by Faith," *Methodist Magazine and Quarterly Review,* 3d ser., 4 (1844): 10–13 (hereafter referred to as *Methodist Magazine*).

74. Ibid., 29.

75. "Keble's *Christian Year*," *Methodist Magazine,* 3d ser., 2 (1842): 458.

sented offended Methodist critics both theologically and socially. Virtually no part of the Tractarian endeavor escaped Methodist censure. Theologically it undermined Protestantism, and devotionally it substituted sentiment for piety. Thus, as one Methodist writer observed, the meaning of the movement was all too clear: "If, therefore, the Church of Rome be the man of sin and the antichrist, the preceding facts show most distinctly how the term *false prophet* attaches to the Church of England."[76] The rise of the Oxford Movement could only be a sign that the great mystical battle of Armageddon that would pit the Antichrist against the church could not be far off.

The Old School Presbyterians, as the more conservative and confessional branch of the Presbyterian Church, also had few problems in formulating a response to Tractarianism. The attitude reflected in Charles Hodge's often repeated boast that no new idea ever came out of Princeton Seminary left them in a secure position from which to challenge Tractarianism. For them as well as for the Methodists the Tracts were a direct threat to the Protestant faith, particularly in their alleged emphasis on sacraments over preaching. They too attacked the new ideas of baptismal justification and the related issue of the rule of faith.[77] Yet for the confessionalist Old School writers the issue was very simple. The true doctrine of the Church of England was to be found in the Articles of Religion, a work they had always viewed as supportive of Calvinism, and hence the Oxford divines were apostates from the true doctrine of the Church of England. Having abandoned their confession, they had fallen upon wrong teaching just as, by implication, the New School Presbyterians had done in their deemphasizing of the Westminster Confession.[78]

One enters a radically different theological environment when one turns to the Unitarian response to Tractarianism. Throughout the first four decades of the nineteenth century Unitarianism had reigned unchallenged in maritime Massachusetts, particularly in the area around

76. "Tracts for the Times," *Methodist Magazine,* 3d ser., 1 (1841): 89.

77. See the book note on McIlvaine's *Justification by Faith, Biblical Repertory,* 2d ser., 12 (1840): 457–58; "Justification by Faith," ibid., 2d ser., 16 (1844): 561–70; and *Correspondence Between The Right Rev. Bishop Doane . . . and the Rev. H. A. Boardman . . . on the Alleged Popish Character of the "Oxford Divinity"* (Philadelphia, 1841).

78. Conversely, Old School writers were extremely wary of attempts to attack the Oxford writers that ignored the formal confessional position of the Church of England. See, for example, Hodge's review of Albert Barnes's "The Position of the Evangelical Party in the Episcopal Church" (to be discussed below), in *Biblical Repertory,* 2d ser., 16 (1844): 319–23.

Boston, dutifully ministered to the leading Brahmin families. Yet Boston Unitarianism had experienced two challenges at the end of the 1830s. The first was the famous outbreak of Transcendentalism, best reflected in Ralph Waldo Emerson's critique of "corpse cold Unitarianism"; a second challenge entailed a vigorous resurgence of the Episcopal Church in eastern Massachusetts. This latter trend would long continue; from 1840 to 1900 the number of Episcopal communicants in Boston alone would double every twenty years. Factors involved in this growth include what one scholar has called the seeming bankruptcy of Unitarianism as well as the growing interest in both art and English culture.[79] All of these themes played a part in the Unitarian response to Tractarianism.

Up to the time of the Tracts, Unitarian writers generally took little notice of American Episcopal writings, which lacked the sophistication of Unitarian works, and they evidenced no strong attraction to Hobartian theology.[80] They did, however, recognize the appeal of Episcopal piety. In marked contrast with the Methodist dismissal of Keble's poetry as upper-class sentimentalism, a Unitarian reviewer praised it as "sweet, solemn, and touching," and further that it "has added richly to the stores of Christian poetry, and that many a Christian, of whom he [Keble] can know nothing, will bless him through the year for the aid and solace which his poetry has imparted."[81] Indeed, they showed a particular attraction for Tractarian poetry with its touches of romantic sensibilities and its harking back to an earlier age. "We are moved to believe," one added, "that the Oxford Movement owes much more of its diffusion to its poetry than to its theology."[82] The sentimental appeal of the Tractarian poets was not lost on Unitarian readers. Nor was the attempt to incorporate forms and connect the worship of the church with outward beauty. They willingly acknowledged that in this regard Episcopalians had a far easier time than evangelicals: "When forms are less regarded, the

79. Peter W. Williams, "A Mirror for Unitarians: Catholicism and Culture in Nineteenth-Century New England Literature," (Ph.D. diss., Yale University, 1970), 204–16. Scholars such as Ann Douglas and T. Jackson Lears in *No Place of Grace* (New York, 1981) have linked this growth to the phenomenon of feminization and the appeal of sentiment and ritual over traditional Protestant introspection.

80. See, for example, the particularly condescending attitude of the reviewer in "The Publications of Bishop Hopkins," *Christian Examiner,* 3d ser., 2 (1836): 354–69.

81. "Keble's *Christian Year,*" *Christian Examiner,* 3d ser., 1 (1835): 169–70.

82. [Samuel Osgood], "The Poet of Puseyism," *Christian Examiner,* 3d ser., 17 (1843): 45.

tendency is to forget outward beauty, and make religion either so metaphysical as to appeal solely to the intellect, or so practical as to address the conscience to the neglect of the imagination."[83]

Yet in the final analysis Tractarianism was at best only a romantic dream, "and we prefer broad daylight and this working-day world."[84] Their romantic attraction never blinded Unitarian critics to the religious and social dangers implied in the teachings of the Tracts. For Unitarians, the religious threat lay not in the Tracts' assault on issues such as justification by faith, but in the Tractarian vision of the church, which seemed to inspire bigotry and obscurantism. The Tractarians' pride in the unchanging stability of their church left little room for tolerance of others. The exclusivity that some Anglo-Catholic writers called for, including even warnings against marrying outside the church, reflected an elevation of the importance of the Anglican Church that "neither her learning nor her labors warrant her assuming."[85] Puseyism ultimately opposed free inquiry just as its worship of the past led it to oppose all innovations and to feel far more at home in the twelfth century than in the nineteenth. Finally, Tractarian religion seemed to be pitted against reason in a way that was disturbing to the reason-respecting Unitarians.[86]

Of even greater importance were the social consequences of Tractarianism. Oxfordism was the religion of a dreamer, not of a man of the world: "It is a religion to make quiet and dreaming men think it a virtue to be quiet and to dream."[87] In contrast to the passionate this-worldliness inculcated by the Unitarians of the period, this new religious spirit appeared to them to have no practical application. It set its face not forward but backward and accordingly had little to offer to the utilitarian modern age. Modern individuals demanded of religion that it advance the progress of the human race, yet Oxfordism seemed little concerned with such practical issues. For this reason one writer compared the appeal of the Tracts with the appeal of the Transcendentalists and linked both with the desire to escape the responsibility of the age—one through nature and blue skies and the other through glorious buildings and ancient rites. Yet the attempt must end in

83. Ibid., 47–48.
84. Ibid., 54.
85. [Ephraim Peabody], "Oxfordism and the English Church," *Christian Examiner*, 4th ser., 1 (1844): 56.
86. See, for example, [George E. Ellis], "Tracts for the Times," *Christian Examiner*, 3d ser., 9 (1839): 176 ff.
87. "Oxfordism and the English Church," 52.

failure. "Sad poet," he advised, "there is no abiding place for you in this age, and you must find an angel guide to a more congenial sphere."[88]

The success of the Tracts in Britain lay in their conservative appeal to the privileged and powerful classes, who had the most to gain in the maintenance of the established church. Yet in the eyes of Boston Unitarians, Whigs to their toes, such an appeal to tradition would never take root in America since it had no affinities with republicanism. The present growth of the movement in America could be explained through secondary causes such as its novelty and its appeal to stability, yet the movement could never really become part of the freedom-loving American scene.[89] Finally, for Boston Unitarians the greatest threat that the Tractarians posed was neither theological nor devotional but concerned their undermining of the sovereignty of the individual, which was the true heritage of the Reformation. Past eras had erred in falsely claiming that the church was the true climax of the gospel message and that "the individual exists for the church." In actuality it was the opposite that was the case, and just as American democracy had overcome the older European notion that the individual existed for the state, so the role of the American churches must be to oppose the theological corollary and rather proclaim that the church should be subservient to the individual.[90] American politics and the American churches were called to provide a common defense against any assault on the centrality of the individual.

For official Unitarian spokesmen in the 1840s questions of theology often gave way to broader issues of the social role and importance of the faith. In their professed attraction to the romantic piety of the new movement, combined with their opposition to its obscurantism and its undermining of the importance of the individual, they reflected a far different response to the threat of the Tracts than the one found in the more theologically conservative denominations.

Perhaps the most vigorous anti-Tractarian criticism emanated from the Congregationalists, and in particular from the *New Englander*, a journal based in New Haven that in part continued to provide a forum for New England Congregationalism. That Congregationalists would feel threatened by the Episcopal Church is not sur-

88. "Poet of Puseyism," 51, 54.
89. "Oxfordism and the English Church," 65–73.
90. [Ezra Stiles Gannett], "The Church," *Christian Examiner,* 4th ser., 3 (1845): 81–82.

prising. In New Haven, for example, the Episcopal Church had increased by over 300 percent in the two and a half decades after 1820,
and the entire diocese was almost doubling in size every decade.[91]

Thus the Episcopal crisis of the 1840s provided a golden opportunity for Congregational writers to challenge the smugness that had
characterized so much of the Episcopal apologetic of the 1830s. With
great glee they contrasted the Episcopal boasts of unity and orthodoxy
with the apparent divisions between high and low church and the
strange doctrines coming forth from Oxford. Yet they did more.
Their criticism included a radical assault on the Episcopal system as a
whole and the expulsion of it from the ranks of the evangelical churches. The liturgical worship of the Episcopal Church might be conducive to impressive effects, but it had nothing to do with true piety
and indeed, substituted ritual for the true worship of the invisible
God. Nor could their piety be considered evangelical. The denial of
the necessity for a conversion and the willingness to attack institutions
such as the Temperance Society made the church a refuge for "Unitarians and Universalists, the nothingarians, the rum sellers and rum
drinkers, and all other classes that are corrupt in principle and practice."[92] By comforting its members rather than challenging them, the
Episcopal Church was an ark of safety—but only for loose livers
desirous of escaping judgmental criticism. During the height of the
controversy over the Onderdonk brothers, one writer cattily noted,

> Had Bishop Hobart, instead of warning Bishop H. U. Onderdonk
> to avoid the "popular *religious* excitements termed revivals of re-
> ligion," exhorted him, by engaging in the temperance reformation,
> to avoid the excitement caused by drinking wine and brandy, that
> unhappy prelate might not have come to an end so disgraceful to
> himself, and so mortifying to the Episcopal Church.[93]

Yet perhaps the boldest criticism of this type was not made by a
Connecticut Congregationalist but by the famous New School Pres-

91. For figures, see *Journals of the Annual Convention of the Diocese of Connecticut
from 1792–1820* (New Haven, 1842), 126; and the *Journals* of 1836 and 1847. Horace
Bushnell, among other Connecticut clergymen, was concerned about this rapid
growth, and Barbara Cross has suggested that his modifications on the question of
Christian nurture were a response to this challenge: see *Horace Bushnell: Minister to a
Changing America* (Chicago, 1958), 41–42, 56–57.

92. [Leverett Griggs], *Looking Glass for High Churchmen: Reflecting the Moral
Phases of High-Churchism in Connecticut* (New Haven, 1843), 13.

93. "Dr. Stone's Memoir of Bishop Griswold," *New Englander* 3 (1845): 238.
Emphasis in original.

byterian Albert Barnes in an important essay published in the *New Englander* in 1844, "The Position of the Evangelical Party in the Episcopal Church." In this essay Barnes boldly proclaimed, "IT HAS NEVER BEEN POSSIBLE PERMANENTLY TO CONNECT THE RELIGION OF FORMS WITH EVANGELICAL RELIGION."[94] Because of its very nature the Episcopal Church could never have a truly evangelical movement. Institutions such as revivals and prayer meetings were not endemic to it, but entered it only through contact with other churches. Furthermore even professed evangelical Episcopalians shared in the exclusive spirit usually associated with the high church wing. No Episcopal clergy would open up his church to clergy from other denominations, nor even combine in open worship with other evangelicals. Since true evangelicalism was so antithetical to the Episcopal system Barnes called on Episcopal evangelicals to decide whether their first loyalty would lie with their church or with their common evangelical faith.

Barnes and the other writers offered an even more far-reaching critique and claimed that the Episcopal Church was at odds not only with evangelicalism but also with the American way of life and the spirit of the age:

> This is an age of freedom, and men *will* be free. The religion of forms is the stereotyped wisdom or the folly of the past, and does not adapt itself to the free movements, the enlarged views, the varying plans of this age. The spirit of this age demands that there shall be freedom of religion; that it shall not be fettered or suppressed; that it shall go forth to the conquest of the world.[95]

Furthermore they argued that since the genius of America worked against everything aristocratic and monarchical, America could never be a fertile ground for the growth of such an alien movement. Episcopalians could never appeal to the different groups that made up the American public; not to the pioneers, nor to those who desired a warmhearted, zealous, and ardent religion, nor even to those who

94. Barnes, "Position of the Evangelical Party . . ." *New Englander* 2 (1844): 120. Emphasis in original. Barnes's essay was later both republished as a tract and included in his *Miscellaneous Essays and Reviews,* 2 vols. (New York, 1855). The editorials opposing it from the *Episcopal Recorder* were also republished in tract form in *Remarks on Mr. Barnes Inquiry . . . ,* 5th ed. (Philadelphia, 1872). For a background to Barnes's essay, see Edward Bradford Davis, "Albert Barnes, 1793–1870: An Exponent of New School Presbyterianism," (Th.D. diss., Princeton Theological Seminary, 1961), 262–67.

95. Barnes, "Position of the Evangelical Party," 142. Emphasis in original.

wanted an intellectual religion united with evangelical principles. Only those very few who desired an intellectual religion without evangelical principles would find themselves drawn to the Episcopal system. The church chiefly attracted only those who were uncomfortable with American egalitarianism and those who wanted a visible mark of higher station within the egalitarian culture.[96]

Alarmed by the Oxford threat, these individuals responded by calling for a great evangelical crusade, a Protestant league to crush the threat. With strikingly military metaphors they proclaimed, "To all the divisions of this evangelical army we give the right hand of fellowship, and pledge ourselves to a hearty cooperation in this warfare."[97] Yet for all its fervor it was a crusade more linked through a common dislike for Tractarianism on social, political, and psychological grounds than by any of the theological issues so exhaustively debated in the preceding decades. The religion of forms versus the religion of the spirit was the key element, and around this cause the memory of the Pilgrims was draped as a protective banner. The call went out for all the sons of the Pilgrims "to return to the churches of our Pilgrim Fathers, where the concern is not for liturgies and creeds, but the Bible and the Bible only."[98] From the days of Elizabethan England (the argument continued), Arminianism, or the party of Laud and of ecclesiastical government, had been at war with popular rights within both the church and the state. Absolutism rather than republicanism was the political ideal of episcopacy. "Prelacy is by nature a hater of all popular rights," one proclaimed; "it opposes every essential principle of republicanism."[99] The Puritan heritage had produced the distinct American patriotism and love of liberty, and it was the obligation of the descendents of the Puritans to oppose any revival of prelacy.

This call for a crusade against episcopacy, so strikingly reminiscent of the movement before the American Revolution, did not even exclude the Unitarians. As one Congregationalist writer suggested, it was finally time to heal the division between the Unitarians and the Orthodox. Rather than standing by idly while individual members slipped off one by one into the Episcopal Church, allured by the culture and prestige of the communion, the time had come to seek the

96. "The Episcopal Church," *New Englander* 3 (1845): 336–40.
97. "Peck on the Rule of Faith," *New Englander* 2 (1844): 308.
98. "Chapin's 'Primitive Church,'" *New Englander* 1 (1843): 491. On this theme, see as well Edwin Hall, *The Puritans and Their Principles* (New York, 1847).
99. "Comparative Influence . . . ," *New Englander*, 514.

reunion "of our dissevered community in a common evangelical faith, and under the simple democratic forms, which were dear to our fathers, and deemed by them scriptural and authoritative."[100] All children of the Pilgrims could agree on the necessity of freedom of thought, the value of free institutions, and the veneration of the Pilgrims. In the face of such solidarity even issues such as human depravity and the nature of the atonement could be overcome.

Though nothing substantive ever came of this offer, the issue of Tractarianism clearly led a number of New England Congregationalists to plumb for an evangelical common ground largely independent of the theology that had characterized it earlier. The shift from theological to social and political argument can be clearly seen in one of the more conservative New England theologians of the period, Edwards Amassa Park. Park is best remembered as the last of the "consistent Calvinists" and arch-defender of the New England theological tradition stemming from Jonathan Edwards. Yet even he, when called upon to answer the threat of the Oxford Movement, offered a critique that was far more social than theological. He rejected the new Oxford theology not for its opposition to Edwards or Taylor but because its narrow sectarianism inevitably clashed with the broad and liberal spirit of the nation: "This is American Christianity. It is in sympathy with the broadness of our lakes, the expanse of our prairies, the length of our rivers, the freeness of our government, the very genius of our whole social organization. A narrow minded religionist is no true countryman of ours."[101] Park's argument centered not on a theological issue such as justification by faith but rather on an appeal for the preservation of American liberty that transcended theological division and that argued instead that religious and political despotism inevitably went hand in hand. Similarly, his chief criticism of the advanced ritual and ceremonial that often was associated with the Tractarians was not only that it was unscriptural, but even more that it was inimicable to republican simplicity: "The genius of a popular government is that of plain rites. It is the aristocracy and the peasantry who love ostentatious observances; but we have not much of either a recognized aristocracy or of a peasantry."[102] In response to the ad-

100. "Unitarian and Episcopal Affinities," *New Englander* 3 (1845): 559.

101. Edwards Amassa Park, *A Discourse Delivered in Boston Before the Pastoral Association . . .* (Andover, 1844), 10. On the broader aspects of Park's thought, see Anthony Cecil, *The Theological Development of Edwards Amassa Park: Last of the "Consistent Calvinists"* (Missoula, Mont., 1974).

102. Ibid., 19.

vanced ceremony of Tractarian worship Park was even willing to urge a new style of preaching having more in common with modern American oratory than with traditional reformation practices. He suggested that a concern for pulpit eloquence be extended even to hand gesticulation, that pulpits be lowered so as not to barricade the preacher from the congregation, and that ministers abandon the use of the Geneva gown, which too often hid the bodily eloquence of the preacher.[103]

That theologians such as Park and Barnes should strive to meet the Tractarian challenge in such a nontheological way, by instead stressing the inconsistency of Tractarianism with a general American ethos, suggests that even while there was still formal acceptance of the traditional doctrines that characterized the evangelicalism of two decades before, there was also perhaps a growing recognition that the emotional power and appeal of American evangelicalism was no longer in its theology. Scarcely heard were the narrowly theological issues raised by Nathaniel William Taylor merely thirty years before to answer Hobart. Concepts such as Americanism, morality, freedom, progress, and an invocation of the Pilgrim past now seemed to carry more emotional clout than theological ideas of grace and faith. This is particularly noticeable when the Congregationalist response is contrasted with the far more theological critique of Old School Presbyterians and Methodists. Even three decades before the often discussed demise of New England theology, religious journalists seemed to sense that "Americanism" had replaced the Saybrook Platform as the emotional glue of New England Congregationalism.

Such a reduction did not go unnoticed by Episcopal respondents, particularly some of the young and precocious ones. The identification of evangelicalism with Americanism led some of the bolder to glory in the implicit claim that catholic Christianity, as reflected in the Oxford Movement, was not American:

> No sir—yours may be "American Christianity" but it is not Catholic Christianity. It may be "in sympathy with the broadness of the lakes, the expanse of the prairies, the length of the rivers," but I would have Christianity—one and universal,—symbolized by the ocean itself— girdling the whole world with its flood, into which the "rivers may go down and be healed."[104]

103. Ibid., 28–29. All of these suggestions were later to be incorporated in the new style of preaching that Henry Ward Beecher was to introduce at his Plymouth Church, Brooklyn. See Clifford E. Clark, Jr., *Henry Ward Beecher: Spokesman for a Middle-Class America* (Urbana, Ill., 1978), 31–32, 88–89.

104. [C. Cole], *A Letter to Professor Edwards A. Park* . . . (Boston, 1844), 9.

Catholic Christianity was posited as a direct alternative to the restricted nature of American Christianity, increasingly robbed of its universality and transcendence. The ramifications of this critique, and how it suggests an altering of the American high church tradition, belong to the next chapter.

6

The Passing of a Tradition

IN 1855, IN A LAUDATORY REVIEW OF ONE OF JOHN HENRY HOPKINS'S current volumes, the writer concluded his panegyric by prophesying, "By the scholars of a future age, the name of Bishop Hopkins will rank with Chillingworth, Hall, Barrow, and Taylor as a worthy and successful defender with them of the same great principles against the same unscrupulous adversaries."[1] In an ironic way this prediction proved all too true since within a decade of his death in 1868 all of Hopkins's works had gravitated to the dusty bowels of theological libraries, and there, together with the volumes of William Chillingworth, Isaac Barrow, and the others, they have remained ever since, largely unread. This chapter enumerates and briefly sketches some of the intellectual and social factors that led to this decline in interest in the Hobartian high church synthesis in the decades after the suspension of Onderdonk.

I

The intraepiscopal furor that raged for much of the 1840s and that entailed long trials and acrid debates deeply troubled Episcopalians from all points of the theological compass. For forty years, whenever a church or chapel had been consecrated, Psalm 122 had dutifully been

---

1. "Book Notes," "'The End of Controversy' Controverted . . . ," *The Church Review and Ecclesiastical Register* 8 (1855): 147 (hereafter referred to as *Church Review*). This journal was founded in 1849 and for twenty years served as the leading voice of the older high church viewpoint.

recited with its evocation, "O pray for the peace of Jerusalem, . . . Peace be within thy walls, and plenteousness within thy palaces," and as it has already been shown, the importance of unity—both as a blessing in itself and as a sign of God's grace—was never far from the thoughts of a large number of Episcopalians.[2] The theological crisis between high church and evangelical Episcopalians threatened the ecclesiastical unity more than any other crisis the church had yet faced, and one glance into the chasm of division convinced many thoughtful individuals that some new basis for a comprehensive peace was necessary if the church were to remain united.

On the further question of how such a comprehensiveness might be accomplished, however, no general agreement existed. An old pragmatic churchman like Calvin Colton offered perhaps the simplest remedy. Having been attracted to the Episcopal Church as a result of its placidity in the midst of the evangelical frenzy of the 1830s, Colton could only respond with dismay to the theological discord of the 1840s. The source of division lay for him in the willingness of certain Episcopalians to abandon the historic role of their church in favor of the new Tractarian ideas. In their desire to mirror Oxford theology and exalt the dignity of the episcopacy and the primitive witness, they lost sight of the fact that the true genius of the American Episcopal Church was its constitutionality.[3] Hobart, it should be remembered, had always made a sharp distinction between episcopacy as a divine institution and as a form of church government. In the former mode it was absolute, but in the latter the American episcopacy was republican and popular. American Tractarians had lost sight of this paradox in Hobart's thought, and because of this they had seriously weakened the constitutional fiber of the church. The assembly of the church, Colton insisted, not the primitive tradition, had to possess final authority if the church were to survive:

> The past is a legitimate field of research, for verifying and vindicating the general economy, the faith, the principles, and the usages of the American Episcopal Church, in all that was recognized, adopted and established at her organization; but not for adding anything in either of the above named particulars, without the consent of the church expressed in the form of legislation.[4]

2. See "The Form of Consecration of a Church or Chapel," in *The Book of Common Prayer* . . . (Hartford, 1847), 304.

3. Calvin Colton, *The Genius and Mission of the Protestant Episcopal Church in the United States* (New York, 1853), 174–75.

4. Ibid., 164.

Only by elevating the authority of church legislation over that of the primitive tradition could Episcopalians escape the anarchy of division that plagued other American Protestant churches.

For Colton, the discord racking the Episcopal Church had not merely ecclesiastical ramifications but dire social ones as well. The church did not exist to be an end in itself but rather to serve society, and in the American situation this entailed acting as a counterweight to the centrifugal tendencies of evangelical Protestantism. Yet the heightened ecclesiology undergirding the Tracts threatened the social function of the church. If taken to its logical conclusion the ecclesiology would lead not only to the separation of the Episcopal Church from the evangelical denominations but also from American society and culture. Such a course would be disastrous since

> a church does not exist for itself alone, or chiefly, but for the world around it. Its mission is to the world, and if it does not gain the world, its mission fails of its great end. If it fails for want of adaptation in the means employed, so far as they consist in non-essentials, it is a fault of a grave character.[5]

The great mission of the Episcopal Church, as a bulwark of peace and order standing against the flood of change, ran the risk of being sacrificed through an overapplication of high church principles. In this view Colton mirrors the similar criticism leveled against Tractarianism by conservative English critics, that the church's primary responsibility was to the society at large. In Colton's critique of Tractarianism one can see the unmistakable dismembering of the Hobartian emphasis on both catholic truth and social order. Whereas in the 1830s the theological principles undergirding the high church position and the desired goal of religious concord had seemed to go hand in hand, by the 1850s they now seemed mutually exclusive. Facing this dilemma, Colton unhesitatingly opted for the side of peace and concord. To recover religious peace, he concluded, the Episcopal Church had to return to its true role—that of an *American* church, united and ordered by a general legislative body, that could offer "a refuge to that numerous class of persons, who have been tossed to and fro on the turbulent sea of religious agitation, and who have become tired of agitation."[6] The key to unity was the willingness to subordinate theological opinions on nonessentials for the sake of the social importance of the church.

5. Ibid., 213.
6. Ibid., 302.

Still another and more important solution to the issue of comprehensiveness was the famous Memorial presented to the House of Bishops in 1853 by a group of clergymen, the most important being William A. Muhlenberg.[7] For them as well as for Colton the Episcopal Church seemed to be losing sight of its mission and indulging instead in divisive feuding. In an American religious environment already suffering from denominational divisiveness, new forms of unbelief, and a newly invigorated Roman Catholic threat, it was the height of irresponsibility for Episcopalians to dissipate their energy in intra-denominational disputation.[8] Like Colton, the Memorialists argued that the Episcopal Church had a responsibility to the entire society, but unlike him they saw this responsibility as the providing of leadership in the American religious environment rather than being a bastion of peace and order. The catholicity in which Episcopalians gloried, they suggested, ought not to be considered as a mark of separation but instead as a gift to be shared. Instead of the old attitude of apostolic exclusivity, the Memorialists called for a new burst of noblesse oblige in which the Episcopal Church could take the lead in uniting the divided religious landscape and reaching out to the growing numbers of unchurched in the urban centers. The Episcopal Church, however, was institutionally ill-adapted to respond to this new challenge. The church was too confined both socially and geographically to accomplish this great end of unity. Furthermore the structure and inflexibility of its liturgy prevented it from addressing adequately the questions and concerns of daily life. Indeed, one contributor related the case of a cleric who, when asked to give thanks for an escape from drowning, was forced to make do with the collect for "A Safe Return from Sea"!

To alleviate this situation the Memorialists proposed two distinct types of reforms. First, they called for certain changes in the liturgy that would make it more flexible in worship, in particular the freedom

7. Because of the large amount of good secondary literature already written on the subject of the Memorial Movement, in this chapter the movement will be only briefly sketched. For more extended discussion, see E. R. Hardy, Jr., "Evangelical Catholicism: W. A. Muhlenberg and the Memorial Movement," *HMPEC* 13 (1944): 155–92; Anne Ayres, *The Life and Work of William Augustus Muhlenberg* (New York, 1880); and Alvin W. Skardon, *Church Leader in the Cities: William Augustus Muhlenberg* (Philadelphia, 1971). On one of the important aspects of the movement, the rise of religious sisterhoods, see the article by V. Nelle Bellamy, "Anne Ayres," in *Notable American Women,* ed. E. T. James, 3 vols. (Boston, 1971), 1:74–75.

8. For a copy of the Memorial, see *An Exposition of the Memorial of Sundry Presbyters* . . . (New York, 1854), 1.

to divide the services of Morning Prayer, the Litany, and Ante-Communion, at the time usually done as one single service. They also called for more freedom in the choice of lessons and prayers, and greater liberty in the use of nonliturgical prayers. The manner in which Episcopal worship was usually performed prevented it from attracting a wider social spectrum of worshippers and contributed to the limited social appeal of the church. Muhlenberg in his own innovative Church of the Holy Communion had for a number of years striven to make Episcopal worship socially and aesthetically more appealing by introducing candles and flowers and other such enrichments into the sanctuary. Yet the Memorialists went further and called for a new extension of the church's apostolic ministry:

> [it] is believed that men can be found among the other bodies of Christians around us, who would gladly receive ordination at your hands, could they obtain it, without that entire surrender which now be required of them. . . . [These are] men who could not bring themselves to conform in all particulars to our prescriptions and customs, but yet sound in faith, and who, having the gifts of preachers and pastors, would be able ministers of the New Testament. . . . The extension of orders to the class of men contemplated (with whatever safeguards, not infringing on evangelical freedom, your wisdom deem expedient) appears to your petitioners to be a subject supremely worthy of your deliberation.[9]

By extending the gift of apostolic ministry beyond the confines of the Episcopal denomination, Episcopalians could make a bold contribution to the cause of a united Evangelical Catholicism, which Muhlenberg saw as the desired end of Protestantism.

As even its contemporaries recognized, the importance of the Memorial lay not in the particular answers it offered, but in the new set of issues it raised and in the new vision it suggested for the Episcopal Church. The ecumenical dimension of the Memorial died a quiet death and provoked little interest among other Protestants. The practical suggestions concerning worship and ritual, however, gained wide acceptance, and in particular the emphasis on broadening the social appeal of the church. Although the attractiveness of the Memorial transcended party distinctions, scholars have noted that the more liberal members of the evangelical camp were its strongest supporters, and many have interpreted the movement as part of a first stirring of a liberal spirit, usually associated with the name of F. D. Maurice,

9. Ibid., 2.

whose sermons were often reprinted in the *Evangelical Catholic,* the leading newspaper of the movement.[10]

Yet the furor over the Memorial has often hidden the fact that even among high church writers there were increasing signs of a recasting of the older arguments in an attempt to find a new and more comprehensive basis of appeal. The Episcopal system was still proclaimed to be superior to the rest of modern American Protestantism, but for somewhat different reasons than it had been earlier.

Nowhere can this new appreciation of the importance of the Episcopal system be so clearly seen as in a series of articles published in the *Churchman* signed simply W.A.[11] In part W.A. continued the older high church defense of the veracity of Episcopal piety in the face of evangelical attacks upon it. He pointedly contrasted evangelical piety, which rested upon a conversion experience, with Episcopal piety. Evangelical piety erred in its basing assurance not upon the external and objective parts of providence, such as church, sacrament, and atonement, but instead upon a subjective perception of a direct and sensible contact with God by the soul. This led all too many individuals into a constant debate over feelings as well as helped to spawn that peculiar genre of "romances" entitled "religious biographies," which consisted in "the stories of pious people who did not do so much but felt so good and talked so well."[12] Following the manner of the general Tractarian critique of evangelical rhetoric, he suggested that evangelicals used words so freely and lushly that they reduced their framework of meaning to the individual subjective experience. Episcopalians were free from this rhetorical and subjective emphasis. Their religious language was firmly tied to the external and objective work of Christ and to the life of the church.[13]

10. Skardon, *Church Leader,* 171–74.

11. W. A. may have been William Adams (1807–80), a graduate of General Seminary, one of the three missionary founders of Nashotah House, and long-time teacher of systematic divinity at that institution. Adams had been greatly affected by the new theological currents stemming from the Oxford Movement as well as impressed by the need for the Episcopal Church to set aside its social and geographical isolation. A letter from Samuel Seabury to Adams (9 October 1845, Seabury Family Papers, NYHS) refers to a series of letters Adams had written for the *Churchman,* and this private letter bears strong similarities in language and sentiment to the public comments made by Seabury concerning W.A.'s letters. See *Churchman* 15 (November 1, 1845): 138.

12. *Churchman* 14 (May 25, 1844): 46; 15 (September 13, 1845): 109.

13. Certain parallels can be drawn between W.A.'s arguments and the implicit critique of evangelical rhetoric in Isaac William's Tract 80, "On Reserve in Commu-

Yet it is in his description of the true nature of the Episcopal Church that one can most clearly see a new spirit, one far different from that of the earlier Hobartians. He argued that it was the folly of the eighteenth century to assume that individuals stood alone and separate from others and by implication that the church was simply an aggregation of individuals. Whereas high church writers had not fallen into this error they had succumbed to a similar one. All too often in the older high church apologetic the church had been reduced to an aggregation of right doctrine.[14] These writers had elevated the doctrine of apostolic succession, but in doing so had made it a superadded principle, divorced from the true essence of the church. This misunderstanding concerning the true nature of the church contributed to a fundamental weakness in traditional high church preaching. Rather than preaching on the reality of the church the older high church school had contented itself in preaching on its doctrines. The emphasis on doctrine rather than incorporation in the church (which would by implication entail adhesion to doctrine) tied the appeal of the apologetic to the rational acceptance of the doctrine. This approach undermined the attractiveness of the church for all but the well educated and literary, who could perceive the connection between doctrine and life. By emphasizing instead the reality of the ecclesia, the church could broaden its appeal and reach out to many for whom questions such as apostolic succession had little importance. Furthermore by emphasizing the primary existential importance of incorporation into the church the two great apologetical attractions of the Episcopal Church during the Hobartian era—the liturgy and worship on the one hand and the apostolic order on the other—could be united in the broader notion of the church as primary historic and existential reality.

One sees in W. A. also the elevating of the importance of the doctrine of the incarnation, a doctrine which would be highly important for Anglican theology in the next century. Just as the reality of the church gave reality to the meaning of individual doctrines, so it shed special meaning on the reality of the incarnation:

> He that is in the Church, to him the inheritance is a sense and feeling of "Christ came in the flesh," which renders the reception of all the distinctive doctrines an easy and natural thing to him, and he that

---

nicating Religious Knowledge," 73–82. For an interesting discussion of Williams and reserve, see G. B. Tennyson, *Victorian Devotional Poetry*, 47 ff.

14. On this point he echoes John Henry Newman's famous criticism of American high church theology in "The American Church," *British Critic*, 334–40.

leaves the Church he leaves behind him all sense and feeling of that fact; and all the doctrines which depend upon these can be proved to him by no scripture, no reason, no argument.[15]

By losing sight of the church, evangelicals had also lost sight of the power of the incarnation, and with it the belief in a universal humanity that had been sanctified by Christ's partaking of its nature. It was this reality of the church and the incarnation that ultimately separated Episcopalians from even orthodox evangelicals. Orthodox doctrines like the atoning work of Christ became simply barren shells of their true selves without an appreciation of the importance of the incarnation. Thus whereas orthodox evangelicals had for decades wrestled with reconciling God's justice and honor in the atonement, for Episcopalians it became simply the finest flowering of the "mercy and love . . . hope and true tenderness, which naturally take their rise from God incarnate, God our brother in the flesh."[16]

Hence the great responsibility of the Episcopal Church was to preserve its unity. Divided, it would fail in its witness to the importance of the incarnation, and on even a more practical level a division of its resources would mean it could never accomplish its mission of continued extension. W.A. acknowledged that everything in American evangelical society seemed to conspire against it: "the spirit of the age is averse to ecclesiastical unity"; yet it was the challenge of the church not to succumb to this outside pressure.[17] In order to escape division he, as well, joined the chorus of voices calling for a new spirit of comprehension: "[What is necessary] is not organization, not legislation, but freedom from incumbrance; free room for the growth that is in the Church, a knowledge in both clergy and laity of the roots of that growth, [and] a confidence in its vitality."[18] The practical importance of the Episcopal Church was of too great moment to be squandered on infighting and schism.

Such themes were also picked up in many of the writings of George Washington Doane, who after the loss of the Onderdonk brothers was probably the most vocal high church bishop in America. Like W.A., the correspondent for the *Churchman*, Doane recognized that the individualism and atomization of evangelical society required in response more than morality and doctrine. "All of Christianity is

15. "Distinctive Principles," *Churchman* 15 (August 2, 1845): 86.
16. Ibid.
17. *Churchman* 14 (June 29, 1844): 66.
18. Ibid.

not doctrine," he maintained. "He who knows the heart knows better how to draw it to Himself. Ours is a *social nature;* and the Framer of it works by social means for our salvation. If it were doctrine only that were needed, he might have written it upon the skies or on our hearts."[19] For Doane the importance of a common communion and fellowship lay in the appeal it made to the social nature of humanity, a nature increasingly threatened by the development of modern society. The contribution the Episcopal Church could make to the spiritual needs of the age was a continuing theme in his preaching. In contrast with the rapid progress of the "age of steam and stir and strife," which threatened to desensitize the soul and isolate the individual, the church's appointed role was to protect the souls of its members and to remind the bustling age that man was not meant to be alone, but rather that humanity had a social nature that was satisfied only in the communion of the church: "Man has a social nature. The church was made for man as he is social in his nature, that so his social nature may be one with God."[20] Indeed, Doane's emphasis upon themes such as community and sensitivity suggest that for him an almost symbiotic relationship existed between the church and the surrounding culture. In the face of a growing loss of community and sensitivity in the public sphere of urban Victorian culture, Doane called for the church to become the reservoir of these ideals.[21]

Because of Doane's preoccupation with the social nature of humanity it is not surprising that he placed a far greater emphasis upon worship than earlier writers had, so much so that the line between the spiritual and the therapeutic values of worship became even less visible than before. In supporting the idea of daily worship, he described such a half hour of thoughtfulness and silence as "a healthful atmosphere

19. "The Pentecostal Pattern" (Fourth Episcopal Charge, 1842), *Works*, 2:126. Emphasis added.

20. Doane, *Works*, 2:373.

21. The question of American Victorianism and its influence on church life is an issue of great complexity and is at present the subject of much discussion. On American Victorianism, see Daniel Walker Howe, "American Victorianism as a Culture," *American Quarterly* 27 (1975): 507–32. On the question of Victorianism and the churches, see the literature surrounding the religious views of the descendents of Lyman Beecher: in particular, Clark, *Henry Ward Beecher;* Marie Caskey, *Chariot of Fire: Religion and the Beecher Family* (New Haven, 1978); and William G. McLoughlin, *The Meaning of Henry Ward Beecher* (New York, 1970). Henry Ward Beecher has increasingly been interpreted as an important figure in the shift from an evangelical piety centered on conversion to a piety centered on nature, home, and nurture.

. . . an atmosphere of peace."[22] He praised the holiness, reverence, and devotion of religious worship for its offer of an escape from the temptations of the world. "Here for a time we escape from it. Here for a time we breathe the atmosphere of heaven."[23] The church's true role was to be an oasis offering fellowship and spiritual sensitivity, and hence the locus of its concern ought not to be in noisy controversy but in the private gentleness of the sanctuary, school, and family. All of these themes would play an important role in the transformation of main line Protestantism in the decades following the Civil War, as all churches attempted to adapt both intellectually and institutionally to the rise of urban America. But the combination of the social makeup of the Episcopal Church and the crisis of the Tracts led Episcopalians such as Doane to explore such an alternative earlier than did many of his Protestant contemporaries.

A practical ramification of this change in high church sensibilities can be seen in Doane's critique of Muhlenberg's Memorial. For earlier Hobartians catholicity had been largely defined as the possession of apostolic order, and accordingly Moravians had usually been granted catholic status because of their possessing bishops. Yet Doane's rejection of Muhlenberg's call for extending apostolic succession beyond the confines of the Episcopal Church reflected the new appreciation that more than episcopal succession was necessary for a truly evangelical catholic church: "the *worship* of the church is its very essence."[24] True incorporation in the body of Christ could be achieved in no other way than through prayer and sacrament.

Doane's recasting of the high church appeal to make it meet more successfully the needs of a new social milieu can be seen most clearly in the radically different roles he saw for the laity and the clergy. The ethos preached by Doane to the schoolboys of Burlington College seems at times like a parodic echo of *Tom Brown's School Days*. To succeed in the bustling Amercian society they were encouraged to be "as men who dare." The age of enterprise in which they lived called for action and dedication, and "they that do nothing will be swept away, like the dry branches when the equinox is up."[25] Yet how different was the advice he gave to his clergy. Their role was to be not as men who

22. Doane, *Works,* 1:453.

23. Ibid., 454.

24. "The Church Sufficient, Through the Cross, For the Salvation of the World" (Eighth Episcopal Charge, 1854), *Works,* 2:236. Emphasis in original.

25. "Baccalaureate Address at the Second Annual Commencement at Burlington College," *Works,* 4:25–27.

dared, but as men who sympathized. The true minister had to have the ability to enter into the sorrows and joys and difficulties of others. To accomplish this the minister had to possess not the virtues of the court nor of the marketplace nor of the legislature but rather the gifts of thoughtfulness and prayer in an age in which both were in anything but abundance.[26] For Doane as well as for many other Victorians the place where these two worlds could meet was in the institution of the family, and the church must reach out to the world through the institution of the family. With almost Machiavellian directness, he advised his clergy, "You must win them by consideration for their personal comfort. You must win them by being interested in their personal interests. You must win them by sympathy with their domestic joys and sorrows. You must win them through their children."[27] All of these themes—the practical usefulness of worship, the sharp distinction between lay and clerical roles, and the importance of sentiment in undergirding lay allegiance—had been present as early as Hobart, but Doane extended them to an unprecedented degree. His views were indicative of a broad shift in the high church viewpoint. In Doane and W.A. one sees exemplified a subtle transformation of the high church position. A concern for comprehension and the social relevance of the church (viewed in personal terms) led to a retreat from the arena of public controversy and to a far greater emphasis on worship, prayer, and a dynamic ecclesiology.

II

To explain, however, the shift in sensibilities and the gradual loss of appeal of the Hobartian synthesis it is necessary to go beyond the concern for comprehension and church unity. In the decades after the 1840s a flurry of intellectual and social factors, together comprising a changed milieu both inside and outside of the Episcopal Church,

26. "Jesus of Nazareth . . . The Model for the Church and the Ministry," *Works*, 2:374.
27. Ibid., 2:375. On the significance of the family in this period, see Kirk Jeffrey, "The Family as Utopian Retreat from the City," *Soundings* 55 (1972): 21–41. For a brief discussion of the historical roots of this phenomenon and an analysis of its decline in the twentieth century, see Christopher Lasch, *Haven in a Heartless World: The Family Besieged* (New York, 1977), 3–21 in particular.

highlighted key weaknesses in the synthesis and finally contributed to its demise.[28]

As has been suggested, the theological world crafted by the proponents of the Hobartian high church tradition contained a peculiar amalgam of elements from many phases of Anglican post-Restoration development. From the great seventeenth-century Caroline scholars such as Pearson and Bull they inherited their trust in the fathers of the early church; from eighteenth-century supernatural rationalists they learned their view of revelation; from eighteenth-century high church writers they gained their concern for an ecclesiology dependent upon the episcopate, as well as a fideistic intellectualist strain, due to the influence of John Hutchinson on these apologists; and from the moralist-latitudinarian tradition they gleaned more of an appreciation for the importance of reason and morality than at times they might have wanted to admit. All of these strands were tenuously held together in large part by a common aversion to Calvinism and enthusiasm, and together they composed a mosaic of authorities enshrined in an established corpus of books. Although high churchmen offered no firm definition on most issues, their amalgam did serve for setting perimeters on the theological discussion. The widening of the theological debate beginning in the 1840s, however, so increased the agenda of discussion that the old perimeter of authorities simply proved inadequate. The reorganization of the high church position that began in earnest in the 1840s necessitated a reconsideration of many of the authorities who seemed to be out of sympathy with the new intellectual and theological concerns. As early as 1840 the *Churchman* felt obliged to warn its readers of the theological weaknesses present in the seventeenth-century Anglican theologian William Chillingworth, who had long been considered a bulwark in the Anglican apologetic.[29] As high church interest moved away from issues like apostolic succession and toward questions like the real presence in the holy eucharist, the theological viewpoint represented by Hooker and even Waterland became extremely constraining. Furthermore the new understanding of the Anglican past posited by the Oxford writers also undermined the American Episcopal catalogue of authorities. The Tractarian argument that the English church had fallen into near fatal slumber in the

28. Nowhere is the demise so clearly seen as in the dates in which the various volumes by Hobart went out of print: *An Apology for Apostolic Order* (1856): *A Companion for the Altar* (1857); *A Companion for the Book of Common Prayer* (1859); *A Companion for the Festivals and Fasts of the Protestant Episcopal Church* (1877).

29. *Churchman* 10 (October 3, 1840): 118.

century and a half between the Caroline divines and 1833 proposed a radical division between seventeenth- and eighteenth-century authorities unknown theretofore in American Episcopal thought. As the Tractarian periodization became more and more popular, indirectly aided no doubt by the traditional lack of appreciation of each generation for its immediate predecessors, the importance of the seventeenth-century authorities increased while that of the eighteenth century decreased.

Furthermore the same factors that were at work in England forging a new alternative to the Tractarian/evangelical impasse were also at work in America. A longing for ecclesiastical comprehensiveness, a concern for better incorporating into the religious life the new philosophical spirit represented by Coleridge, and a desire for the churches to begin addressing the great social problems of the day all came together in a loosely defined position known as Broad Churchmanship. We have already seen that as early as 1840 individuals like Caleb S. Henry had found themselves attracted to both the new Oxford theology and the philosophical ideas stemming from Coleridge. In the decades that followed, the new philosophical spirit began to take on even greater importance. Henry, for example, by 1860 had largely rejected the empirical-historical theology of the early Hobartians and also the precedence they gave to rational doctrine over moral sentiment. In Henry's later writings one sees an increased appreciation for philosophical idealism, the importance of the moral constitution, the absolute priority of the benevolent nature of God, and a preference in religion for issues of practical living over those of doctrine. Looking back, perhaps with a hint of autobiography, he could reflect,

> Meanwhile, as Time has been making changes in everything, so it has made orthodoxy among us Churchmen less harsh than it was. . . . [T]he benevolent hope of the final restoration of all men to goodness, and of the conversion of the Evil One, is not as shocking to the minds of good Churchmen as it once was; and the avowal of it does not put a man out of the pale of their charitable thoughts, in the way it used to.[30]

Even persons not as involved in the new philosophy as Henry could feel the attraction of the Broad Church appeal, particularly the empha-

30. Caleb S. Henry, *Dr. Oldham's Talk at Greystones* (New York, 1872), v. On his interest in idealism, see p. 118. See, too, his edition of Victor Cousin's *Elements of Psychology* (4th ed., New York, 1856). For an extended discussion of this phase in Henry's thought, see Wells, *Three Christian Transcendentalists,* 49–95.

sis upon the belief that God had created and redeemed all in Christ and all of the practical ramifications derived from this belief. George Templeton Strong, upon perusing F. D. Maurice's *Theological Essays,* candidly admitted in his diary, "I think the Broad Church appeal is more likely to *tell* on men and to be felt in the church than either the High Church or Evangelical party."[31] Increasingly the older sources and debates seemed strangely out of date.

Yet nothing undermined the Hobartian synthesis more than the growing historical consciousness. The importance of the discovery of history for the nineteenth century is hard to overemphasize. Originating in late eighteenth-century Germany, the growing awareness of the participation of individuals and cultures in the historical process became a hallmark of nineteenth-century Western civilization. "The historical method," as one scholar has noted, "meant the study of social phenomena of all kinds, institutions, customs, beliefs as the natural product of a given time and place."[32] The Enlightenment tendency of evaluating history from an abstract, rational criterion came increasingly to be rejected in favor of the attempt to understand individuals and societies contextually. Such an approach, however, drastically clashed with the prevailing high church belief that the witness of the primitive church could be used as a pattern of perfection.[33] It was on this very issue that John Henry Newman had abandoned Anglicanism for Roman Catholicism rejecting the older apostolic argument in favor of the continuity of theological development, and in light of it asked his famous question that if Athanasius and Ambrose were to come back to life, where would they find such continuity. Yet the Hobartian view of the past also was criticized by Philip Schaff in his *What is Church History?* Schaff, the great representative of the Mercersburg Theology and the individual usually deemed the father of American church history, had much praise for the Anglican High Church tradition. He lauded the Puseyites for joining with the Mercersburg critique of the rationalist, subjectivist, and sectarian strains in

31. Strong, *Diary* (1854), 2:170–71.

32. Walter E. Houghton, *The Victorian Frame of Mind, 1830–1870* (New Haven, 1957), 14–15. Studies of the rise of historical consciousness abound and continue to multiply. See Herbert Butterfield, *Man on His Past: The Study of the History of Historical Scholarship* (Cambridge, 1955); Peter Gay and Victor G. Wexler, eds., *Historians at Work,* vol. 3 (New York, 1975); and Hayden V. White, *Metahistory: The Historical Imagination in Nineteenth-Century Europe* (Baltimore, [1973]).

33. See Duncan Forbes, *The Liberal Anglican Idea of History* (Cambridge, 1952), 105.

American Protestantism.[34] Yet the subtitle of his essay on church history, *A Vindication of the Idea of Doctrinal Development,* hinted at one of the basic points of difference. In a critique of seventeenth-century Anglican patristic scholarship, Schaff observed,

> The English Episcopalians in particular, made it their business to establish a perfect identity between the primitive Church and their own. In this effort they showed themselves often more unhistorical, and less favourable to the idea of development, than even the Romanists themselves. So, for example, the learned *Dr. George Bull,* in his celebrated Defence of the Nicene Creed, undertakes to show that the ante-Nicene fathers taught in the full all that this creed contains, and that all differences which appear in the case are formal only, not affecting the substance at any point.[35]

The positing of a golden age led to both a dishonesty about inconsistencies in the historical record and to a basic misreading of the significance of other epochs in the history of the church by an undermining of the idea of historical continuity.[36] This theme was harped on by Schaff's associate John W. Nevin, who found the Episcopal reliance on the idea of a pure church an arbitrary contrivance: "Alas the whole theory is as brittle as glass, and falls to pieces with the first tap of the critic's hammer."[37] The historical apologetic of high church authors not only created a chasm between historical eras, but ignored the fact that even in the "pure" age beliefs such as purgatory, celibacy, the intercession of the saints, and the use of relics had been accepted.

High church writers were shocked and disturbed by Newman's and Schaff's views on development. Newman, for them, seemed to suggest that the entire enterprise of patristic controversy was fruitless since what finally mattered was not "Catholic consent" but "Roman authority."[38] Schaff, on the other hand, fell into the error of linking the

34. Philip Schaff, *The Principles of Protestantism* (Chambersburg, Pa., 1845), 122–23.

35. Philip Schaff, *What is Church History? A Vindication of the Idea of Doctrinal Development* (Philadelphia, 1846), 51. Emphasis in original.

36. Schaff also criticized the concept of development put forth by John Henry Newman in his *Essay on the Development of Christian Doctrine.* On this question, see Kathryn Johnson's astute and perceptive analysis in "The Mustard Seed and the Leaven: Philip Schaff's Confident View of Christian History," *HMPEC* 50 (1981): 157–70 in particular.

37. John W. Nevin, "Early Christianity," *Mercersburg Review* 3 (1851): 487–88.

38. *Churchman* 15 (November 27, 1845): 170–71. For an extended critique of Newman, Nevin, and Newman's question of Ambrose, see "Value of the Christian Fathers," *Church Review* 4 (1852): 497–522.

orthodox and the heretics in a schema that saw all church history as the development of the moral government of God.[39] In doing so, high church critics suggested, Schaff at times seemed to succumb to the errors of modern pantheism, by viewing the different periods of history as connected through the increasing realization of the idea of humanity.[40] Development seemed to embody all the theological evils that the high church feared most, not the least because of the blow it leveled to any appeal to the normative value of the primitive church.

If this were not a serious enough challenge to the idea of the pure church, the theological tensions within Episcopalianism also began to bend the concept sorely out of shape. The precise duration of the period of the "pure" church had never been completely defined. For T. C. Brownell, bishop of Connecticut, the pure church extended only through the first two centuries, yet for others it was seen continuing through the fifth or even the eighth centuries.[41] As a result of the Oxford Movement, many began to chafe at a restricted definition of the pure church. What they desired was not a Schaff-like concept of development, but instead the including of as much of the Middle Ages as possible within the normative period—both to include the entire period of the ecumenical councils and to provide support for certain medieval (in contrast to apostolic) practices.[42] The eagerness among some to extend the era of the pure church, however, led to a serious problem, since many of the practices and teachings of the seventh and eighth centuries were not only difficult to reconcile with earlier teachings, but also seemed too often to be colored by the superstition generally associated with the Middle Ages.[43] If the church were pure in practice and doctrine in the eighth century, the question then became when was it ever corrupt? Caught between an increased recognition of the idea of doctrinal development and the rising interest among some to extend the pure church into the medieval period, the old concept of the pure church, long the touchstone of the Hobartian apologetic, became less and less credible.

39. For an implicit critique of Schaff on this point, see "Neander as Church Historian," *Church Review* 3 (1850): 241–44.

40. "The Pantheistic Movement," *Church Review* 1 (1848): 560.

41. For Brownell's narrow definition of the pure church, see *Errors of the Times* (Hartford, 1843).

42. Such was the direction Hurrell Froude gave to the Oriel circle. See Newman's assessment, *Apologia Pro Vita Sua* (London, 1879), 24–25.

43. Hopkins, in *"The End of Controversy" Controverted*, went to great length cataloging what seemed to him to be the growing rise of ecclesiastical corruption from the fourth century onward. See 1:59–194.

Furthermore these changes in the applicability of the apostolic argument became exacerbated through a subtle change in ecclesiology that began in the 1840s and increased rapidly in significance. As has already been emphasized, the central core of the Hobartian high church tradition had been the office of the bishop and the appeal to apostolic order. Bishops such as Hobart, Hopkins, and Onderdonk saw themselves as modern day Cyprians, standing as patriarchs over their dioceses, governing them with firmness and protecting and defending them from disorder from within and assault from without. After the 1840s, however, the succeeding generation of high church apologists, while in no way denying the importance of the episcopacy (and indeed an appeal to the apostolic succession continued to have a major role in their apologetical repertoire), nonetheless found the office of the episcopate existentially less central. In large part this shift can be explained in light of certain practical factors. As a diocese grew larger, and contained more clergy, the influence of the bishop became less immediate. Second, as other scholars have noted, the decades after 1841 witnessed a marked drop in the number of high church clerics raised to the episcopate both in England and America. Although the situation in America was nowhere near as extreme as that in England, where a policy of marked disfavor was urged by Prince Consort Albert, George DeMille has calculated that only one-third of the American bishops elected in the decade after *Tract 90* were high church, and none of these were outstanding leaders.[44] Often the situation occurred where Tractarian clergy found themselves in open conflict with their bishops. A wit of the time put into verse this ambiguous Tractarian relationship with bishops:

> He talketh much of discipline,
> yet when the shoe doth pinch,
> This most obedient duteous son
> will not give way an inch;
> Pliant and obstinate by turns,
> what'ere may be the whim,
> He's only for the Bishop
> when the Bishop is for him.

A belief in apostolic succession did not necessarily mean an acceptance

44. DeMille, *Catholic Movement*, 69. On the English situation, see W. J. Sparrow Simpson, "The Revival from 1845 to 1933," in *Northern Catholicism: Centenary Studies of the Oxford and Parallel Movements*, ed. N. P. Williams (New York, 1933), 43.

of episcopal authority.[45] Nor was this attitude limited simply to England. When in Boston the Church of the Advent, a congregation founded by a group of persons influenced by the new spirit of worship, attempted to introduce an altar cross and candles, the bishop of the diocese, Manton Eastburn, refused to set foot in the church. The decision by the General Convention in 1856, which required that a bishop visit each of his congregations at least once every three years and that he could not legally refuse to do so out of disagreement with a parish's worship or theology, hinted at a new understanding of the episcopate. The office was to reflect that same position of comprehension toward which the church as a whole had been falteringly heading.[46]

At the same time this decline in the centrality of the episcopate hinted at a further shift in high church self-understanding. Broadly speaking, if the central image in the high church imagination during the Hobartian period had been the patriarchal bishop governing from his apostolic office, for later high churchmen the central image became the priest serving at the altar. The famous cry of the English anti-ritualists, "It is the Mass that matters," would have appeared as a terrible anachronism in the Hobartian period.[47] Questions concerning eucharistic theology and the voluminous debates over vestments and ceremonials such as candles, the mixed chalice, and the eastward position while celebrating the holy communion were to capture the interest of a generation of young ecclesiastical ritualists. All of these new concerns pointed to a far greater concern for the sacerdotal role of the priest than for the apostolic role of the bishop.

III

The Hobartian framework came under attack not only from the European-based theological arena, but also from forces closer to home via new understandings of the meaning of American nationhood and destiny. During the first few decades of the century the Hobartian

45. The wit was Sydney Smith, canon of St. Paul's Cathedral, London. Cited in Horton Davies, *Worship and Theology in England* (Princeton, 1961), 3:275.

46. Harry Croswell, *A Memoir of the late Rev. William Croswell, D.D., Rector of the Church of the Advent* (New York, 1853), 340–480. *The Parish of the Advent in the City of Boston: A History of One Hundred Years* (Boston, 1944), 6–46.

47. Quoted in T. A. Lacey, *The Anglo-Catholic Faith* (London, [1926]), 140.

social vision had been slowly set forth. Inspired by a vision of the pre-Constantinian church, it combined a firm conviction that ecclesiology and theology were the criteria by which all moral sentiment had to be evaluated (which effectively relegated sentiment to piety and worship) with a strong suspicion against cooperating with either other churches or political movements. How this vision failed in responding to the challenges of midcentury America remains to be considered.

It has already been suggested that beneath the level of surface agreement the Anglican tradition provided two contrasting visions of social involvement, which have been labelled the apostolic and the English models. The apostolic vision tended to identify the church with the pre-Constantinian community and hence set its highest priority on church purity and independence. The English vision, which was an inheritance of the English religious establishment, saw instead a far more positive role for the church in support of the state and reflected a spirit of ecclesiastical noblesse oblige. It linked squire and parson in a common end. The decision by Hobart and his supporters to advocate vigorously the former vision stemmed at least in part from the practical recognition that the strong anglophobia of the early national period called for an elaboration of an Episcopal "story" that could serve as an alternative to an unpopular identification of the Episcopal Church with the English establishment. Thus on his return from England in 1825, for example, Hobart pointedly emphasized the close connection of the American Episcopal church with the primitive church and its superiority in its present condition to the established Church of England. The desire for the radical independence of the church vis-à-vis the state lay behind the very public rejection by Hobartians of any secular use of church buildings.[48]

The suspicion of things English, or at least of the Tory England of crown and altar as compared to the Whig and nonconformist England, was long in dying. Philip Hone, writing in 1837, could still recall those days when "men were afraid to wear a red watch ribbon, lest it might be taken for a symbol of Toryism and bring the wearer a broken head"; and even as late as the 1830s an Episcopal college like Kenyon in Ohio was still considered by the surrounding countryside

---

48. See, for example, the continuing concern with this question in William H. Moore, *The History of St. George's Church, Hempstead, Long Island* (New York, 1881), 228–30.

to be a British outpost.[49] Yet the growing interest in English intellectual and cultural trends began to seriously undermine the last vestiges of anglophobia, particularly among the urban business and professional classes, many of whom found themselves attracted to the Episcopal Church as a bastion of English culture.[50] The Episcopal willingness to glorify its English connection perhaps reached its antebellum zenith with the visit of Albert Edward, Prince of Wales, to America in 1860. The New York Episcopal community held a special service in his honor at Trinity Church, and there all the fine points of republican ideology were temporarily set aside. The prince was assured of the American Episcopal belief that God alone was "the only ruler of princes."[51] Yet it is in the sermon preached by George Washington Doane upon his return from England in 1841 that one can most clearly see the psychological distance traversed in the sixteen years since Hobart's similar sermon. For Doane, the visit to England was a veritable "pilgrimage," and it convinced him of the close spiritual connection between the two realms. In place of Hobart's sense of republican suspicion of the English establishment, Doane emphasized the closeness of the two churches. A community of faith and intercourse connected

49. Tuckerman, *Hone,* 1:243; Caswall, *American Church,* 415. Most of the present discussions of nineteenth-century Anglo-American relations in the antebellum period have accepted the claim found in Frank Thistlethwaite's important study *The Anglo-American Connection in the Early Nineteenth Century* (Philadelphia, [1959]) that the basic Anglo-American connection during these years was the evangelical and Whig connection, which perhaps culminated in the great meeting of the Evangelical Alliance in 1846. As this study has in several places suggested, however, American high church Episcopalians had a completely different set of relations connecting them intellectually and culturally with England and served as an important conduit of British thought into America. Though the evidence is only sketchy, the American suspicion of this Anglican/Tory England was far slower dying than was the suspicion of England in general.

50. For a contemporary account of this movement, see "Unitarian and Episcopal Affinities," *New Englander,* 557. For three slightly differing modern interpretations of this phenomenon, see Williams, "A Mirror for Unitarians," who in part links it to a reaction against immigration; Lears, *No Place of Grace,* who sees its roots in antimodernist and elitist feeling; and Mara Nacht Mayor, "Norton, Lowell, and Godkin: A Study of American Attitudes Toward England, 1865–1885" (Ph.D. diss., Yale University, 1969), who sees it as being derived from both contact with the English and English culture and from a disillusionment with the American political scene.

51. Dix, *History of Trinity,* 4:470. See too G. T. Strong's more jaundiced view of the event, *Diary,* 3:52.

both churches and both nations. "Are we not the sons of Englishmen?" he asked. "Is not the English character our inheritance? Are not their triumphs our trophies? . . . [T]rue Americans have English hearts!"[52]

Yet with this shift in sentiment the apostolic identification and the significance of the apostolic metaphor could not help but be weakened, since the English attraction began to surpass that of the apostolic. Even the model of the bishop was affected.[53] Yet perhaps the area in which this new sentiment played its most crucial role was in the growth of the boarding school movement. The history of this movement and the leadership provided by the Episcopal Church has been told elsewhere.[54] Yet it is important to emphasize how broad a cultural gap separated the Carthage of Cyprian and the Rugby of Arnold. In response to the pedagogical need for nurturing "gentlemen, scholars, patriots, and Christians," even a high church figure like Doane dramatically lowered the high wall that Hobart had so carefully erected between the domains of the church and the state. In the first commencement of Burlington College he emphasized its role as a "nursery for Young Americans" and the need of keeping the "secular festivals" such as the Fourth of July and Washington's Birthday.[55] Indeed, to play the role of the American Rugby it became necessary to treat themes such as patriotism and duty in a far more serious and conscientious way than earlier. Doane's willingness to do so reflected a recognition even among high church leaders of the need to adapt to the new conditions. The expanding vision of the role of the Episcopal Church in American society led to a gradual curtailment of the extreme separation between church and state that the Hobartian apostolic metaphor had assumed.

Of far greater importance in the reassessment of Episcopal social attitudes was the crisis over union and slavery that swept over the Republic in the 1850s and 1860s. The general Episcopal predilection

52. Doane, "Glorious Things of the City of God," *Works,* 4:538. Emphasis in original. Doane, although extreme, was not alone in these sentiments. As one English visitor noted, "The more an American Christian reveres and appreciates England, the more he is drawn to the Daughter Church of England which he finds so firmly planted . . . in his own country." *Recent Recollections of the Anglo-American Church in the United States,* 2 vols. (London, 1861), 2:105.

53. See the quotation by the Presbyterian clergyman Cortlandt Van Rensselaer in Doane, *Works,* 1:324.

54. See James McLachlan, *American Boarding Schools: A Historical Study* (New York, 1970), 172 ff.

55. Doane, *Works,* 4:13.

for avoiding political issues and the high church suspicion of the reform movements of the evangelical united front that have already been outlined in chapter 4 continued to provide the framework within which Episcopalians in large part responded to these issues.[56]

For most of the same reasons that were suggested earlier, Episcopalians of all theological complexions were loathe to raise as a point of debate the question of slavery. The fear of ecclesiastical schism; the strong intersectional, personal, and ecclesiastical connections; and the general preoccupation with questions of churchmanship all combined to keep the question of slavery out of public discussion.[57] The addition to these factors of the continual threat of national division in the decade between the Great Compromise of 1850 and the secession of South Carolina made the continuation of ecclesiastical union seem even more essential. John C. Calhoun had earlier warned,

> The chords that bind the states together are not only many but various in character. . . . The strongest of those of a spiritual and ecclesiastical nature consisted in the unity of the great denominations. . . . [T]he Episcopal Church is the only one of the four great Protestant denominations which remains unbroken and entire. . . . If the agitation goes on . . . there will be nothing to hold the states together except force.[58]

Such advice had not been lost on Episcopalians themselves. Throughout the 1850s there continued a strong Episcopal self-awareness of the social importance of the undivided Episcopal Church. As one journalist put it, the church was "one of the few conservative elements left."[59] A journal like the *Churchman,* for example, throughout the 1850s continually called for unity in both church and state. Yet this overriding concern for church unity bears striking parallels to a broad-

56. Not, of course, that there had ever been unanimity as to the principle upon which the propensity was to be based. For some it had largely been a pragmatic attitude, justified largely through its usefulness in avoiding schism. For others, it had stemmed from a principled belief that Jerusalem could have nothing to do with Athens. Up to the beginning of the war, however, both attitudes contributed to the lack of political discussion.

57. T. M. Clark in his *Reminiscences,* 136, relates a humorous anecdote about his attempt to include the subject of slavery, in a modest way, in the Pastoral Letter that was to have been issued by the House of Bishops in 1859. As a result of his suggestion the entire letter was cancelled.

58. Quoted in Chester Forrester Dunham, *The Attitude of the Northern Clergy Toward the South, 1860–1865* (Toledo, Ohio, 1942), 1–2.

59. "Sermons for Servants," *Church Review* 4 (1851): 381.

er political phenomenon which some cultural historians have argued had become extremely pervasive in the years before the Civil War.[60] The threat of secession led political moderates to cleave ever more closely to the memory of the Founding Fathers and the fact of union, yet in doing so they often lost sight of the moral meaning for which the Union stood. This can help explain the great outpouring of concern for church unity during these troubled years. The unity of the church became more and more valued during the troubled decade of the 1850s, and all other issues were seen to be of decidedly lesser concern. One practical result of such an attitude was that Episcopal churches increasingly became havens for Democrats and Doughfaces, who were attracted to the church because of the lack of sectional strife found there. Even Southeners who were not themselves Episcopalians often joined Episcopal congregations while sojourning in the North so as to be assured of not having to hear abolitionist sermons.[61] Yet just as was the case in the national ideology, the price of this unity was a willingness to abandon any elevated moral vision for the church, an abandonment which all too often appeared to stem more from a desire to avoid debate than from any established principle. As Caleb Henry sadly noted in explaining to a correspondent why his bishop had rebuked him for having taken a public stand against the extension of slavery, "As to Slavery Extension he is undoubtedly a sheer indifferentist;— but bitterly opposed in his own private feeling . . . to *all* agitation on the question of Slavery—especially to all attempts to arouse the moral sense of the North, particularly in our Church, *against* it."[62]

The firing on Fort Sumter, as is well known, created a tremendous metamorphosis in religious opinion throughout the North. Emanating from countless Protestant pulpits and presses was a call for the preservation of liberty in America, not simply on patriotic grounds, but as a cause laced with millennial significance.[63] To call the great

---

60. See, for example, Paul C. Nagel, *One Nation Indivisible: The Union in American Thought* (New York, 1964), 184–96. See too, by the same author, *This Sacred Trust: American Nationality, 1798–1898* (New York, 1971), 129–94.

61. *Recent Recollections,* 2:249–51.

62. C. S. Henry to Richard H. Dana, 26 November 1864, in Wells, *Three Christian Transcendentalists,* 199.

63. On the response of northern clerics, see Dunham, *Northern Clergy,* passim, and R. L. Stanton, *The Church and the Rebellion* . . . (New York, 1864). The two most provocative accounts of the millennial significance of the conflict are James Moorhead, *American Apocalypse, Yankee Protestants and the Civil War, 1860–1869* (New Haven, 1978); and Timothy Smith's now classic *Revivalism and Social Reform: American Protestantism on the Eve of the Civil War* (Nashville, 1957).

crusade mentality that gripped so much of northern evangelical Protestantism the last hurrah of the evangelical enterprise is only a slight
exaggeration. Postmillennialism, or the belief that it was the responsibility of Christians to help in preparing the way for the Kingdom of
God, and the long-standing sense of America's peculiar destiny in this
regard—stemming from Jonathan Edwards's famous *Thoughts on the
Revival of Religion*—came together one final time. The combination
created a burst of energy and enthusiasm that saw the Civil War as part
of the final, apocalyptic battle.[64] Julia Ward Howe's famous vision of
the coming of the Lord and the nations being gathered before his
judgment seat gave a poetic witness to the emotional power this apocalyptic vision could entail.

That on the formal level high church Episcopalians would seem
somewhat intellectually uncertain in this highly charged atmosphere is
not surprising. Their comparative freedom from millennial speculation and their traditional concern for ecclesiology rather than national
destiny had for decades made them suspicious of the evangelical
crusade mentality. The continuing suspicion is suggested from many
of the formal diocesan pronouncements at the beginning of the war
that strove to walk that fine line between ecclesiastical neutrality and
open support for the war.[65] As would be expected, on the individual
level the clerical response to the political crisis varied. The editor of the
Churchman, who had invested so much emotion in the cause of peace,
terminated his journal a fortnight after Fort Sumter. Having argued
that the war was a result of the dilapidated state of church discipline, he
could only hope, "If then, this unity of primitive organization in
Christ's Kingdom on earth were once more established, might we not
hope to restore to our country the blessing of peace and prosperity
which, under the Divine sanction and by the guidance of the Holy
Ghost, would remain forever?"[66] On the other hand, William R.
Whittingham, living in Maryland, lent support (as a private person, he
emphasized, and not as bishop) to the attempt to keep Maryland in the
Union.[67]

Yet it is often forgotten how on the practical level this linking of
religion and nationhood proved strongly attractive even to many high

64. Moorhead, *American Apocalypse,* 58.
65. See, for example, the address by Horatio Potter, bishop of New York, for
1861, in which the war was mentioned only in order to contrast it with the peace and
heavenly rest offered by the church. *JDNY of 1861,* 77–80.
66. "The Church and the Country," *Churchman* 31 (May 2, 1861): 81.
67. Brand, *Life of Whittingham,* 2:7–8.

church laity. Once again the example of George Templeton Strong, the New York layman, may be instructive. For Strong, who had earlier entertained himself with dreams of a Columbia College recast in the model of Oxford, the impending crisis of union had been a painful and troubling experience. With the attack on Fort Sumter a burst of patriotic enthusiasm overcame him that washed away the careful Hobartian distinctions between church and state. As a vestryman of Trinity Church, New York, he decided that a flag should fly from the Gothic tower of that building, and his personal reflections on the significance of the action are illuminative. He recognized that it was

> an unprecedented demonstration, but these are unprecedented times; not only good in itself, as a symbol of the sympathy of the Church Catholic with all movements to suppress privy conspiracy sedition, but a politic move for Trinity Church at this memorable hour of excitement. . . . [T]he ideas of Church and State, Religion and Politics, have been practically separated so long that people are specially delighted with any manifestation of the Church's sympathy with the State and recognition of our national life on any fitting occasion. This flag was a symbol of the truth that the Church is no esoteric organization, no private soul saving society; that it has a position to take in every great public national crisis, and that its position is important.[68]

In Strong's reflections one can observe a fundamental flaw implicit in the Hobartian social position. The demand for an almost sectarian division of church and state in a nongathered communion such as the Episcopal Church that contained such a large number of socially and politically active members could be maintained only through a strict psychological compartmentalization on the personal level of religious and political concerns. The psychological jolt produced by the crisis of union led Strong to jettison this compartmentalization. The mobilization of will, both on the individual and social levels, called for an integration of the great concerns of religion and nationhood.

The issue of the proper relation of the church to the state in a time of national crisis became the subject of debate at the General Convention of 1862. Its opening less than a fortnight after the carnage of the

---

68. Strong, *Diary,* 3:124–26. The question of flags on church buildings continued to be an issue of symbolic importance, and General Seminary was sharply criticized for its refusal to fly a flag over its buildings. See Dawley, *General Theological Seminary,* 196–97.

battle of Antietam and scarcely more than a week after Abraham Lincoln had issued his Emancipation Proclamation gave it an importance far greater than that of most general conventions.[69] As the strongly pro-Union *New York Times* and Horace Greeley's *New York Daily Tribune* called for a strong statement of support for the war effort, the *New York Daily Herald* warned darkly of the ramifications of any political involvement by the convention. For fourteen days the convention wrestled with the issue of the church and the war, until a final resolution was passed. Although mild from the perspective of the support for the Union shown by other denominations, both the resolution and the accompanying Pastoral Letter clearly broke from the long Episcopal tradition of political noninvolvement. The setting aside of a proposal that rejected any introduction of secular and national interests into the legislature of the Christian church and which called upon the Episcopal Church to be "a true ark of refuge into which the multitudes of the wise and good would gladly come for refuge from the storm and tempest of worldly interest" indicated the change in sentiment.[70] A few years earlier such an expression of apostolic exclusivity would have been overwhelmingly approved, but in the midst of the crisis of union the sentiment seemed no longer tenable. Even the delegates from such traditional high church bastions as New York and Connecticut refused to go along with the proposal. The Hobartian paradox, or the linking of an almost sectarian theology and social vision to an inclusive, socially assimilated denomination, became a casualty of the crisis of union. Composed by a committee of nine, the final resolution accepted by the convention firmly placed the Episcopal Church behind the movement to restore the Union.[71] In the Pastoral Letter issued by the House of Bishops after long debate— which was required to be read in all the churches—the support of the Union cause became even more explicit. Phrases from the English national religious heritage like "sedition, privy conspiracy, and re-

---

69. A number of contemporary witnesses commented on the great concern shown by non-Episcopalians at the time to make sure that the Episcopal Church at that critical moment would give firm support to the Union. See Hopkins, Jr., *Life of Hopkins*, 325–30, and [W. C. Doane], "The General Convention of 1862," *Church Review* 15 (1863): 104–05. The convention was further complicated by politics. Horatio Seymour was a lay delegate from western New York. At the time he was the Democratic candidate for governor of New York and a leading critic of the Lincoln administration.

70. *JGC., 1862*, 89.

71. Ibid., 51–53.

bellion" and long passages from the Elizabethan homily "Against Willful Rebellion" pepper the letter, which concluded in affirming,

> We have now brethren . . . ascertained a basis of principle and duty on which we may heartily rejoice in all the active and energetic loyalty with which the members of our Churches, in union with their fellow citizens . . . are sustaining the Government in its vast efforts to reinstate the rightful control of its laws, wherever they have been disowned.[72]

Yet while this letter was being solemnly read to the united convention, the chair of the presiding bishop remained empty in mute protest. For an individual like John Henry Hopkins, the presiding bishop at the convention, the willingness of the church to take sides in the national conflict was a gross abandonment of its historic role. In a public protest delivered to the House of Bishops, he lamented the church's entrance into the realm of political questions. In the long-established high church model, his argument was structured around precedent from the early church and emphasized the distinction between one's duty as church member and as citizen: "And while I maintain a fast allegiance to the State, I am bound to maintain the infinitely more solemn and sublime allegiance to my omnipotent Lord and Master in such wise, that I may not confound the lines of demarcation which He has placed between them."[73]

Hopkins's refusal to participate in the public reading of the Pastoral Letter was a fitting symbol of the inability of the older tradition to accept the weakening of the rigid boundary between church and nation. Hobart, Bowden, How, and others of that generation would have clearly understood and sympathized with the principle involved. Yet a perusal of the list of delegates who supported the new view reads like a who's who of the influential figures in the postbellum Episcopal Church. Francis Vinton, soon to become professor of ecclesiastical polity at General Seminary; M. A. DeWolfe Howe, later the bishop of central Pennsylvania, William S. Perry, the famous historian of the Episcopal Church; and Edward A. Washburn, one of the most important leaders in the postbellum American Broad Church movement; all rejected the isolation of ecclesiastical concerns from those of the nation. Furthermore throughout the country younger clergy like Henry

72. *A Pastoral Letter of the House of Bishops of the Protestant Episcopal Church* . . . (New York, 1862), 11.

73. The "Protest" is printed in the appendix of Hopkins, Jr., *Life of Hopkins,* 464.

Codman Potter, who would later become a famous bishop of New York, found the continuing sectarian mentality of the Episcopal Church frustrating.[74] Many would have probably agreed with Phillips Brooks's private assessment of the convention: "Its shilly-shallying was disgraceful. It was ludicrous, if not sad, to see those old gentlemen sitting there for fourteen days, trying to make out whether there was a war going on or not, and whether if there was it would be safe for them to say so."[75] Perry Miller has noted that one of the casualties of the crisis of union involved the whole genre of legal discourse, which suffered from a "vulgarization" because of the support it gave to causes such as the Dred Scott decision. It appears that among many younger Episcopalians the traditional high church schema suffered from a similar vulgarization during these troubled years.[76]

Perhaps the most difficult factor to assess in the undermining of the Hobartian system is the role played by the wartime debate over the question of slavery. Daniel Walker Howe's observation concerning the problem of slavery within Unitarianism—that is, that it was a crisis not simply because it pitted the intellectual leadership of the church against the economic elite that made up the laity, but also because it highlighted a basic uncertainty and indirection within the leadership itself—is equally applicable to the Episcopal situation.[77] Because of this indirection, Episcopalians, far more than any other Protestant group, never really addressed the horror of American slavery.

Whereas before the war there had been scarcely any difference in public opinion between high church and low church commentators on the question of slavery, during the war this no longer proved to be the case. The Episcopal evangelical prewar position had stemmed largely from the concern not to alienate southern Episcopal evangelicals. When secession and the division within the church between North and South ended this concern, Episcopal evangelicals often moved closer to the sensibilities concerning slavery shown by their Protestant neighbors. As suggested in chapter 4, however, among high church writers the question of slavery had been much more closely connected to key theological attitudes, and in particular to the priority of primitive evidence over modern moral sentiment. From the high church

74. George Hodges, *Henry Codman Potter* (New York, 1915), 48–49.

75. Brooks to William Brooks, 23 October 1862, in A. V. G. Allen, *Life and Letters of Phillips Brooks,* 3 vols. (New York, 1901), 1:428.

76. Miller, *Life of the Mind,* 155.

77. Daniel Walker Howe, *The Unitarian Conscience, Harvard Moral Philosophy, 1805–1861* (Cambridge, Mass., 1970), 270.

perspective immediate abolition could all too easily be dismissed as part of the rejected evangelical crusade. Even in the midst of the war, the connections between abolition and modern Puritanism could not be forgotten. In commenting on both, one Episcopalian observed, "The innate idea of 'mission' so inwrought into the very framework and texture of the Puritan, makes him of necessity, whatever his character, a professional 'Reformer,' this is his vocation; in other words he becomes a meddler in other peoples' business."[78]

This is not to say that Episcopalians as individuals were oblivious to the increasing crisis over slavery. Indeed, scarcely any individual living through a decade that witnessed the publication of Harriet Beecher Stowe's *Uncle Tom's Cabin,* the travail of civil war in "Bleeding Kansas," and the furor aroused over the Dred Scott decision could have been untouched by the question. George T. Strong, for example, continued to grapple with the peculiar high church dilemma over slavery. He acknowledged that slavery was universally condemned "from London to Vienna," yet he still could find no theological justification for such condemnation. As the decade progressed and as events highlighted even more boldly the catastrophic effect of slavery on the Union, Strong strove to hang on to a barely defensible paradox. Slavery could be defended in the abstract, yet in its southern existence, he concluded, it was "the greatest crime on the largest scale known in modern history . . . a blasphemy *not in word,* but in systematic action against the spirit of God."[79]

Just as with the question of the Union, the firing on Fort Sumter and the later call for emancipation strained to the breaking point the fragile paradox upon which the Hobartian social vision rested. Not only Episcopal social thought but the Hobartian theological method itself felt the effect of this challenge. In this context, the appearance of works by Samuel Seabury and John Henry Hopkins on the question of slavery take on a new light. Seabury's and Hopkins's volumes both defended southern slavery and both caused a serious scandal both inside and outside of the church.[80] More important, however, both

78. [N. S. Richardson], "The Union, the Constitution, and Slavery," *Church Review* 15 (1863): 545.

79. Strong, *Diary* (1856), 2:278, 304–05. Emphasis added.

80. Hopkins treated the question of slavery in four works: *Slavery: Its Religious Sanction, Its Political Dangers, And the Best Mode of Doing it Away* (Buffalo, N.Y., 1851); *The American Citizen: His Rights and Duties . . .* (New York, 1857); *The Bible View of Slavery* (New York, 1861); and *A Scriptural, Ecclesiastical, and Historical View of Slavery . . .* (New York, 1864). In addition to occasional editorials, Seabury's

show a continuation of the earlier high church attitude. For Hopkins in particular the issue of slavery was ultimately tied to the larger question of the priority of the ancient witness over modern views of morality. As with so many other questions that he and other high church writers had investigated, the issue of slavery was examined in light of scripture, of the teachings of the early church through sources like Tertullian, Jerome, Augustine, and Chrysostom, and of biblical commentators from the Reformation to the beginning of the nineteenth century. Weighed by these criteria, the antislavery movement was deemed an innovation based more on modern views of morality than upon the objective record of revelation:

> And who are we that, in our modern wisdom, we presume to set aside the Word of God, and scorn the example of the divine Redeemer, and spurn the preaching and conduct of the apostles, and invent for ourselves a "higher law" than . . . Holy Scriptures? . . . Who are we that virtually blot out the language of the sacred record, and dictate to the majesty of heaven what He shall regard as sin and reward as duty? Who are we that are ready to trample on the doctrines of the Bible, and tear to shreds the Constitution of our country? . . . Woe to the Union when the blind become leaders of the blind! Woe to the man who dares to strive against his Maker![81]

The travail of the nation could be directly attributed to the abandonment of the truth of scripture and tradition, and for one final time the message of Vincent of Lerins was invoked to chastise innovation: *quod semper, quod ubique, quod ab omnibus.*

Yet what distinguished the works of Hopkins and Seabury was the implicit acknowledgment that in the heightened emotional atmo-

---

main contribution was *American Slavery Distinguished from the Slavery of English Theorists and Justified by the Law of Nature* (New York, 1861). On the controversy provoked, see (among others) [M. A. DeWolfe Howe], *A Reply to a Letter of Bishop Hopkins . . .* (Philadelphia, 1864); [Leonard Marsh], *A Review of a "Letter . . ." by Vermonter* (Burlington, 1861); Frances Anne Kemble, *The Views of Judge Woodward and Bishop Hopkins on Negro Slavery in the South* (Philadelphia, 1863); John R. Bolles, *A Reply to Bishop Hopkins' View of Slavery and a Review of the Times* (Philadelphia, 1865); Daniel R. Goodwin, *Southern Slavery in its Present Aspects . . .* (Philadelphia, 1864); *The Bible View of Slavery Reconsidered . . .* (Philadelphia, 1863); and *Bishop Hopkins' Letter on Slavery Ripped Up . . .* (New York, 1863). Hopkins's *Bible View of Slavery* in particular became the center of a large controversy when it was reprinted in 1863 as a campaign tract by the Democratic Party in the gubernatorial election in Pennsylvania. One hundred sixty-three Episcopal clergy, including Bishop Alonzo Potter, signed a formal protest.

81. Hopkins, *Bible View of Slavery,* 16–17.

sphere, an *Athanasius contra mundum* attitude could not be relied upon. The elevation of the importance of the conscience had become so pervasive that any pitting of revelation against moral sentiment would convince few individuals and threaten for many more the authority of the revelation itself. Even an Episcopal clergyman like Caleb Henry could forthrightly proclaim, "Show me a revelation that contradicts the necessary convictions of reason and conscience—and I reject it."[82] The issue of the morality of slavery had to be addressed or the fundamental question of the authority of revelation would be lost, since it was becoming clear that revelation for most could not stand without the support of reason and morality. As Seabury explained in a letter, the abolitionists had thrown down a gauntlet:

> many of them, both men and women of strong minds and popular talents, persistently offered the issue; slavery is *per se* either morally wrong or morally right: if morally wrong it must and ought to fall, and the Constitution and the Bible and all else that protects it deserve to be buried with it in a common grave: if morally right prove it to be so by arguments drawn from reason and we will no longer carp at the Constitution and the Bible, but will unite with you in your efforts to meliorate its conditions and reform its abuses.[83]

This recognition that the theological issue could not proceed without first addressing the moral question led Seabury in *American Slavery* into the foreign fields of contract law and racial theory. It had to be demonstrated that the law of God did not contradict the law of nature. Even Hopkins recognized the need for including amateur sociological analysis of southern life along with his evidence from the early church; and for the sake of preserving the authority of the revelation, he argued that slavery was not only theologically right, but also, when properly understood, not antithetical with reason and conscience. Yet such arguments in Hopkins—for example, his justification of the whipping post by an appeal to the scourge with which Christ drove the money changers out of the temple—were invariably weak and seem to flow more from a concern for consistency in argument than from any heartfelt belief.[84]

82. Caleb S. Henry, *Patriotism and the Slaveholders' Rebellion* (New York, 1861), 16.

83. Samuel Seabury to Alonzo Potter, 14 March 1864, Seabury Family Papers, NYHS. This extremely important letter sheds essential light on the fundamental purpose behind Seabury's argument.

84. Hopkins, *Bible View of Slavery*, 29.

As suggested earlier, the Hobartian position on the question of slavery bears more marks of having been reached from the inner consistency of argument than from reason. For those, however, whose vision was not tied so closely to the theological/ecclesiological matrix of the strict Hobartian viewpoint, the endeavors of Hopkins and Seabury seemed to be a reductio ad absurdum of the entire line of argument. The revolution of opinion among northern Protestants during the course of the war concerning the question of slavery has been noted by many scholars. Slavery was increasingly seen as an intolerable blemish on the millennial visage of the American Republic. Episcopalians, particularly the laity who as a group were far more sensitive to national trends than the clergy, were not aloof to these changes. For a layman like George Templeton Strong, a person who could express sentiments such as those found in the works of Hopkins and Seabury was hopelessly out of touch with the national mood:

> He does not see how times have changed and how fast they are changing. He looks on the great national movement that is growing stronger every day and already controls the conduct of the war just as he looked on the ravings of the little knot of philanthropes and infidels that constituted the Abolition Society twenty-five years ago. . . . [He] learns nothing and forgets nothing.[85]

For Strong, the revolution in political and social reality made ideas and arguments untenable that before the war would have been readily accepted.[86] The new understanding, however, was impossible from within the high church position without overriding long cherished principles. A layman like Strong could do so, but for clergy like Hopkins and Seabury, who were more concerned with theological consistency, the price was too high to pay.

A number of critics recognized that the issue boiled down to the question of theology and included in their critiques an attack on the underlying Hobartian assumptions. Again and again Hopkins in particular was accused of preferring a dead external creed which petrified the mind from all appeals to a higher nature rather than the true spirit of the gospel.[87] By having the creed stand sentinel over the heart the true essence of Christianity was lost. The most elaborate refutation

85. Strong, *Diary* (1864), 3:392. In this quote Strong referred to his friend Gulian Verplanck, yet it generally reflects his wider opinion on the question.

86. Strong, for example in a diary entry in early 1861, praised Seabury's *American Slavery:* see 3:96–97.

87. "Immorality in Politics," *North American Review* 98 (1864): 111.

was offered by Daniel R. Goodwin, an Episcopal clergyman and provost of the University of Pennsylvania. Responding to Hopkins's claim that a sin had to violate an expressed law of God that had been revealed in scripture as interpreted by the primitive church, Goodwin suggested that any violation of the law of reason and conscience could be considered a sin against God, whether explicitly forbidden by a divine command or not. "The revealed law of God," he argued, "is not substituted for the moral law written in man's heart and conscience."[88] The high church methodology fundamentally erred when it found itself more interested in historical evidence than in eternal truth: "What men who adhere obstinately to the letter, like the Bishop, never comprehend . . . [is] that Christianity is not a set of rules in detail, like the law of Moses, but a system of great principles, working as a Divine leaven in the heart and conscience of men and nations."[89]

Timothy Smith has suggested that by the 1850s the crisis over slavery had already begun shaking a large number of evangelicals away from a simple reliance on the literal reading of scripture.[90] A parallel phenomenon can be observed in the Episcopal Church vis-à-vis the issue of the authority of the primitive church. The emphasis upon the independence of the primitive witness and its function in judging modern innovations had been a boon to Episcopal apologists in the 1830s, but by the 1860s and the crisis over slavery the same methodological assumption had become a heavy yoke. History, as well as scripture, it came to be argued, had to be interpreted on the level of spirit rather than merely letter, and the modern conscience could not be blithely ignored. The *Athanasius contra mundum* mentality that had been a heritage of the Hobartian tradition was weighed in the balance and found wanting. How much the question of slavery contributed to the collapse of the Hobartian methodology is difficult to assess, particularly since serious flaws had emerged in it before the question of slavery served to popularize these flaws. Yet for many it was the immediate issue of slavery that led to a questioning of the Hobartian view of apostolic exclusivity, and once the break had been made and the intellectual confines of the synthesis had been thrown off, it became difficult in retrospect to recall the importance the strictures had played in the earlier synthesis. Writing a scant thirty years afterward, one denominational historian, in explaining the position taken by

88. Goodwin, *Southern Slavery*, 199.
89. Marsh, *Review of a Letter*, 13.
90. Smith, *Revivalism and Social Reform*, 216–18.

Hopkins on slavery and the war, simply concluded that he was one "to rest content in precedent rather than to profoundly study ultimate principles."[91] Such a comment suggests not only that the Hobartian era of high church Episcopal thought was over, but that it was, from the next generation's perspective, scarcely comprehensible.

IV

The increasing disarray in the theological presuppositions undergirding the Hobartian high church position created a vacuum within the church that led to an increased emphasis upon worship and devotion both on theological and pastoral levels. As had been the case at other times in the history of Anglicanism, the worship tradition provided the continuity during the period of theological reorganization. Indeed, such a redirection had already been hinted at by the increased emphasis on worship in individuals like Doane and Muhlenberg. Both Doane's concern for the social nature of the believer and Muhlenberg's concern for extending the church presupposed that it was in the realm of worship that the Episcopal Church's real contribution to American society lay. In the debates over daily worship and the aesthetic enrichment of worship as well as in the rise of free churches that could extend the outreach of the denomination's worship the Episcopal Church began taking on those concerns that would characterize it in the postbellum era. All of these emphases on architecture, aesthetics, prayer, and nonrational forms of communication had been themes present in the earlier Hobartian devotional writings, yet they became improved upon and deepened through the influences of the Oxford Movement, ritualism, romanticism, and the general movement away from dogma and toward ceremonial that characterized main line Protestantism generally in the latter part of the nineteenth century.[92] Nowhere can the new attitude be so clearly seen as in the collect for the Transfiguration composed by William Reed Huntington and included in the prayerbook revision of 1892: "O God, who on the mount didst reveal to chosen witnesses thine only-begotten Son wonderfully transfigured, in raiment white and glistering, Mercifully grant that we, being delivered from the disquietude of this world, may be permitted to behold the King in his beauty." As Doane had earlier suggested, the

91. Tiffany, *History of the Protestant Episcopal Church,* 501.
92. Lears, *No Place of Grace,* 184–92.

importance of worship in the urban Victorian milieu was precisely in its ability to provide an escape from "disquietude" and to open the participants to holiness and beauty.

Such an attitude bespoke an even more important shift in the self-understanding of the purpose of the church. No longer did it seem that its primary responsibility was to maintain its identity in the midst of an aggressive evangelical culture, as it had seemed to the Hobartians earlier in the century. The Episcopal Church was neither as weak as it had been, nor was the cultural force of evangelicalism so strong after the Civil War. The effect of the war and reconstruction, intellectual changes like Darwinism that divided evangelicals into conservative and liberal camps, and the social issues involved in the rise of urban America all served to weaken the dominance of evangelicalism after the war. With the church's identity no longer under siege, the great concern for a large number of Episcopalians in the last third of the nineteenth century was the need to address the intellectual and social concerns of Victorian society. For such a task the dogmatic rigor of the Hobartian synthesis was ill-suited. It had neither the intellectual flexibility to expand and address the new concerns for evolution, history, and philosophical idealism that characterized the later period nor did it have the breadth of social vision to address adequately the social questions of the day. By the postwar period, the religious tradition that was rooted in the seventeenth and eighteenth centuries and was eagerly adopted by American high church writers at the turn of the century had run its course. Dying gradually with its last defenders, it became within a generation a dead theology and a discarded vision.

Epilogue

The change in the tenor and spirit of both the Episcopal Church and the high church movement within it after the Civil War was marked. The new high church concerns for ritualism and a more elaborated eucharistic theology made a work like Hobart's *Companion for the Altar* extremely out of date.[1] Furthermore the end of the decade of the 1860s witnessed not only the death of John Henry Hopkins, but also the rebirth of the *Churchman*. The same newspaper, however, that once had been the great defender of the rigid apostolic argument now served as the champion of the call for a spirit of comprehension within the Episcopal Church. Even the *Church Review* by the late 1860s had begun abandoning the "Vincentian Rule" (to the lament of its former editor) in order to follow as well the "mistaken plea of the Church comprehensiveness."[2] Although there were continuers of the old tradition, the later history of the Episcopal Church became more and more the history of the heirs of the Tractarians and the descendents of the Broad Church movement of F. D. Maurice. The opinion expressed by one presbyter in 1874 became increasingly a common assumption:

1. Indeed, Hobart's name was invoked in opposition to these new trends. See *A Voice From the Past. Two Letters from Bishop White to the Rev. John Henry Hobart, D.D.* . . (Philadelphia, 1879). Nor was Seabury any more sympathetic to these new trends. See Samuel R. Johnson, *A Discourse . . . in Memory of Samuel Seabury, D.D.* (New York, 1873), 42–43. Hopkins did defend the new rituals in his famous *The Law of Ritualism* . . . (New York, 1866); but he used a very singular set of arguments which have little in common with the bulk of the pro-ritualist literature. See Mullin, "Ritualism, Anti-Romanism, and the Law," 386–88.

2. Cited in Henry Mason Baum, "Nathaniel Smith Richardson," *Church Review* 42 (1883): 308.

Instead of restriction I think we need larger liberty. The idea is too generally entertained that the Bishops of the Church are alone responsible within their dioceses in regard to the doctrine and worship of the Church. There is undoubtedly such a responsibility, but it does not overshadow that of the presbyters of the Church. And the great need, in my opinion, is now to strengthen this feeling of the responsibility of the presbyters of the Church, in accordance with their ordination vows, so to present the doctrine and ritual of the Church as in their view may be most conducive to the glory of God and the salvation of their fellow men."[3]

All of these sentiments had little in common with the intellectual assumptions that made up the intellectual milieu of Hobartianism.

For those familiar with the broader history of American religion the general story of post–Civil War theological collapse is, of course, familiar. Virtually every theological synthesis that had been so carefully crafted during the early nineteenth century by the 1880s was to fall apart like Oliver Wendell Holmes's "One Hoss Shay," and those few which did not collapse found themselves driven into a dogmatic defensive perimeter. An intellectual curtain has descended dividing the antebellum world and the modern religious consciousness. Just as few modern day Episcopalians read Hobart (except out of historical curiosity), few Congregationalists read Nathaniel William Taylor and Moses Stuart, and few Presbyterians read Albert Barnes. The transformation of philosophy, the rise of modern developmental history, sociological change, and even the travail of the Civil War all rang the death knell on the antebellum high church synthesis, just as similar factors would lead to the revolt by the Andover liberals and others in the decades to follow.

Nor will students of American religion be surprised at the collapse of the Hobartian attempt at apostolic separation in the social realm. As Ralph Waldo Emerson has noted, "no dissenter rides in his coach for three generations; he infallibly falls into the Establishment," and the high church vision of social assimilation coupled with ecclesiastical exclusivity did not last even three generations.[4] In the case of the Episcopal Church inclusive piety triumphed over exclusive eccle-

3. John Cotton Smith, "Limits of Legislation in Regard to Doctrine and Ritual," *Authorized Report of the Proceedings of the First Congress of the Protestant Episcopal Church . . .* (New York, 1875), 15.
4. Emerson is quoted in this regard in Frederick Tolles's classic *Meeting House and Counting House: The Quaker Merchants of Colonial Philadelphia, 1682–1763* (Chapel Hill, 1948), 141.

siology. Whether this should be viewed as a tragedy or a triumph perhaps depends on how an individual comes down on the always thorny question of Christ and culture. Nonetheless, it has been a question that Catholic, Protestant, Eastern Orthodox, and Jewish groups have been wrestling with ever since.

In many ways the transformation of the American Episcopal Church pointed the way that many other Protestant communions would travel by the end of the nineteenth century. Though none experimented in the use of ritual to the degree that Episcopalians did, an emphasis on worship, sentiment, nurture, and aesthetics all became part of the Protestant attempt to adapt their ministry to the Victorian city. As one Congregationalist at the turn of the next century noted, his church had been compelled into greater emphasis on public worship since "many of our young people, especially the college bred, turn naturally and easily to the Episcopal Church to satisfy their aesthetic, if not their spiritual desires."[5] Yet, as it has been shown, the other aspects of the high church synthesis proved far less permanent, and we must conclude that the Hobartian synthesis failed. It failed both because its view of the nature of revelation and the schema of church history proved unable to adapt to the new intellectual world of the second half of the nineteenth century and also because its social vision could ultimately not be reconciled to the sociological reality of American existence.

Yet the Hobartian high church movement should be judged not by its later failings but by its contemporary purpose. In its antebellum heyday it served as a basic alternative both theologically and socially to evangelicalism. Furthermore the high church movement served as an important conduit of European ideas into America, and without its contributions the intellectual life of the young republic would have been much poorer. The high church vision, though now discarded, should not be forgotten.

---

5. Edwin Whitney Bishop, "Public Worship," in Lewis Bayles Paton, ed., *Recent Christian Progress: Studies in Christian Thought and Work During the Last Seventy-Five Years* (New York, 1909), 370 ff. For a contemporary acknowledgment of the transformation in the worship of other American Protestants, see George Harris, *A Century's Change in Religion* (New York, 1914), 194–202.

Select Bibliography

The abbreviation *HMPEC* is used for
Historical Magazine of the Protestant Episcopal Church

MANUSCRIPT COLLECTIONS

Austin, Texas. Protestant Episcopal Church in the U.S.A. Archives, John Henry Hobart Correspondence.

Austin, Texas. Nathan Williams Papers. Typescript Copy. (Originals at Oneida County Historical Society, Utica, New York)

New Haven, Connecticut. Yale University. Harry Croswell Diaries.

New Haven, Connecticut. Yale University. Protestant Episcopal Bishops Papers.

New York, New York. New-York Historical Society. Benjamin Tredwell Onderdonk Manuscripts.

New York, New York. New-York Historical Society. Miscellaneous Correspondence.

New York, New York. New-York Historical Society. Rufus King Letters.

New York, New York. New-York Historical Society. Seabury Family Papers.

New York, New York. General Theological Seminary. Ashton Collection.

New York, New York. General Theological Seminary. Benjamin I. Haight Manuscripts.

New York, New York. General Theological Seminary. Bishops Collection.

New York, New York. General Theological Seminary. McVickar Family Papers.

New York, New York. General Theological Seminary. Samuel Roosevelt Johnson Papers.

New York, New York. General Theological Seminary. Samuel Seabury Correspondence.

New York, New York. General Theological Seminary. William Berrian Diaries and Correspondence.

SELECT BIBLIOGRAPHY

Princeton, New Jersey. Princeton University. Samuel Miller
Correspondence.

DENOMINATIONAL REPORTS

*Annual Report of . . . the New-York Protestant Episcopal City Missionary
Society.* 1831–45.
*Extracts from the Minutes of the General Assembly of the Presbyterian Church in
the United States of America.* 1802–08.
Journal of the Annual Convention of the Diocese of Vermont. . . . 1833–67.
Journal of the General Convention of the Protestant Episcopal Church. . . . 1844,
1862.
Journal of the Proceedings of the Diocese of Connecticut. . . . 1819–45.
Journal of the Proceedings of the Convention of the Diocese of New York.
*Journal of the Proceedings of the Protestant Episcopal Church in the Diocese of
Western New York.* 1838–46.

NEWSPAPERS AND JOURNALS

Banner of the Cross (Philadelphia, High Church)
Biblical Repertory and Princeton Review (Princeton, Old School Presbyterian)
Boston Recorder (Boston, Congregational)
British Critic and Quarterly Theological Review (London, Tractarian)
Christian Examiner (Boston, Unitarian)
Christian Journal (New York, High Church)
Christian's Magazine (New York, Presbyterian)
Christian Observer (London, High Church)
Christian Register and Moral and Theological Review (New York, High
Church)
Church Journal (New York, Tractarian)
Church Review and Ecclesiastical Register (Conn./New York, High Church)
The Churchman (New York, High Church)
Churchman's Magazine (Conn./New York, High Church)
Episcopal Recorder (Philadelphia, Low Church)
Literary and Theological Review (New York, Calvinist)
Mercersburg Review (Journal of the Mercersburg theologians)
Methodist Magazine and Quarterly Review (New York, Methodist)
New Englander (New Haven, Congregational)
New-York Review (New York, Episcopal/Intellectual)
North American Review
Protestant Episcopalian and Church Register (Philadelphia, High Church)
Quarterly Christian Spectator (New Haven, Congregational)

SELECT BIBLIOGRAPHY

PRIMARY SOURCES

SELECT BIBLIOGRAPHY

PRIMARY SOURCES

Allen, Benjamin. *A Letter to the Right Reverend John Henry Hobart, D.D.* . . . Philadelphia, 1827.

———. *A Second Letter to the Right Reverend John Henry Hobart.* . . . Philadelphia, 1827.

Anthon, Henry. *The True Churchman Warned Against the Errors of the Times.* New York, 1843.

Bacon, Leonard. *Thirteen Historical Discourses.* . . . New Haven, 1839.

Bacon, William. *Regeneration, The New Birth: A Sermon.* Waterloo, New York, 1818.

———. *A Reply to the Layman's Letter.* . . . Waterloo, New York, 1818.

Baird, Washington. *A Discourse on Ordination and Church Polity.* . . . New York, 1844.

Bancroft, George. *History of the United States of America.* . . . 6 vols. New York, 1887.

Barnes, Albert. *Miscellaneous Essays and Reviews.* 2 vols. New York, 1855.

Barnes, Albert, et al. *The Position of the Evangelical Party in the Episcopal Church.* 5th ed. Philadelphia, 1875.

Beach, John. *God's Sovereignty and His Universal Love to Men Reconciled.* . . . Boston, 1747.

Beard, James Franklin, ed. *Letters and Journals of James Fenimore Cooper.* 4 vols. Cambridge, Mass., 1960–64.

Beecher, Lyman. *Autobiography, Correspondences, etc., of Lyman Beecher, D.D.* Edited by Charles Beecher. 2 vols. New York, 1865.

Berrian, William. *An Historical Sketch of Trinity Church, New-York.* New York, 1847.

The Bible View of Slavery Reconsidered. . . . Philadelphia, 1863.

Bishop Hopkins' Letter on Slavery Ripped Up. . . . New York, 1863.

Bolles, John R. *A Reply to Bishop Hopkins' View of Slavery and a Review of the Times.* Philadelphia, 1865.

Bowden, John. *The Essentials of Ordination Stated, In a Letter to a Friend.* . . . New York, 1812.

———. *A Full Length Portrait of Calvinism.* 2d ed. New York, 1809.

———. *A Letter From a Churchman to His Friend in New Haven.* . . . New Haven, 1808.

———. *Two Letters to the Editor of the Christian's Magazine by a Churchman.* New York, 1807.

Bristed, John. *Thoughts on the Anglican and American-Anglo Churches.* New York, 1822.

Brittan, Thomas S. *An Apology for Conforming to the Protestant Episcopal Church.* . . . New York, 1833.

Brownell, Thomas C. *Errors of the Times.* . . . Hartford, 1843.

[219]

Bull, George. *Defensio Fidei Nicaenae.* . . . Oxford, 1685.

[Butler, Thomas C.]. *A Letter to the Rev. James C. Richmond.* . . . New York, 1845.

Caswall, Henry. *America and the American Church.* London, 1839.

Catholicus [pseud.]. *A Letter to Dr. Bushnell, of Hartford, on the Rationalistic, Socinian and Infidel Tendency of Certain Passages in His Address Before the Alumni of Yale College.* Hartford, 1843.

[Chapin, Alonzo Bowen]. *New-Englandism not the Religion of the Bible.* . . . Hartford, 1844.

_____. *Puritanism Not Genuine Protestantism.* . . . New York, 1847.

_____. *Review of the "Tribute to the Pilgrims".* . . . Hartford, 1836.

_____. *The State of Religion in England and Germany Compared.* . . . Hartford, 1844.

_____. *A View of the Organization and Order of the Primitive Church.* . . . New Haven, 1842.

Chase, Philander. *Reminiscences.* 2 vols. 2d ed. Boston, 1848.

Clark, Orin. *The Character and Principles of the Protestant Episcopal Church Vindicated.* . . . Geneva, New York, 1818.

Clark, Thomas M. *Reminiscences.* 2d ed. New York, 1895.

Coit, Thomas W. *Puritanism.* . . . New York, 1845.

[Cole, C.]. *A Letter to Professor Edwards A. Park.* . . . Boston, 1844.

Colton, Calvin. *The Genius and Mission of the Protestant Episcopal Church in the United States.* New York, 1853.

_____. *Protestant Jesuitism: By a Protestant.* New York, 1836.

_____. *Thoughts on the Religious State of the Country, With Reasons for Preferring Episcopacy.* New York, 1836.

Cooper, James Fenimore. *The American Democrat.* Penguin Edition. Baltimore, 1969.

Correspondence Between the Right Reverend Bishop Doane . . . and the Rev. H. A. Boardman . . . on the Alleged Popish Character of the "Oxford Divinity." Philadelphia, 1841.

[Coxe, Arthur C.]. *Revivalism and the Church.* . . . Hartford, 1843.

Croswell, Harry. *A Memoir of the Late Rev. William Croswell, D.D., Rector of the Church of the Advent, Boston.* . . . New York, 1853.

Daubeny, Charles. *A Guide to the Church.* . . . New York, 1803.

A Declaration and Protest of the Wardens and Vestry of Christ Church, Cincinnati. . . . Cincinnati, 1823.

Dickinson, Jonathan. *Sermons and Tracts.* Edinburgh, 1793.

Doane, George Washington. *The Life and Writings of George Washington Doane, D.D., LL.D. . . . with a Memoir by his Son, William Croswell Doane.* 4 vols. New York, 1860–61.

Duer, John. *A Speech . . . Delivered in the Convention of the Protestant Episcopal Church.* New York, 1843.

Duffie, Cornelius. *Sermons by the Late Cornelius Duffie.* . . . New York, 1829.

Duffy, John J., ed. *Coleridge's American Disciples: The Selected Correspondence of James Marsh.* Amherst, 1973.

Dwight, Timothy. *Theology Explained and Defended in a Series of Sermons.* . . . 4 vols. New York, 1851.

Francis, John W. *Old New York: or Reminiscences of the Past Sixty Years.* New York, 1858.

Glorious Triumph of the Truth in the Trial and Conviction of the Pope and His Confederates, the Puseyites. . . . New York, 1844.

Goodwin, Daniel P. *Southern Slavery in its Present Aspects.* . . . Philadelphia, 1864.

[Griggs, Leverett]. *Looking Glass For High Churchmen.* . . . New Haven, 1843.

Haight, Benjamin I. *A Letter to a Parishioner.* . . . New York, 1843.

Hall, Edwin. *The Puritans and Their Principles.* 3d ed. New York, 1847.

Hare, George Emlen. *Christ to Return . . . with a Preface by the Rt. Rev. L. Silliman Ives.* Philadelphia, 1840.

Haswell, Charles H. *Reminiscences of an Octogenarian of the City of New York (1816–1860).* New York, 1896.

Hawes, Joel. *A Tribute to the Memory of the Pilgrims, and a Vindication of the Congregational Churches of New-England.* Hartford, 1830.

Henry, Caleb S. *A Compendium of Christian Antiquities.* Philadelphia, 1837.

––––––. *Dr. Oldham's Talk at Greystones.* New York, 1872.

––––––. *Patriotism and the Slaveholders' Rebellion.* New York, 1861.

Hobart, John Henry. *An Address Delivered Before the Auxiliary New-York Bible and Common Prayer Book Society.* . . . New York, 1816.

––––––. *An Address Delivered Before the New-York Protestant Episcopal Missionary Society.* . . . New York, 1817.

––––––. *An Address, Delivered to the Annual Convention of the Protestant Episcopal Church in the State of New York.* New York, 1823.

––––––. *An Address, Delivered to the Students of the General Theological Seminary.* New York, 1828.

––––––. *An Apology for Apostolic Order and its Advocates.* 2d ed. New York, 1844.

––––––. *The Beneficial Effects of Sunday Schools Considered.* . . . New York, 1818.

––––––. *The Candidate for Confirmation Instructed.* . . . New York, 1826.

––––––. *A Charge to the Clergy of the Protestant Episcopal Church in the State of New York.* New York, 1815.

––––––. *The Charter of the Corporation of Trinity Church Defended against the Attacks of a Late Pamphlet.* . . . 1813. Reprint. New York, 1846.

_____. *The Christian Bishop.* . . . Philadelphia, 1827.

_____. *Christian Sympathy: A Sermon Preached to the Congregation of English Protestants in the City of Rome.* . . . London, 1825.

_____. *The Christian's Manual of Faith and Devotion.* . . . New York, 1849.

_____. *The Church Catechism.* . . . New York, 1826.

_____. *The Churchman. The Principles of the Churchman Explained, in Distinction from the Corruptions of the Church of Rome.* . . . New York, 1819.

_____. *The Churchman's Profession of his Faith and Practice.* . . . New York, 1821.

_____. *The Claims of the Orphan.* . . . New York, 1820.

_____. *The Clergyman's Companion.* . . . New York, 1806.

_____. *A Companion for the Altar: or Week's Preparation for the Holy Communion.* . . . 2d ed. New York, 1809.

_____. *A Companion for the Book of Common Prayer.* 4th ed. New York, 1827.

_____. *A Companion for the Festivals and Fasts of the Protestant Episcopal Church.* . . . 2d ed. New York, 1817.

_____. *Correspondence (Archives of the General Convention,* edited by Arthur Lowndes). 6 vols. New York, 1911–12.

_____. *The Corruptions of the Church of Rome Contrasted with Certain Protestant Errors.* New York, 1818.

_____. *The Duty of the Clergy with Respect to Inculcating the Doctrine of the Trinity.* . . . New York, 1829.

_____. *The Excellence of the Church.* New York, 1810.

_____. *Grammar School and Theological Seminary.* New York, 1814.

_____. *The High Churchman Vindicated.* . . . New York, 1826.

_____. *An Introductory Address on Occasion of the Opening of the General Theological Seminary.* . . . New York, 1822.

_____. *An Introductory Lecture to a Course of Religious Instruction for Young Persons.* New York, 1822.

_____. *The Man of God.* . . . New York, 1828.

_____. *The Moral Efficacy and Positive Benefits of the Ordinances of the Gospel.* New Haven, 1816.

_____. *A Note from Corrector to William Jay.* New York, 1823

_____. *The Old Paths.* . . . New York, n.d.

_____. *On Heavenly Wisdom.* . . . [New York], 1835.

_____. *The Origin, the General Character, and the Present Situation of the Protestant Episcopal Church in the United States of America.* Philadelphia, 1814.

_____. *A Pastoral Letter Addressed to the Clergy and Laity of the Protestant Episcopal Church . . . on the Subject of the Protestant Episcopal Clerical Association.* . . . New York, 1829.

_____. *A Pastoral Letter to the Laity of the Protestant Episcopal Church in the*

State of New York, on the Subject of Bible and Common Prayer Book Societies. New York, 1815.

————. *The Posthumous Works of the Late Right Reverend John Henry Hobart, D.D. . . . with a Memoir of his Life by the Rev. William Berrian, D.D.* 3 vols. New York, 1832–33.

————. *The Reciprocal Duties of Minister and People.* New York, 1830.

————. *A Reply to a Letter Addressed to the Right Rev. Bishop Hobart . . . by Corrector.* New York, 1823.

————. *A Reply to a Letter to the Right Rev. Bishop Hobart . . . by Corrector.* New York, 1823.

————. *A Reply to "An Answer to Bishop Hobart's Pastoral Letter" . . . by Another Episcopalian.* New York, 1815.

————. *The Security of the Nation. . . .* New York, 1815.

————. *Sermons on the Principal Events and Truths of Redemption.* 2 vols. New York, 1824.

————. *The State of the Departed. . . .* New York, 1857. Reprint of 1816 address.

————. *A Statement Addressed to the Episcopalians in the State of New York. . . .* New York, 1812.

————. *The United States of America Compared with some European Countries. . . .* New York, 1825.

————. *The Worship of the Church on Earth, a Resemblance of that of the Church in Heaven. . . .* Philadelphia, 1823.

Hopkins, John Henry. *The American Citizen: His Rights and Duties. . . .* New York, 1857.

————. *Autobiography in Verse: Dedicated to My Children.* Cambridge, Mass., 1866.

————. *The Bible View of Slavery.* New York, 1863.

————. *The Case of the Rev. Mr. Gorham Against the Bishop of Exeter, Considered. . . .* Burlington, Vt., 1849.

————. *The Church of Rome in Her Primitive Purity, Compared with the Church of Rome, at the Present Day. . . .* Burlington, Vt., 1837.

————. *"The End of Controversy" Controverted. . . .* 2 vols. 3d ed. New York, 1855.

————. *An Essay on Gothic Architecture.* Burlington, Vt., 1836.

————. *Fraternal Unity in the Church of God. . . .* New York, 1850.

————. *The History of the Confessional.* New York, 1850.

————. *A Humble but Earnest Address . . . on the Tolerating Among our Ministry of the Doctrines of the Church of Rome.* New York, 1846.

————. *The Missionary Constitution, The Oxford Tracts, and Nestorianism. . . .* Burlington, Vt., 1842.

————. *The Novelties Which Disturb our Peace. . . .* Philadelphia, 1844.

————. *The Primitive Church, Compared with the Protestant Episcopal Church of the Present Day. . . .* 2d ed. Burlington, Vt., 1836.

———. *The Primitive Creed, Examined and Explained.* . . . Burlington, Vt.,
1834.

———. *The Relation of Science and Religion.* . . . Albany, 1856.

———. *A Reply to a Letter of Dr. Seabury.* . . . New York, 1846.

———. *A Scriptural, Ecclesiastical, and Historical View of Slavery.* . . . New
York, 1864.

———. *Scripture and Tradition.* . . . New York, 1841.

———. *Sixteen Lectures on the Causes, Principles, and Results of the British
Reformation.* Phildelphia, 1844.

———. *Slavery: Its Religious Sanction, Its Political Dangers, and the Best Mode
of Doing it Away.* Buffalo, 1851.

———. *The Unity of the Church Consistent with the Divisions of Party.* . . .
New York, 1847.

Hopkins, John Henry, Jr. *The Life of the Late Right Reverend John Henry
Hopkins . . . by One of His Sons.* New York, 1875.

How, Thomas Y. *An Address Delivered Before the Auxiliary New-York Bible
and Common Prayer Book Society.* . . . New York, 1817.

———. *Letters Addressed to the Rev. Samuel Miller, D.D., in Reply to his
Letters Concerning the Constitution and Order of the Christian Ministry.*
Utica, N.Y., 1808.

———. *A Vindication of the Protestant Episcopal Church.* . . . New York,
1816.

[Howe, M. A. DeWolfe]. *A Reply to a Letter of Bishop Hopkins.* . . .
Philadelphia, 1864.

[Irving, William]. *A Word in Season, Touching the Present Misunderstanding in
the Episcopal Church.* New York, 1811.

Jay, John, *Caste and Slavery in the American Church.* New York, 1843.

———. *Facts Connected with the Presentment of Bishop Onderdonk.* . . . New
York, 1845.

———. *Thoughts on the Duty of the Episcopal Church in Relation to Slavery.*
New York, 1839.

———. *To the Rector and Vestry of St. Matthew's Church, Bedford.* [Bedford,
N.Y.], 1863.

Jay, William. *A Letter to the Right Rev. Bishop Hobart, in Reply to the
Pamphlet Addressed to Him by the Author, under the Signature of Corrector.*
New York, 1823.

———. *A Letter to the Right Reverend Bishop Hobart . . . by a Churchman.*
New York, 1823.

———. *A Letter to the Right Reverend Bishop Hobart Occasioned by the
Strictures on Bible Societies.* . . . New York, 1823.

———. *Miscellaneous Writings on Slavery.* Boston, 1853.

———. *A Reply to a Second Letter . . . From the Right Rev. John Henry
Hobart.* . . . New York, 1823.

———. *Strictures on a Pastoral Letter to the Laity of the Protestant Episcopal Church on the Subject of Bible and Common Prayer Book Societies . . . by a Layman.* New York, 1815.

Johnson, Evan M. *The Decline of Religion and its Causes. . . .* Brooklyn, 1836.

———. *Duty to the Church. . . .* Brooklyn, 1841.

Johnson, Samuel. *Samuel Johnson . . . His Career and Writings.* Edited by Herbert and Carol Schneider. 4 vols. New York, 1929.

Jones, Cave. *Dr. Hobart's System of Intolerance. . . .* New York, 1811.

[Jones, William, ed.]. *The Scholar Armed Against the Errors of the Time. . . .* 2 vols. 2d ed. London, 1800.

J.R.O. [pseud]. *A Letter to a Churchman. . . .* New Haven, 1808.

Keble, John. *Occasional Papers and Reviews. . . .* London, 1877.

Kemble, Frances Anne. *The Views of Judge Woodward and Bishop Hopkins on Negro Slavery in the South. . . .* Philadelphia, 1863.

King, Charles. *A Review of the Trial of the Rt. Rev. Benjamin T. Onderdonk, D.D.* New York, 1845.

Laicus [pseud.]. *The Trial Tried: or the Bishop and the Court at the Bar of Public Opinion.* New York, 1845.

The Laugh of the Layman. . . . New York, 1845.

A Letter Addressed to the Episcopalians, and Other Religiously Disposed Persons in Waterloo and its Vicinity. Geneva, 1818.

A Letter to the Honorable and Rev. George Spencer on the Oxford Movement in the United States. New York, 1842.

Linn, William, et al. *A Collection of Essays on the Subject of Episcopacy.* New York, 1806.

"A Looker On" [pseud.]. *Jay's Pamphlet Reviewed.* N.p, n.d.

McIlvaine, Charles. *Oxford Divinity Compared with the Romish and Anglican Churches. . . .* Philadelphia, 1841.

McVic[k]ar, John. *The Early Life and Professional Years of Bishop Hobart.* Oxford, 1838.

———. "Preliminary Essay." In *Aids to Reflection,* Samuel T. Coleridge. New York, 1872.

Marsh, James. "Preliminary Essay." In *Aids to Reflection,* Samuel T. Coleridge. New York, 1840.

———. *The Remains of the Rev. James Marsh, D.D. . . .* Boston, 1843.

[Marsh, Leonard]. *A Review of a "Letter from the Right Rev. John H. Hopkins . . . on the Bible View of Slavery," by a Vermonter.* Burlington, Vt., 1861.

Mason, John M. *The Writings of . . . John M. Mason, D.D. . . .* Edited by Ebenezer Mason. 4 vols. New York, 1832.

Maxwell, William. *A Memoir of the Rev. John Holt Rice, D.D. . . .* Philadelphia, 1835.

Meade, William. *Statement of Bishop Meade in Reply to Some Parts of Bishop Onderdonk's Statement.* . . . New York, 1845.

Miller, Samuel. *A Continuation of Letters Concerning the Constitution and Order of the Christian Ministry.* New York, 1809.

———. *Letters Concerning the Constitution and Order of the Christian Ministry.* . . . New York, 1807.

———. *Memoir of the Rev. John Rodgers, D.D.* . . . Abridged ed. Philadelphia, 1840.

———. *The Utility and Importance of Creeds and Confessions.* . . . Princeton, 1824.

Miller, Samuel. *The Life of Samuel Miller, D.D., LL.D.* 2 vols. Philadelphia, 1869.

[Mines, Flavel Scott]. *A Presbyterian Clergyman Looking for the Church.* New York, 1855.

[Muhlenberg, W. A., et al.] *An Exposition of the Memorial of Sundry Presbyters.* . . . New York, 1854.

Newman, John Henry. *Apologia Pro Vita Sua.* . . . London, 1879.

———. *Lectures on Justification.* . . . London, 1838.

———. *Lectures on the Prophetical Office of the Church.* . . . London, 1837.

Obsequies and Obituary Notices of the Late Right Reverend Benjamin Tredwell Onderdonk. . . . New York, 1862.

Observer [pseud.]. *Review of Bishop B. T. Onderdonk's Address in Respect to a Late Ordination.* Philadelphia, 1843.

Onderdonk, Benjamin T. *An Address . . . at the Funeral of the Rev. Henry J. Feltus, D.D.* . . . New York, 1828.

———. *An Address of the Rt. Rev. B. T. Onderdonk, D.D.* . . . New York, 1843.

———. *The Character of the Protestant Episcopal Church in its Prominent Distinctive Features.* . . . New York, 1831.

———. *The Christian Ministry.* . . . Baltimore, 1839.

———. *Christian Unity.* . . . New York, 1840.

———. *The Church—The Faith—Tradition.* New York, 1844.

———. *The Edifying of the Church.* . . . New York, 1839.

———. *The Episcopal Office.* . . . Utica, N.Y., 1839.

[———]. *A Letter to the Wardens and Vestry of Christ Church, Cincinnati.* . . . New York, 1824.

———. *A Pastoral Letter . . . on the Duty of Aiding in Education for the Holy Ministry, and in the Missionary Operations of the Diocese.* New York, 1839.

———. *A Pastoral Letter to the Clergy and People of his Spiritual Charge.* . . . New York, 1844.

———. *A Plea for Religious Charity Schools.* . . . New York, 1825.

———. *A Sermon . . . at the Consecration of the Rt. Rev. Levi Silliman Ives, D.D.* New York, 1831.

———. *A Sermon Preached in St. James Church . . . Before and For the Benefit of the Domestic and Foreign Missionary Society, of the Protestant Episcopal Church.* New York, 1829.

———. *A Sermon Preached in the Chapel of the General Theological Seminary. . . .* New York, 1831.

———. *A Statement of Facts and Circumstances. . . .* New York, 1845.

———, ed. *Works on Episcopacy.* 2 vols. New York, 1831.

Onderdonk, Henry M. *A History of the Protestant Episcopal Church in the City of New York.* New York, 1843–45.

Onderdonk, Henry Ustick. *An Appeal to the Religious Public. . . .* Canandaigua, N.Y., 1818.

[———, et al.]. *Episcopacy Examined and Reexamined.* New York, 1835.

———. *An Essay on Regeneration.* Philadelphia, 1835.

———. *Sermons and Episcopal Charges.* 2 vols. Philadelphia, 1851.

One Faith: or Bishop Doane vs. Bishop McIlvaine on Oxford Theology . . . by a Presbyterian. 2d ed. Burlington, N.J., 1843.

Osgood, Samuel. *A Letter on the Subject of Episcopacy. . . .* New York, 1807.

Owen, John. *The History of the Origin and First Ten Years of the British and Foreign Bible Society.* 2 vols. London, 1816.

Park, Edwards A. *A Discourse Delivered in Boston Before the Pastoral Association. . . .* Andover, 1844.

A Pastoral Letter of the House of Bishops of the Protestant Episcopal Church. . . . New York, 1862.

Pearson, John. *An Exposition of the Creed. . . .* 2 vols. London, n.d.

Philalethes [pseud.]. *A Letter to Samuel Osgood. . . .* New York, 1807.

Pintard, John. *Letters from John Pintard to his Daughter . . . 1816–1833.* New York, 1940–41.

Plebs, Washington [pseud.]. *A Letter to the Rt. Rev. Bishop Onderdonk. . . .* New York, 1843.

Potter, John. *A Discourse on Church Government. . . .* 5th ed. London, 1838.

Pusey, Edward B. *A Letter to the . . . Lord Bishop of Oxford . . . From the 2nd Oxford edition.* New York, 1839.

Recent Recollections of the Anglo-American Church in the United States, by an English Layman. 2 vols. London, 1861.

Reese, David M. *Humbugs of New York: Being a Remonstrance Against Popular Delusion, Whether in Science, Philosophy, or Religion.* New York, 1838.

Reeves, William. *The Apologies of Justin Martyr . . . with a Commonitory of*

Vincentius Lirinensis Concerning the Primitive Rule of Faith. London, 1709.

A Reply to Bishop Hopkins' Attack on the Temperance Society. . . . Phildelphia, 1836.

Report of the Committee Appointed to Consider the Sentence Upon the Right Rev. Benjamin T. Onderdonk. . . . New York, 1845.

Richmond, James C. *The Conspiracy Against the Late Bishop of New York Unravelled.* . . . New York, 1845.

———. *A Defence of the Ladies.* . . . New York, 1845.

———. *Mr. Richmond's Reply.* . . . New York, 1845.

[———]. *No Church Without a Bishop: or the Controversy Between the Revs. Drs. Potts and Wainwright.* . . . New York, 1844.

Rose, Hugh James. *The State of Protestantism in Germany Described.* . . . 2d ed. London, 1829.

Schaff, Philip. *The Principles of Protestantism as Related to the Present State of the Church.* Chambersburg, Pa., 1845.

———. *What is Church History? A Vindication of the Idea of Doctrinal Development.* Philadelphia, 1846.

Schroeder, John F., ed. *Memorial of Bishop Hobart: A Collection of Sermons on the Death of the Right Reverend John Henry Hobart, D.D., with a Memoir of His Life and Writings.* New York, 1831.

Seabury, Samuel. *American Slavery Distinguished from the Slavery of the English Theories and Justified by the Law of Nature.* New York, 1861.

[———]. *A Full and True Statement of the Examination and Ordination of Mr. Arthur Carey.* New York, 1843.

———. *The Joy of the Saints.* . . . New York, 1844.

———. *The Supremacy and Obligation of Conscience.* . . . New York, 1860.

Smyth, Thomas. *The Prelatical Doctrine of Apostolic Succession Examined.* . . . Boston, 1841.

Spectator [pseud]. *Bishop Onderdonk's Trial: The Verdict Sustained at the Bar of Public Opinion.* New York, 1845.

Sprague, William, ed. *Annals of the American Pulpit.* . . . 9 vols. New York, 1859–69.

Stanton, R. L. *The Church and the Rebellion.* . . . New York, 1864.

Stephens, Archibald John, ed. *The Book of Common Prayer . . . with Notes Legal and Historical.* 3 vols. London, 1849–54.

[Stevens, William]. *A Treatise on the Nature and Constitution of the Christian Church.* . . . London, 1773.

Stone, John S. *A Memoir of the Life of James Milnor, D.D. . . . Abridged by the Author.* New York, [1849].

Strong, George Templeton. *The Diary of George Templeton Strong.* Edited by Allan Nevins and Milton Halsey Thomas. 4 vols. New York, 1952.

Stuart, Moses. *Letters on the Eternal Generation of the Son of God.* . . . Andover, 1822.

Taylor, Nathaniel W. *Regeneration, The Beginning of Holiness in the Human Heart.* New Haven, 1816.

Trapier, Paul. *A Narrative of Facts.* . . . New York, 1845.

The True Issue Sustained. . . . New York, 1843.

Tuckerman, Bayard, ed. *Diary of Philip Hone,* 2 vols. New York, 1899.

Turner, Samuel H. *Autobiography of the Rev. Samuel H. Turner, D.D.* . . . New York, 1863.

———. *A Sermon on the Occasion of the Matriculation of a New Class.* . . . New York, 1832.

Tyng, Stephen H. *A Letter Sustaining the Recent Ordination of Mr. Arthur Carey.* New York, 1843.

Van Vechten, Jacob. *Memoirs of John M. Mason, D.D., S.T.D.* . . . *with Portions of His Correspondence.* New York, 1856.

Verplanck, Gulian. *Essays on the Nature and Uses of the Various Evidences of Revealed Religion.* New York, 1824.

A Voice From the Past. Two Letters From Bishop White to the Rev. John Henry Hobart, D.D. . . . Philadelphia, 1879.

Walworth, Clarence. *The Oxford Movement in America: or Glimpses of Life in an Anglican Seminary.* New York, [1895].

Waterland, Daniel. *Regeneration, Stated and Explained.* . . . Philadelphia, 1829.

———. *The Works of Daniel Waterland, D.D.* . . . 6 vols. London, 1856.

Waylen, Edward. *Ecclesiastical Reminiscences of the United States.* London, 1846.

White, William. *The Case of the Episcopal Churches Considered.* Edited by Richard G. Salomon. N.p., 1954.

———. *Memoirs of the Protestant Episcopal Church.* . . . 2d ed. New York, 1836.

Whittingham, William R., ed. *The Churchman Armed.* New York, 1844.

———. *Count the Cost.* . . . [New York], 1836.

———. *The Ministry Called to Self-Denial.* New York, 1840.

———. *The Priesthood in the Church.* . . . 2d ed. Baltimore, 1843.

Wilberforce, Samuel. *A History of the Protestant Episcopal Church in America.* 2d ed. London, 1846.

Wilson, Bird. *Memoir of the Life of the Right Reverend William White.* . . . Philadelphia, 1839.

Woods, Leonard. *Lectures on Church Government: Containing Objections to the Episcopal Scheme.* New York, 1844.

SELECT BIBLIOGRAPHY

SECONDARY SOURCES

Addleshaw, G. W. O. *The High Church Tradition: A Study in the Liturgical Thought of the Seventeenth Century.* London, [1941].

Ahlstrom, Sydney. *A Religious History of the American People.* New Haven, 1972.

------. *Theology in America: The Major Protestant Voices from Puritanism to Neo-Orthodoxy.* Indianapolis, 1967.

Ainslie, James. *The Doctrines of Ministerial Order in the Reformed Churches of the 16th and 17th Centuries.* Edinburgh, 1940.

Albright, Raymond W. *A History of the Protestant Episcopal Church.* New York, [1964].

Allen, Alexander V. G. *The Life and Letters of Phillips Brooks.* 3 vols. New York, 1901.

Allison, C. F. *The Rise of Moralism: The Proclamation of the Gospel from Hooker to Baxter.* London, 1966.

American State Papers on Freedom in Religion. 3d ed. rev. Washington, D.C., 1943.

Anderson, Philip J. "William Linn, 1752–1808: American Revolutionary and Anti-Jeffersonian." *Journal of Presbyterian History* 53 (1977): 381–94.

Anstice, Henry. *History of St. George's Church in the City of New York: 1752–1811–1911.* New York, 1911.

Ayres, Anne. *The Life and Work of William Augustus Muhlenberg.* New York, 1880.

Bailyn, Bernard. *The Ideological Origins of the American Revolution.* Cambridge, Mass., 1967.

Baltzell, E. Digby. *Philadelphia Gentleman: The Making of a National Upper-Class.* 1958. Reprint. New York, 1964.

Barnes, Gilbert. *The Anti-Slavery Impulse, 1830–1844.* New York, 1933.

Barth, J. Robert. *Coleridge and Christian Doctrine.* Cambridge, Mass., 1969.

Beardsley, E. Edward. *The History of the Episcopal Church in Connecticut. . . .* 2 vols. New York, 1868–69.

Benson, Lee. *The Concept of Jacksonian Democracy: New York as a Test Case.* New York, 1969.

Bercovitch, Sacvan. *The Puritan Origins of the American Self.* New Haven, 1975.

Berk, Stephen E. *Calvinism versus Democracy: Timothy Dwight and the Origins of American Evangelical Orthodoxy.* Hamden, Ct., 1974.

Bodo, John R. *The Protestant Clergy and Public Issues, 1812–1848.* Princeton, 1954.

Boles, John B. *The Great Revival, 1787–1805: The Origins of the Southern Evangelical Mind.* Lexington, Ky., 1972.

Boulger, James Denis. *Coleridge as Religious Thinker.* New Haven, 1961.

Bowen, Desmond. *The Idea of the Victorian Church: A Study of the Church of England, 1833–1889.* Montreal, 1968.

Bozeman, Theodore Dwight. *Protestants in an Age of Science: The Baconian Ideal and Antebellum American Religious Thought.* Chapel Hill, 1977.

Bragg, George F. *A History of the Afro-American Group of the Episcopal Church.* Baltimore, 1922.

Brand, William Francis. *The Life of William Rollinson Whittingham.* 2 vols. New York, 1883.

Brewer, Clifton H. *A History of Religious Education in the Episcopal Church to 1835.* New Haven, 1924.

Brickley, Charles N. "The Episcopal Church in Protestant America, 1800–1860: A Study in Thought and Action." Ph.D. dissertation, Clark University, 1950.

Bridenbaugh, Carl. *Mitre and Sceptre: Transatlantic Faiths, Ideas, Personalities, and Politics, 1689–1775.* New York, 1962.

Brilioth, Yngve. *The Anglican Revival: Studies in the Oxford Movement.* London, 1925.

Brown, Ford K. *Fathers of the Victorians: The Age of Wilberforce.* Cambridge, 1961.

Butterfield, Herbert. *Man on His Past: The Study of the History of Historical Scholarship.* Cambridge, 1955.

Cameron, Kenneth. "Wordsworth, Bishop Doane, and the Sonnets of the American Church." *HMPEC* 11 (1942): 83–91.

Carter, T. T. *Undercurrents of Church Life in the Eighteenth Century.* London, 1899.

Caskey, Marie. *Chariot of Fire: Religion and the Beecher Family.* New Haven, 1978.

Cave, Alfred A. *An American Conservative in the Age of Jackson: The Political and Social Thought of Calvin Colton.* Fort Worth, 1969.

Cecil, Anthony. *The Theological Development of Edwards Amassa Park: Last of the "Consistent Calvinists."* Missoula, Mont., 1974.

Chadwick, Owen. *From Bossuet to Newman: The Idea of Doctrinal Development.* Cambridge, 1957.

————, ed. *The Mind of the Oxford Movement.* Stanford, 1960.

————. *The Victorian Church.* 2 vols. London, [1966–70].

Cherry, Conrad, ed. *God's New Israel: Religious Interpretations of American Destiny.* Englewood Cliffs, N.J., 1971.

Childs, Brevard. *Introduction to the Old Testament as Scripture.* Philadelphia, 1979.

Chorley, E. Clowes. "Benjamin Tredwell Onderdonk, Fourth Bishop of New York." *HMPEC* 9 (1940); 1–51.

————. *Men and Movements in the American Episcopal Church.* New York, 1950.

Church, Richard. *The Oxford Movement: Twelve Years, 1833–1845.* Edited with an introduction by Geoffrey Best. Chicago, 1970.

Clark, Clifford E., Jr. *Henry Ward Beecher: Spokesman for a Middle-Class America.* Urbana, Ill., 1978.

Clark, Kenneth. *The Gothic Revival: An Essay in the History of Taste.* 3d ed. London, 1962.

Clarke, W. K. Lowther. *Eighteenth-Century Piety.* London, 1944.

Conforti, Joseph A. *Samuel Hopkins and the New Divinity Movement.* . . . Grand Rapids, 1981.

Cragg, Gerald. *From Purtianism to the Age of Reason: A Study of Changes in Religious Thought Within the Church of England, 1660–1700.* Cambridge, 1950.

Craven, Wesley Frank. *The Legend of the Founding Fathers.* New York, 1956.

Cross, Arthur L. *The Anglican Episcopate and the American Colonies.* New York, 1902.

Cross, Barbara. *Horace Bushnell: Minister to a Changing America.* Chicago, 1958.

Cross, Whitney R. *The Burned-Over District: The Social and Intellectual History of Enthusiastic Religion in Western New York, 1800–1850.* New York, 1965.

Davies, Horton. *Worship and Theology in England.* Vol. 3: *From Watts and Wesley to Maurice.* Princeton, 1961.

Davis, David Brion. *The Problem of Slavery in the Age of Revolution, 1770–1823.* Ithaca, N.Y., 1975.

––––––. *The Problem of Slavery in Western Culture.* Ithaca, N.Y., 1966.

Davis, Edward Bradford. "Albert Barnes, 1793–1870: An Exponent of New School Presbyterianism." Th.D. dissertation, Princeton Theological Seminary, 1961.

Dawley, Powel Mills. *The Story of the General Theology Seminary.* New York, 1969.

DeMille, George. *The Catholic Movement in the American Episcopal Church.* 2d ed., rev. and enlarged. Philadelphia, 1950.

––––––. *A History of the Diocese of Albany, 1704–1923.* Philadelphia, [1946].

––––––. *St. Thomas Church in the City and County of New York, 1823–1954.* Austin, Tex., 1958.

Dix, Morgan, et al. *A History of the Parish of Trinity Church in the City of New York.* 6 vols. New York, 1898–1962.

Douglas, Ann. *The Feminization of American Culture.* New York, 1977.

Dulles, Foster Rhea. *America Learns to Play: A History of Popular Recreation, 1607–1940.* New York, 1940.

Dunham, Chester Forrester. *The Attitude of the Northern Clergy Toward the South, 1860–1865.* Toledo, Ohio, 1942.

Dwight, Henry Otis. *The Centennial History of the American Bible Society.* New York, 1816.

Ekirch, Arthur A. *The Idea of Progress in America, 1815–1860.* 1944. Reprint. New York, 1964.

Ellis, Joseph. *The New England Mind in Transition.* New Haven, 1973.

Engelder, Conrad James. "The Churches and Slavery: A Study of the Attitudes Towards Slavery of the Major Protestant Denominations." Ph.D. dissertation, University of Michigan, 1964.

Epstein, Barbara Leslie. *The Politics of Domesticity: Women, Evangelism, and Temperance in Nineteenth-Century America.* Middletown, Ct., 1981.

Every, George. *The High Church Party, 1688–1718.* London, 1956.

Faber, Geoffrey. *Oxford Apostles: A Character Study of the Oxford Movement.* London, 1974.

Fairweather, Eugene R., ed. *The Oxford Movement.* New York, 1964.

Ferm, Robert L. *Jonathan Edwards the Younger, 1745–1801.* Grand Rapids, 1976.

Filler, Louis. *The Crusade Against Slavery, 1830–1860.* New York, 1960.

Flanagan, Mary Kathleen, S.C. "The Influence of John Henry Hobart on the Life of Elizabeth Ann Seton." Ph.D. dissertation, Union Theological Seminary, 1978.

Flower, Elizabeth, and Murray G. Murphey. *A History of American Philosophy.* 2 vols. New York, 1977.

Foner, Philip S. *Business and Slavery: The New York Merchants and the Irrepressible Conflict.* Chapel Hill, 1941.

Forbes, Duncan. *The Liberal Anglican Idea of History.* Cambridge, 1952.

Foster, Charles I. *An Errand of Mercy: The Evangelical United Front, 1790–1837.* Chapel Hill, 1960.

Foster, Frank H. *A Genetic History of the New England Theology.* Chicago, 1907.

Fox, Dixon Ryan. *The Decline of Aristocracy in the Politics of New York.* New York, 1919.

————. *Yankees and Yorkers.* New York, 1940.

Frothingham, Octavius B. *Transcendentalism in New England.* Harper Torchbook. New York, 1959.

Gabriel, Ralph Henry. *The Course of American Democratic Thought.* New York, 1940.

Gay, Peter, and Victor G. Wexler, eds. *Historians at Work.* 4 vols. New York, 1972–75.

Goodwin, W. A. R., ed. *A History of the Theological Seminary in Virginia and its Historical Background.* 2 vols. New York, 1923–24.

Gray, Horatio. *Memoirs of the Rev. Benjamin C. Cutler, D.D. . . .* New York, 1865.

Gribbin, William. *The Churches Militant: The War of 1812 and American Religion*. New Haven, 1973.

Griffin, Clifford S. *Their Brother's Keeper: Moral Stewardship in the United States, 1800–1865*. New Brunswick, 1960.

Griffin, Martin. "Latitudinarianism in the Seventeenth-Century Church of England." Ph.D. dissertation, Yale University, 1963.

Gunn, Julien. "Bishop Hobart's Emphasis on Confirmation." *HMPEC* 24 (1955): 294–309.

Gusfield, Joseph R. *Symbolic Crusade: Status Politics and the American Temperance Movement*. Urbana, Ill., 1963.

Guttmann, Allen. *The Conservative Tradition in America*. New York, 1967.

Handy, Robert T. *A Christian America: Protestant Hopes and Historical Realities*. New York, 1971.

Hardy, E. R. "Evangelical Catholicism: W. A. Muhlenberg and the Memorial Movement." *HMPEC* 13 (1944): 155–92.

Haroutunian, Joseph. *Piety versus Moralism: The Passing of the New England Theology*. New York, 1932.

Hartz, Louis. *The Liberal Tradition in America*. New York, 1955.

Hatch, Nathan, and Mark O. Noll, eds. *The Bible in America: Essays in Cultural History*. New York, 1982.

Hatch, Nathan. *The Sacred Cause of Liberty: Republican Thought and the Millennium in Revolutionary New England*. New Haven, 1977.

Hayes, Charles W. *The Diocese of Western New York*. 2 vols. Rochester, 1904.

Haywood, Marshall DeLancey. *Lives of the Bishops of North Carolina.* . . . Raleigh, N.C., 1910.

Heimert, Alan. *Religion and the American Mind: From the Great Awakening to the Revolution*. Cambridge, Mass., 1966.

Hodge, Archibald A. *The Life of Charles Hodge, D.D., LL.D.* New York, 1880.

Hodges, George. *Henry Codman Potter.* . . . New York, 1915.

Hogue, William M. "The Novel as a Religious Tract: James Fenimore Cooper—Apologist for the Episcopal Church." *HMPEC* 40 (1971): 5–26.

Holmes, David L. "The Episcopal Church and the American Revolution." *HMPEC* 41 (1978): 261–91.

———. "The Making of the Bishop of Pennsylvania, 1826–1827." *HMPEC* 41 (1972): 225–62; 42 (1973): 171–97.

Holtby, R. T. *Daniel Waterland, 1683–1740: A Study in Eighteenth-Century Orthodoxy*. Carlisle, U.K., 1966.

Hood, Fred J. *Reformed America: The Middle and Southern States, 1783–1837*. University, Ala., 1980.

Horwitz, Morton. *The Transformation of American Law, 1780–1860.* Cambridge, Mass., 1977.

Houghton, Walter E. *The Victorian Frame of Mind, 1830–1870.* New Haven, 1957.

Hovenkamp, Herbert. *Science and Religion in America, 1800–1860.* Philadelphia, 1978.

Howe, Daniel W. "American Victorianism as a Culture." *American Quarterly* 27 (1975): 507–32.

———. *The Political Culture of the American Whigs.* Chicago, 1979.

———. *The Unitarian Conscience: Harvard Moral Philosophy, 1805–1861.* Cambridge, Mass., 1970.

Howe, M. A. DeWolfe. *Memoirs of the Life and Services of the Rt. Rev. Alonzo Potter. . . .* Philadelphia, 1871.

Hunt, John. *Religious Thought in England from the Reformation to the End of the Last Century. . . .* 3 vols. London, 1870–73.

Jacob, Margaret. *The Newtonians and the English Revolution, 1689–1720.* Ithaca, N.Y., 1976.

Jeffrey, Kirk. "The Family as Utopian Retreat from the City: The Nineteenth-Century Contribution." *Soundings* 55 (1972): 21–41.

Johnson, Kathryn. "The Mustard Seed and the Leaven: Philip Schaff's Confident View of Christian History." *HMPEC* 50 (1981): 117–70.

Johnson, Paul. *A Shopkeeper's Millennium: Society and Revivals in Rochester, New York, 1815–1837.* New York, 1978.

Kammen, Michael. *People of Paradox: An Inquiry Concerning the Origins of American Civilization.* New York, 1972.

Kantrow, Alan. "Anglican Custom, American Consciousness." *New England Quarterly* 52 (1979): 307–25.

Keller, Charles R. *The Second Great Awakening in Connecticut.* New Haven, 1942.

Kinloch, Hector. "Anglican Clergy in Connecticut, 1701–1785." Ph.D. dissertation, Yale University, 1959.

Kirk, Russell. *The Conservative Mind: From Burke to Santayana.* Chicago, 1953.

———. *The Roots of American Order.* LaSalle, Ill., 1974.

Knox, Ronald. *Enthusiasm: A Chapter in the History of Religion, with Special Reference to the XVII and XVIII Centuries.* Oxford, 1950.

Krout, John Allen. *The Origins of Prohibition.* New York, 1925.

Lacey, T. A. *The Anglo-Catholic Faith.* London, [1926].

Lamont, William. *Godly Rules: Politics and Religion, 1603–1660.* London, 1969.

Langstaff, John Brett. *The Enterprising Life: John McVickar: 1787–1868.* New York, 1961.

Lasch, Christopher. *Haven in a Heartless World: The Family Besieged.* New York, 1977.

Lears, T. Jackson. *No Place of Grace: Anti-Modernism and the Transformation of American Culture, 1880–1920.* New York, 1981.

Liddon, H. P. *Life of Edward Bouverie Pusey.* . . . 4 vols. London, 1893–97.

Lipson, Dorothy Ann. *Freemasonry in Federalist Connecticut.* Princeton, 1977.

Loetscher, Lefferts A. "The Problem of Christian Unity in Early Nineteenth-Century America." *Church History* 32 (1963): 3–16.

Loveland, Clara O. *The Critical Years: The Reconstitution of the Anglican Church in the United States of America.* Greenwich, Ct., 1956.

Lowndes, Arthur. *A Century of Achievement: The History of the New-York Bible and Common Prayer Book Society for One Hundred Years.* 2 vols. New York, [1909].

Ludlum, David M. *Social Ferment in Vermont.* Montpelier, Vt., 1948.

McAdoo, H. R. *The Spirit of Angelicanism: A Survey of Anglican Theological Method in the Seventeenth Century.* London, 1965.

McConnell, S. D. *The History of the American Episcopal Church.* . . . New York, 1890.

McLachlan, James. *American Boarding Schools: A Historical Study.* New York, 1970.

MacLear, James F. "The 'True American Union' of Church and State: The Reconstruction of the Theocratic Tradition." *Church Histroy* 28 (1959): 41–59.

McLoughlin, William G. *The Meaning of Henry Ward Beecher.* . . . New York, 1970.

———. *Modern Revivalism: Charles Grandison Finney to Billy Graham.* New York, 1959.

———. *Revivals, Awakenings and Reform: An Essay on Religion and Social Change in America, 1607–1977.* Chicago, 1978.

McNeill, John T., and James Hastings Nichols. *Ecumenical Testimony: The Concern for Christian Unity within the Reformed and Presbyterian Churches.* Philadelphia, 1974.

McVickar, William. *The Life of the Rev. John McVickar, S.T.D.* . . . New York, 1872.

McWilliams, John P., Jr., *Political Justice in a Republic: James Fenimore Cooper's America.* Berkeley, 1972.

Manross, William W. "The Episcopal Church and Social Reform." *HMPEC* 12 (1943): 339–66.

———. *The Episcopal Church in the United States, 1800–1840.* New York, 1938.

———. *A History of the American Episcopal Church.* New York, 1935.

Marsden, George. *The Evangelical Mind and the New School Presbyterian Experience.* New Haven, 1970.

Martin, William Evans. "The Question of the Validity of Lay Baptism: Its Antecedents, Theological Foundations, and Influence in the History of the Church of England." Ph.D. dissertation, University of Notre Dame, 1977.

Mason, A. J. *The Church of England and Episcopacy.* Cambridge, 1914.

Mathews, Donald G. *Religion in the Old South.* Chicago, 1977.

———. "The Second Great Awakening as an Organizing Process." *American Quarterly* 21 (1969): 23–43.

———. *Slavery and Methodism: A Chapter in American Morality, 1780–1845.* Princeton, 1965.

Mathews, Lois K. *The Expansion of New England.* New York, 1909.

Mayor, Mara Nacht. "Norton, Lowell, and Godkin: A Study of American Attitudes Toward England, 1865–1885." Ph.D. dissertation, Yale University, 1969.

Mead, Sidney. *The Lively Experiment: The Shaping of Christianity in America.* New York, 1963.

———. *Nathaniel William Taylor, 1786–1858: A Connecticut Liberal.* Chicago, 1942.

———. *The Nation with the Soul of a Church.* New York, 1975.

———. *The Old Religion in the Brave New World: Reflections on the Relation Between Christendom and the Republic.* Berkeley, 1977.

Memorial of St. Mark's Church in the Bowery. New York, 1899.

Miller, Howard. *The Revolutionary College: American Presbyterian Higher Education, 1707–1837.* New York, 1976.

Miller, Perry. *The Life of the Mind in America.* New York, 1965.

Mills, Frederick V., Sr. *Bishops by Ballot: An Eighteenth-Century Ecclesiastical Revolution.* New York, 1978.

———. "The Protestant Episcopal Churches in the United States, 1783–1789: Suspended Animation or Remarkable Recovery?" *HMPEC* 46 (1977): 151–70.

Moore, William H. *The History of St. George's Church, Hampstead, Long Island. . . .* New York, 1881.

Moorhead, James. *American Apocalypse: Yankee Protestants and the Civil War, 1860–1869.* New Haven, 1978.

Morgan, Edmund S. *The Gentle Puritan: A Life of Ezra Stiles.* New Haven, 1962.

———. "The Puritan Ethic and the American Revolution." *William and Mary Quarterly,* 3d ser., 24 (1967): 3–43.

Mulder, John M., and John F. Wilson, eds. *Religion in American History: Interpretive Essays.* Englewood Cliffs, [1978].

Mullin, Robert Bruce. "Biblical Critics and the Battle Over Slavery." *Journal of Presbyterian History* 61 (1983): 210–26.

_____. "Ritualism, Anti-Romanism, and the Law in John Henry Hopkins." *HMPEC* 50 (1981): 377–90.

Murray, Andrew E. *Presbyterians and the Negro: A History.* Philadelphia, 1966.

Murrin, John. "Anglicizing an American Colony: The Transformation of Provincial Massachusetts." Ph.D. dissertation, Yale University, 1966.

Nagel, Paul C. *One Nation Indivisible: The Union in American Thought.* New York, 1964.

_____. *This Sacred Trust: American Nationality, 1798–1898.* New York, 1971.

New, John F. H. *Anglican and Puritan: The Basis of Their Opposition, 1558– 1640.* Stanford, 1964.

Newman, Richard K. "Yankee Gothic: Medieval Architectural Forms in the Protestant Church Buildings of Nineteenth-Century New England." Ph.D. dissertation, Yale University, 1949.

Nichols, James H. *Romanticism in American Theology: Nevin and Scaff at Mercersburg.* Chicago, 1961.

Nichols, Robert H., and James H. Nichols. *Presbyterianism in New York State. . . .* Philadelphia, [1963].

Niebuhr, H. Richard. *Christ and Culture.* New York, 1951.

_____. *The Kingdom of God in America.* Harper Torch Book. New York, 1959.

Nye, Russel B. *The Cultural Life of the New Nation, 1776–1830.* New York, 1960.

O'Connell, Margaret Norheim. " 'A Spirit Afloat': The Impact of the Oxford Movement in America." Ph.D. dissertation, University of Chicago, 1962.

O'Connell, Marvin R. *The Oxford Conspirators: A History of the Oxford Movement.* New York, 1969.

O'Grady, John. *Levi Silliman Ives: Pioneer Leader in Catholic Charities.* New York, 1933.

Orr, Robert R. *Reason and Authority: The Thought of William Chillingworth.* Oxford, 1967.

Overton, John H., and Frederic Relton. *The English Church, From the Accession of George I. to the End of the Eighteenth Century.* London, 1906.

Overton, John. *The Evangelical Revival of the Eighteenth Century.* London, 1891.

Paton, Lewis Bayles, ed. *Recent Christian Progress: Studies in Christian Thought and Work During the Last Seventy-Five Years.* New York, 1909.

Peck, Kenneth M. "The Oxford Controversy in America: 1839." *HMPEC* 33 (1964): 49–63.

Peck, William George. *The Social Implications of the Oxford Movement.* New York, 1933.

[Perkins, Joshua Newton]. *History of St. Stephen's Parish in the City of New York, 1805–1905.* New York, 1906.

Pochman, Henry A. *German Culture in America: Philosophical and Literary Influences, 1600–1900.* Madison, Wisc., 1952.

Popkin, Richard C. *The History of Scepticism from Erasmus to Descartes.* Assen, 1960.

Pratt, James Webb. *Religion, Politics and Diversity: The Church-State Theme in New York History.* Ithaca, N.Y., 1967.

Prichard, Robert W. "Nineteenth-Century Episcopal Attitudes on Predestination and Election." *HMPEC* 51 (1982): 23–51.

Prickett, Stephen. *Romanticism and Religion: The Tradition of Coleridge and Wordsworth in the Victorian Chruch.* New York, 1976.

Ratner, Lorman. *Powder Keg: Northern Opposition to the Anti-Slavery Movement, 1831–1840.* New York, 1968.

Reardon, Bernard M. G. *From Coleridge to Gore: A Century of Religious Thought in Britain.* London, 1971.

Reynolds, David S. "The Feminization Controversy: Sexual Stereotypes and the Paradoxes of Piety in Nineteenth-Century America." *New England Quarterly* 53 (1980): 96–108.

Richards, Leonard L. *"Gentlemen of Property and Standing": Anti-Abolition Mobs in Jacksonian America.* New York, 1970.

Richey, Russell E., ed. *Denominationalism.* Nashville, 1977.

Rorabaugh, W. J. *The Alcoholic Republic: An American Tradition.* New York, 1979.

Rosenberg, Carol Smith. *Religion and the Rise of the American City: The New York City Mission Movement, 1812–1870.* Ithaca, N.Y., 1971.

Ryan, John K., and E. D. Benard. eds. *American Essays for the Newman Centennial.* Washington, D.C., 1947.

Saloman, Richard. "The Episcopate and the Carey Case. . . ." *HMPEC* 18 (1949): 240–81.

Sanders, Charles R. *Coleridge and the Broad Church Movement. . . .* Durham, N.C., 1942.

Scott, Donald M. *From Office to Profession: The New England Ministry, 1750–1850.* Philadelphia, 1978.

Skardon, Alvin W. *Church Leader in the Cities: William Augustus Muhlenberg.* Philadelphia, 1971.

Smith, Elwyn A., ed. *The Religion of the Republic.* Philadelphia, 1971.

Smith, H. Shelton. *Changing Conceptions of Original Sin: A Study in American Theology Since 1750.* New York, 1955.

Smith, Timothy D. *Revivalism and Social Reform: American Protestantism on the Eve of the Civil War.* Nashville, 1957.

Smythe, George Franklin. *A History of the Diocese of Ohio until the Year 1918*. Cleveland, 1931.

Spann, Edward K. *The New Metropolis: New York City, 1840–1857*. New York, 1981.

Stange, Douglas C. *Patterns of Antislavery Among American Unitarians, 1831–1860*. Rutherford, N.J., 1977.

Staudenraus, P. J. *The African Colonization Movement, 1816–1865*. New York, 1961.

Steiner, Bruce. *Samuel Seabury, 1729–1796: A Study in the High Church Tradition*. Athens, Ohio, 1971.

Stephen, Leslie. *History of English Thought in the Eighteenth Century*. 2 vols. New York, 1876.

Stewart, William Rhinelander. *Grace Church and Old New York*. New York, 1924.

Stokes, Anson Phelps. *Church and State in the United States*. . . . 3 vols. New York, 1950.

Stowe, Walter H., ed. *The Life and Letters of Bishop William White*. . . . New York, [1937].

Swatos, William H. *Into Denominationalism: The Anglican Metamorphosis*. [Storrs, Ct.], 1979.

Sweet, William W. *Religion on the American Frontier*. Vol. 2: *The Presbyterians*. 1936. Reprint. New York, 1964.

Sykes, Norman. *Church and State in England in the Eighteenth Century*. 1934. Reprint. Hamden, Ct., 1962.

———. *Edmund Gibson, Bishop of London, 1669–1748: A Study in Politics and Religion in the Eighteenth Century*. London, 1926.

———. *From Sheldon to Secker: Aspects of English Church History, 1660–1768*. Cambridge, 1959.

———. *William Wake, Archbishop of Canterbury, 1657–1737*. 2 vols. Cambridge, 1957.

Temple, Sydney A., Jr. *The Common Sense Theology of Bishop White*. . . . New York, 1946.

Tennyson, G. B. *Victorian Devotional Poetry*. Cambridge, Mass., 1981.

Thistlethwaite, Frank. *The Anglo-American Connection in the Early Nineteenth Century*. Philadelphia, [1959].

Tiffany, Charles C. *A History of the Protestant Episcopal Church in the United States of America*. New York, 1895.

Tolles, Frederick. *Meeting House and Counting House: The Quaker Merchants of Colonial Philadelphia, 1682–1763*. Chapel Hill, 1948.

Toon, Peter. *Evangelical Theology, 1833–1856: A Response to Tractarianism*. London, 1979.

Tuckerman, Bayard. *William Jay and the Constitutional Movement for the Abolition of Slavery.* New York, 1894.

Tulloch, John. *Rational Theology and Christian Philosophy in England in the Seventeenth Century. . . .* 2 vols. London, 1872.

Tuveson, Ernest L. *Redeemer Nation: The Idea of America's Millennial Role.* Chicago, [1968].

Vander Stelt, John. *Philosophy and Scripture: A Study in Old Princeton and Westminster Theology.* Marlton, N.J., 1978.

Walworth, Clarence. *Reminiscences of Edgar P. Wadhams, First Bishop of Ogdensburg.* New York, [1893].

Webb, C. C. J. *Religious Thought in the Oxford Movement.* London, 1928.

Wells, David, and John D. Woodbridge, eds. *The Evangelicals. . . .* 2d eds. rev. Grand Rapids, 1977.

Wells, Ronald Vale. *Three Christian Transcendentalists.* Rev. ed. New York, 1972.

Welter, Rush. *The Mind of America, 1820–1860.* New York, 1975.

Wertenbaker, Thomas J. *Princeton, 1746–1896.* Princeton, 1946.

Wertz, Richard W. "John Henry Hobart, 1775–1830: Pillar of the Episcopal Church." Ph.D. dissertation, Harvard University, 1967.

Wharton, Anne Hollingsworth. *Social Life in the Early Republic.* Philadelphia, 1902.

White, Edwin G. *Inter-relation of Personality and Institution as Exemplified in the Membership of the Protestant Episcopal Church.* East Lansing, Mi., 1934.

White, Hayden V. *Metahistory: The Historical Imagination in Nineteenth-Century Europe.* Baltimore, [1973].

Willey, Basil. *Nineteenth-Century Studies: Colerdige to Matthew Arnold.* Harper Torchbook. New York, 1966.

Williams, N. P., ed. *Northern Catholicism: Centenary Studies in the Oxford and Parallel Movements.* New York, 1933.

Williams, Peter W., "A Mirror for Unitarians: Catholicism and Culture in Nineteenth-Century New England Literature." Ph.D. dissertation, Yale University, 1970.

Wilson, James Grant, ed. *The Centennial History of the Protestant Episcopal Church in the Diocese of New York, 1785–1885.* New York, 1886.

Wilson, John F., ed. *Church and State in American History.* Boston, 1965.

Wilson, Major L. *Space, Time and Freedom: The Quest for Nationality and the Irrepressible Conflict, 1815–1861.* Westport, Ct., 1974.

Woolverton, John F. "Philadelphia's William White: Episcopal Distinctiveness and Accommodation in the Post-Revolutionary Period." *HMPEC* 43 (1974): 279–96.

Yolton, John. *John Locke and the Way of Ideas*. [London], 1956.

Zabriskie, Alexander, ed. *Anglican Evangelicalism*. Philadelphia, 1943.
_____. "The Rise and Main Characteristics of the Anglican Evangelical Movement in England and America." *HMPEC* 12 (1943): 83–115.
Zimmer, Anne Y. .*Jonathan Boucher, Loyalist in Exile*. Detroit, 1978.

Index